"THERE CAN BE NO DOUBT THAT THIS IS THE BEST TEXT OF THE HISTORY OF PHILOSOPHY NOW AVAILABLE IN ENGLISH"
The Historical Bulletin

"Fr. Copleston presents in this volume a comprehensive survey of ancient philosophy . . . He discusses the matter at hand in a fresh and interesting as well as in an accurate and authoritative manner . . . This work is highly recommended."
The Catholic Historical Review

"A detailed, clear and judicious account of ancient philosophy from the Pre-Socratics down to Neo-Platonism, based on adequate knowledge of the sources and of the most important secondary material." *The Journal of Philosophy*

"Fr. Copleston writes with ease and lucidity, and his book should be valuable not merely as a text book but as an introduction to Christian philosophy for the general reader."
Pax

". . . broad-minded and objective, comprehensive and scholarly, unified and well-proportioned . . . No thinker with any claim to distinction in ancient philosophy is dismissed. . . . We cannot recommend too highly the adoption of Fr. Copleston's book as a manual in Catholic seminaries, colleges and universities." *Thought*

"Fr. Copleston has written an authoritative, well-documented history which the reader can trust. Although his work is far from being a 'popularization', it is not ponderous and has an easy style which makes for pleasant reading." *The Thomist*

"The author's desire to be objective and fair is evidenced throughout by his painstaking recourse to primary sources and by a spirit of impartiality and tolerance in his critical appraisals." *Theological Studies*

A History of Philosophy

VOLUME I

Greece and Rome

PART I

by Frederick Copleston, S.J.

NEW REVISED EDITION

IMAGE BOOKS
A Division of Doubleday & Company, Inc.
Garden City, New York

Image Books Edition 1962
by special arrangement with The Newman Press

PRINTING HISTORY
The Newman Press Edition published December, 1946

1st printing	December, 1946
2nd printing	September, 1948
3rd printing	December, 1950
4th printing	July, 1953
5th printing	October, 1955
6th printing	July, 1957
7th printing	July, 1959
8th printing	October, 1960

Image Books Edition published February, 1962

DE LICENTIA SUPERIORUM ORDINIS:
Franciscus Mangan, S.J., Praep. Prov. Angliae
NIHIL OBSTAT:
C. Lattey, S.J., Censor Deputatus
IMPRIMATUR:
✠ Thomas, Archiepiscopus Birmingamiensis
Die 17 Martii 1944

TO MY BROTHER

CONTENTS

PREFACE

There are so many histories of philosophy already in existence that it seems necessary to give some explanation why one has added to their number. My chief motive in writing this book, which is designed to be the first volume of a complete history of philosophy, has been that of supplying Catholic ecclesiastical seminaries with a work that should be somewhat more detailed and of wider scope than the text-books commonly in use and which at the same time should endeavour to exhibit the logical development and inter-connection of philosophical systems. It is true that there are several works available in the English language which (as distinct from scientific monographs dealing with restricted topics) present an account, at once scholarly and philosophical, of the history of philosophy, but their point of view is sometimes very different from that of the present writer and of the type of student whom he had in mind when writing this book. To mention a "point of view" at all, when treating of the history of philosophy, may occasion a certain lifting of the eyebrows; but no true historian can write without some point of view, some standpoint, if for no other reason than that he must have a principle of selection, guiding his intelligent choice and arrangement of facts. Every conscientious historian, it is true, will strive to be as objective as possible and will avoid any temptation to distort the facts to fit a preconceived theory or to omit the mention of certain facts simply because they will not support his preconceived theory; but if he attempts to write history without any principle of selection, the result will be a mere chronicle and no real history, a mere concatenation of events or opinions without understanding or *motif*. What would we think of a writer on

English history who set down the number of Queen Elizabeth's dresses and the defeat of the Spanish Armada as facts of equal importance, and who made no intelligent attempt to show how the Spanish venture arose, what events led to it and what its results were? Moreover, in the case of an historian of philosophy, the historian's own personal philosophical outlook is bound to influence his selection and presentation of facts or, at least, the emphasis that he lays on certain facts or aspects. To take a simple example. Of two historians of ancient philosophy, each may make an equally objective study of the facts, e.g. of the history of Platonism and Neo-Platonism; but if the one man is convinced that all "transcendentalism" is sheer folly, while the other firmly believes in the reality of the transcendental, it is hardly conceivable that their presentation of the Platonic tradition should be exactly the same. They may both narrate the opinion of the Platonists objectively and conscientiously; but the former will probably lay little emphasis on Neo-Platonic metaphysics, for instance, and will indicate the fact that he regards Neo-Platonism as a sorry ending to Greek philosophy, as a relapse into "mysticism" or "orientalism," while the other may emphasise the syncretistic aspect of Neo-Platonism and its importance for Christian thought. Neither will have distorted the facts, in the sense of attributing to philosophers opinions they did not hold or suppressing certain of their tenets or neglecting chronology or logical interconnection, but all the same their pictures of Platonism and Neo-Platonism will be unmistakably different. This being so, I have no hesitation in claiming the right to compose a work on the history of philosophy from the standpoint of the scholastic philosopher. That there may be mistakes or misinterpretations due to ignorance, it would be presumptuous folly to deny; but I do claim that I have striven after objectivity, and I claim at the same time that the fact that I have written from a definite standpoint is an advantage rather than a disadvantage. At the very least, it enables one to give a fairly coherent and meaningful account of what might otherwise be a mere jumble of incoherent opinions, not as good as a fairy-tale.

From what has been said, it should be clear that I have written not for scholars or specialists, but students of a certain type, the great majority of whom are making their first acquaintance with the history of philosophy and who are studying it concomitantly with systematic scholastic philosophy, to which latter subject they are called upon to devote the greater part of their attention for the time being. For the readers I have primarily in mind (though I should be only too glad if my book should prove of any use to others as well) a series of learned and original monographs would be of less use than a book which is frankly designed as a text-book, but which may, in the case of some students, serve as an incentive to the study of the original philosophical texts and of the commentaries and treatises on those texts by celebrated scholars. I have tried to bear this in mind, while writing the present work, for *qui vult finem, vult etiam media*. Should the work, therefore, fall into the hands of any readers who are well acquainted with the literature on the history of ancient philosophy, and cause them to reflect that this idea is founded on what Burnet or Taylor say, that idea on what Ritter or Jaeger or Stenzel or Praechter have said, let me remind them that I am possibly quite well aware of this myself, and that I may not have agreed uncritically or unthinkingly with what the scholar in question says. Originality is certainly desirable when it means the discovery of a truth not hitherto revealed, but to pursue originality for the sake of originality is not the proper task of the historian. I willingly acknowledge my debt, therefore, to those men who have shed lustre on British and Continental scholarship, to men like Professor A. E. Taylor, Sir David Ross, Constantin Ritter, Werner Jaeger and others. In fact, it is one of my excuses for writing this book that some of the manuals which are in the hands of those for whom I am writing have paid but scant attention to the results of modern specialist criticism. For my own part, I should consider a charge of making insufficient use of such sources of light a more reasonable ground for adverse criticism, than a charge of making too much use of them.

Grateful thanks are due to the Encyclopaedia Britannica Co., Ltd., for permission to use diagrams taken from Sir Thomas Little Heath's article on Pythagoras (14th edit.); to Professor A. E. Taylor (and Messrs. Macmillan & Co., Ltd.) for his generous permission to utilise so freely his study on Forms and Numbers in Plato (reprinted from *Mind in Philosophical Studies*); to Sir David Ross and Messrs. Methuen & Co. for kind permission to incorporate his table of the moral virtues according to Aristotle (from *Aristotle*, p. 203); to Messrs. George Allen & Unwin, Ltd., for permission to quote a passage from the English translation of Professor Nicolai Hartmann's *Ethics* and to utilise a diagram from that work; to the same publishers and to Dr. Oscar Levy to make some quotations from the authorised English translation of Nietzsche's works (of which Dr. Levy is editor); to Messrs. Charles Scribner's Sons (U.S.A.) for permission to quote the translation of Cleanthes' Hymn to Zeus by Dr. James Adam (from Hicks' *Stoic and Epicurean*); to Professor E. R. Dodds and the S.P.C.K. for permission to utilise translations found in *Select Passages Illustrating Neo-Platonism* (S.P.C.K. 1923); and to Messrs. Macmillan & Co., Ltd., for permission to quote from R. L. Nettleship's *Lectures on the Republic of Plato*.

References to the pre-Socratic philosophers are given according to the fifth edition of Diels' *Vorsokratiker* (D. in text). Some of the fragments I have translated myself, while in other cases I have (with the kind permission of Messrs. A. & C. Black, Ltd.) adopted the English translation given by Burnet in his *Early Greek Philosophy*. The title of this work is abbreviated in reference to E.G.P., and *Outlines of the History of Greek Philosophy*, by Zeller–Nestle–Palmer, appear generally as *Outlines*. Abbreviations for the titles of Platonic dialogues and the works of Aristotle should be sufficiently obvious; for the full titles of other works referred to recourse may be had to the first Appendix at the end of the volume, where the abbreviations are explained. I have mentioned a few works, by way of recommendation, in the third Appendix, but I do so simply for the practical convenience of the type of student for whom I have primarily written; I do not dignify the short list of books with the title of bibliography and I disclaim any intention of giving a bibliography, for the simple reason that anything approaching a full bibliography (especially if it took into account, as it ought to do, valuable articles in learned periodicals) would be of such an enormous size that it would be quite impracticable to include it in this work. For a bibliography and a survey of sources, the student can turn to e.g. Ueberweg-Praechter's *Die Philosophie des Altertums*.

AUTHOR'S FOREWORD
TO REVISED EDITION

My thanks are due to the Rev. T. Paine, S.J., the Rev. J. Woodlock, S.J., and the Reader of Messrs. Burns Oates and Washbourne, Ltd., for their valuable assistance in the correction of misprints and other errors of form which disfigured the first impression, and for their suggestions in regard to the improvement of the index. Some slight additions to the text have been made, as on pp. 146-147, and for these I am entirely responsible. The necessity of producing a second edition without delay has prevented me from making more extensive changes in the text.

Chapter One

INTRODUCTION

1. Why Study the History of Philosophy?

1. We would scarcely call anyone "educated" who had no knowledge whatsoever of history; we all recognise that a man should know something of the history of his own country, its political, social and economic development, its literary and artistic achievements—preferably indeed in the wider setting of European and, to a certain extent, even World history. But if an educated and cultured Englishman may be expected to possess some knowledge of Alfred the Great and Elizabeth, of Cromwell and Marlborough and Nelson, of the Norman invasion, the Reformation, and the Industrial Revolution, it would seem equally clear that he should know something at least of Roger Bacon and Duns Scotus, of Francis Bacon and Hobbes, of Locke, Berkeley and Hume, of J. S. Mill and Herbert Spencer. Moreover, if an educated man is expected to be not entirely ignorant of Greece and Rome, if he would be ashamed to have to confess that he had never even heard of Sophocles or Virgil, and knew nothing of the origins of European culture, he might equally be expected to know something of Plato and Aristotle, two of the greatest thinkers the world has ever known, two men who stand at the head of European philosophy. A cultured man will know a little concerning Dante and Shakespeare and Goethe, concerning St. Francis of Assisi and Fra Angelico, concerning Frederick the Great and Napoleon I: why should he not be expected also to know something of St. Augustine and St. Thomas Aquinas, Descartes and Spinoza,

Kant and Hegel? It would be absurd to suggest that we should inform ourselves concerning the great conquerors and destroyers, but remain ignorant of the great creators, those who have really contributed to our European culture. But it is not only the great painters and sculptors who have left us an abiding legacy and treasure: it is also the great thinkers, men like Plato and Aristotle, St. Augustine and St. Thomas Aquinas, who have enriched Europe and her culture. It belongs, therefore, to a cultured education to know something at least of the course of European philosophy, for it is our thinkers, as well as our artists and generals, who have helped to make our time, whether for good or ill.

Now, no one would suppose that it is a waste of time to read the works of Shakespeare or contemplate the creations of Michelangelo, for they have intrinsic value in themselves which is not diminished by the number of years that have elapsed between their deaths and our own time. Yet no more should it be considered a waste of time to study the thought of Plato or Aristotle or St. Augustine, for their thought-creations abide as outstanding achievements of the human spirit. Other artists have lived and painted since the time of Rubens, but that does not lessen the value of Rubens' work: other thinkers have philosophised since the time of Plato, but that does not destroy the interest and beauty of his philosophy.

But if it is desirable for all cultured men to know something of the history of philosophic thought, so far as occupation, cast of mind and need for specialisation permit, how much more is this not desirable for all avowed students of philosophy. I refer especially to students of the Scholastic Philosophy, who study it as the *philosophia perennis*. That it is the *philosophia perennis* I have no wish to dispute; but it did not drop down from Heaven, it grew out of the past; and if we really want to appreciate the work of St. Thomas Aquinas or St. Bonaventure or Duns Scotus, we should know something of Plato and Aristotle and St. Augustine. Again, if there is a *philosophia perennis*, it is only to be expected that some of its principles should be operative in the minds even of philosophers of modern times, who may seem at first sight to stand far from St. Thomas Aquinas. And even if this were not so, it would be instructive to observe what results follow from false premises and faulty principles. Nor can it be denied that the practice of condemning thinkers whose position and meaning has not been grasped or seen in its true historic setting is greatly to be deprecated, while it might also be borne in mind that the application of true principles to all spheres of philosophy was certainly not completed in the Middle Ages, and it may well be that we have something to learn from modern thinkers, e.g. in the field of Aesthetic theory or Natural Philosophy.

2. It may be objected that the various philosophical systems of the past are merely antique relics; that the history of philosophy consists of "refuted and spiritually dead systems, since each has killed and buried the other." [1] Did not Kant declare that Metaphysic is always "keeping the human mind in suspense with hopes that never fade, and yet are never fulfilled," that "while every other science is continually advancing," in Metaphysic men "perpetually revolve round the same point, without gaining a single step"? [2] Platonism, Aristotelianism, Scholasticism, Cartesianism, Kantianism, Hegelianism—all have had their periods of popularity and all have been challenged: European Thought may be "represented as littered with metaphysical systems, abandoned and unreconciled." [3] Why study the antiquated lumber of the chamber of history?

Now, even if all the philosophies of the past had been not only challenged (which is obvious) but also refuted (which is not at all the same thing), it still remains true that "errors are always instructive," [4] assuming of course that philosophy is a possible science and is not *of itself* a will-o'-the-wisp. To take an example from Mediaeval Philosophy, the conclusions to which Exaggerated Realism lead on the one hand and those to which Nominalism lead on the other hand indicate that the solution of the problem of universals is to be sought in a mean between the two extremes. The history of the problem thus serves as an experimental proof of the thesis learnt in the Schools. Again, the fact that Absolute Idealism has found itself incapable of providing any adequate explanation of finite selves, should be sufficient to deter anyone from embarking on the monistic path. The insistence in modern philosophy on the theory of knowledge and the Subject-Object relation should, despite all the extravagances to which it has led, at any rate make it clear that subject can no more be reduced to object than object to subject, while Marxism, notwithstanding its fundamental errors, will teach us not to neglect the influence of technics and man's economic life on higher spheres of human culture. To him especially who does not set out to learn a given system of philosophy but aspires to philosophise *ab ovo*, as it were, the study of the history of philosophy is indispensable, otherwise he will run the risk of proceeding down blind alleys and repeating the mistakes of his predecessors, from which a serious study of past thought might perhaps have saved him.

3. That a study of the history of philosophy may tend to induce a sceptical frame of mind is true, but it must be remembered that the fact of a succession of systems does not prove that any one philosophy is erroneous. If X challenges the position of Y and abandons it, that does not by itself prove that the position of Y is untenable, since X may have abandoned it on insufficient grounds or have adopted false premisses, the development of which involved a departure from the philosophy of Y. The world has seen many religions—Buddhism, Hinduism, Zoroastrianism, Christianity, Mohammedanism, etc., but that does not prove that Christianity is not the true Religion; to prove that, a thorough refutation of Christian Apologetics would be necessary. But just as it is absurd to speak as if the existence of a variety of Religions *ipso facto* disproved the claim of any one religion to be the true Religion, so it is absurd to speak as though the succession of philosophies *ipso facto* demonstrated that there is no true philosophy and can be no true philosophy. (We make this observation, of course, without meaning to imply that there is no truth or value in any other religion than Christianity. Moreover, there is this great difference between the true [revealed] Religion and the true philosophy, that whereas the former, as revealed, is necessarily true in its totality, in all that is revealed, the true philosophy may be true in its main lines and principles without reaching completion at any given moment. Philosophy, which is the work of the human spirit and not the revelation of God, grows and develops; fresh vistas may be opened up by new lines of approach or application to new problems, newly discovered facts, fresh situations, etc. The term "true philosophy" or *philosophia perennis* should not be understood to denote a static and complete body of principles and applications, insusceptible of development or modification.)

2. Nature of the History of Philosophy

1. The history of philosophy is certainly not a mere con-
geries of opinions, a narration of isolated items of thought
that have no connection with one another. If the history of
philosophy is treated "only as the enumeration of various
opinions," and if all these opinions are considered as of equal
value or disvalue, then it becomes "an idle tale, or, if you will,
an erudite investigation." [5] There is continuity and connection,
action and reaction, thesis and antithesis, and no philosophy
can really be understood fully unless it is seen in its historical
setting and in the light of its connection with other systems.
How can one really understand what Plato was getting at
or what induced him to say what he did, unless one knows
something of the thought of Heraclitus, Parmenides, the
Pythagoreans? How can one understand why Kant adopted
such an apparently extraordinary position in regard to Space,
Time and the Categories, unless one knows something of
British empiricism and realises the effect of Hume's sceptical
conclusions on the mind of Kant?

2. But if the history of philosophy is no mere collection of
isolated opinions, it cannot be regarded as a continual progress or even a spiral ascent. That one can find plausible
instances in the course of philosophic speculation of the
Hegelian triad of thesis, antithesis and synthesis is true, but it
is scarcely the task of a scientific historian to adopt an *a
priori* scheme and then to fit the facts into that scheme.
Hegel supposed that the succession of philosophic systems
"represent the necessary succession of stages in the development" of philosophy, but this can only be so if the philosophic thought of man is the very thinking of the "World-
Spirit." That, practically speaking, any given thinker is limited as to the direction his thought will take, limited by the
immediately preceding and the contemporary systems (limited
also, we might add, by his personal temperament, his education, the historical and social situation, etc.) is doubtless true;
none the less he is not determined to choose any particular
premisses or principles, nor to react to the preceding philosophy in any particular way. Fichte believed that his system followed logically on that of Kant, and there is certainly
a direct logical connection, as every student of modern philosophy is aware; but Fichte was not *determined* to develop
the philosophy of Kant in the particular way he did. The

succeeding philosopher to Kant might have chosen to re-examine Kant's premises and to deny that the conclusions which Kant accepted from Hume were true conclusions; he might have gone back to other principles or excogitated new ones of his own. Logical sequence there undoubtedly is in the history of philosophy, but not *necessary* sequence in the strict sense.

We cannot, therefore, agree with Hegel when he says that "the final philosophy of a period is the result of this development, and is truth in the highest form which the self-consciousness of spirit affords of itself." [6] A good deal depends, of course, on how you divide the "periods" and what you are pleased to consider the final philosophy of any period (and here there is ample scope for arbitrary choice, in accordance with preconceived opinion and wishes); but what guarantee is there (unless we first adopt the whole Hegelian position) that the final philosophy of any period represents the highest development of thought yet attained? If one can legitimately speak of a Mediaeval period of philosophy, and if Ockhamism can be regarded as the final main philosophy of that period, the Ockhamist philosophy can certainly not be regarded as the supreme achievement of mediaeval philosophy. Mediaeval philosophy, as Professor Gilson has shown, [7] represents a *curve* rather than a straight line. And what philosophy of the present day, one might pertinently ask, represents the synthesis of all preceding philosophies?

3. The history of philosophy exhibits man's search for Truth by the way of the discursive reason. A Neo-Thomist, developing St. Thomas' words, *Omnia cognoscentia cognoscunt implicite Deum in quolibet cognito*, [8] has maintained that the judgment always points beyond itself, always contains an implicit reference to Absolute Truth, Absolute Being. [9] (We are reminded of F. H. Bradley, though the term "Absolute" has not, of course, the same meaning in the two cases.) At any rate we may say that the search for truth is ultimately the search for Absolute Truth, God, and even those systems of philosophy which appear to refute this statement, e.g. Historical Materialism, are nevertheless examples of it, for they are all seeking, even if unconsciously, even if they would not recognise the fact, for the ultimate Ground, the supremely Real. Even if intellectual speculation has at times led to bizarre doctrines and monstrous conclusions, we cannot but have a certain sympathy for and interest in the struggle of

the human intellect to attain Truth. Kant, who denied that Metaphysics in the traditional sense were or could be a science, none the less allowed that we cannot remain indifferent to the objects with which Metaphysics profess to deal, God, the soul, freedom;[10] and we may add that we cannot remain indifferent to the human intellect's search for the True and the Good. The ease with which mistakes are made, the fact that personal temperament, education and other apparently "fortuitous" circumstances may so often lead the thinker up an intellectual cul-de-sac, the fact that we are not pure intelligence, but that the processes of our minds may frequently be influenced by extraneous factors, doubtless shows the need for religious Revelation; but that should not cause us to despair altogether of human speculation nor make us despise the *bona-fide* attempts of past thinkers to attain Truth.

4. The present writer adheres to the Thomistic standpoint that there is a *philosophia perennis* and that this *philosophia perennis* is Thomism in a wide sense. But he would like to make two observations on this matter: (a) To say that the Thomist system is the perennial philosophy does not mean that that system is closed at any given historical epoch and is incapable of further development in any direction. (b) The perennial philosophy after the close of the Mediaeval period does not develop merely alongside of and apart from "modern" philosophy, but develops also in and through modern philosophy. I do not mean to suggest that the philosophy of Spinoza or Hegel, for instance, can be comprehended under the term Thomism; but rather that when philosophers, even if they would by no means call themselves "Scholastic," arrive by the employment of true principles at valuable conclusions, these conclusions must be looked on as belonging to the perennial philosophy.

St. Thomas Aquinas certainly makes some statements concerning the State, for example, and we have no inclination to question his principles; but it would be absurd to expect a developed philosophy of the modern State in the thirteenth century, and from the practical point of view it is difficult to see how a developed and articulate philosophy of the State on scholastic principles could be elaborated in the concrete, until the modern State had emerged and until modern attitudes towards the State had shown themselves. It is only when we have had experience of the Liberal State and of the

Totalitarian State and of the corresponding theories of the State, that we can realise all the implications contained in the little that St. Thomas says on the State and develop an elaborated Scholastic political philosophy applicable to the modern State, which will expressly contain all the good contained in the other theories while renouncing the errors. The resultant State-philosophy will be seen to be, when looked at in the concrete, not simply a development of Scholastic principle in absolute isolation from the actual historical situation and from intervening theories, but rather a development of these principles in the light of the historical situation, a development achieved in and through opposing theories of the State. If this point of view be adopted, we shall be enabled to maintain the idea of a perennial philosophy without committing ourselves, on the one hand, to a very narrow outlook whereby the perennial philosophy is confined to a given century, or, on the other hand, to an Hegelian view of philosophy, which necessarily implies (though Hegel himself seems to have thought otherwise—inconsistently) that Truth is never attained at a given moment.

3. How to Study the History of Philosophy

1. The first point to be stressed is the need for seeing any philosophical system in its historical setting and connections. This point has already been mentioned and does not require further elaboration: it should be obvious that we can only grasp adequately the state of mind of a given philosopher and the *raison d'être* of his philosophy if we have first apprehended its historical *point de départ*. The example of Kant has already been given; we can understand his state of mind in developing his theory of the *a priori* only if we see him in his historical situation *vis-à-vis* the critical philosophy of Hume, the apparent bankruptcy of Continental Rationalism and the apparent certainty of mathematics and the Newtonian physics. Similarly, we are better enabled to understand the biological philosophy of Henri Bergson if we see it, for example, in its relation to preceding mechanistic theories and to preceding French "spiritualism."

2. For a profitable study of the history of philosophy there is also need for a certain "sympathy," almost the psychological approach. It is desirable that the historian should know something of the philosopher as a man (this is not possible in the case of *all* philosophers, of course), since this

will help him to feel his way into the system in question, to view it, as it were, from inside, and to grasp its peculiar flavour and characteristics. We have to endeavour to put ourselves into the place of the philosopher, to try to see his thoughts from within. Moreover, this sympathy or imaginative insight is essential for the Scholastic philosopher who wishes to understand modern philosophy. If a man, for example, has the background of the Catholic Faith, the modern systems, or some of them at least, readily appear to him as mere bizarre monstrosities unworthy of serious attention, but if he succeeds, as far as he can (without, of course, surrendering his own principles), in seeing the systems from within, he stands much more chance of understanding what the philosopher meant.

We must not, however, become so preoccupied with the psychology of the philosopher as to disregard the truth or falsity of his ideas taken in themselves, or the logical connection of his system with preceding thought. A *psychologist* may justly confine himself to the first viewpoint, but not an *historian* of philosophy. For example, a purely psychological approach might lead one to suppose that the system of Arthur Schopenhauer was the creation of an embittered, soured and disappointed man, who at the same time possessed literary power and aesthetic imagination and insight, and *nothing more;* as though his philosophy were simply the manifestation of certain psychological states. But this viewpoint would leave out of account the fact that his pessimistic Voluntaristic system is largely a reaction to the Hegelian optimistic Rationalism, as it would also leave out of account the fact that Schopenhauer's aesthetic theory may have a value of its own, independent of the *kind of man* that propounded it, and would also neglect the whole problem of evil and suffering which is raised by Schopenhauer's system and which is a very real problem, whether Schopenhauer himself was a disappointed and disillusioned man or not. Similarly, although it is a great help towards the understanding of the thought of Friedrich Nietzsche if we know something of the personal history of the man, his ideas can be looked at in themselves, apart from the man who thought them.

3. To work one's way into any thinker's system, thoroughly to understand not only the words and phrases as they stand, but also the shade of meaning that the author intended to convey (so far as this is feasible), to view the details of

the system in their relation to the whole, fully to grasp its genesis and its implications, all this is not the work of a few moments. It is but natural, then, that specialisation in the field of the history of philosophy should be the general rule, as it is in the fields of the various sciences. A specialist knowledge of the philosophy of Plato, for instance, requires besides a thorough knowledge of Greek language and history, a knowledge of Greek mathematics, Greek religion, Greek science, etc. The specialist thus requires a great apparatus of scholarship; but it is essential, if he is to be a true historian of philosophy, that he should not be so overwhelmed with his scholarly equipment and the details of learning, that he fails to penetrate the spirit of the philosophy in question and fails to make it live again in his writings or his lectures. Scholarship is indispensable but it is by no means enough.

The fact that a whole lifetime might well be devoted to the study of one great thinker and still leave much to be done, means that anyone who is so bold as to undertake the composition of a continuous history of philosophy can hardly hope to produce a work that will offer anything of much value to specialists. The author of the present work is quite conscious of this fact, and as he has already said in the preface, he is not writing for specialists but rather utilising the work of specialists. There is no need to repeat again here the author's reasons for writing this work; but he would like once more to mention that he will consider himself well repaid for his work if he can contribute in some small degree, not only to the instruction of the type of student for whom the work is primarily designed, but also to the broadening of his outlook, to the acquirement of a greater understanding of and sympathy with the intellectual struggle of mankind, and of course to a firmer and deeper hold on the principles of true philosophy.

4. Ancient Philosophy

In this volume we treat the philosophy of the Greeks and Romans. There can scarcely be much need for dwelling on the importance of Greek culture: as Hegel says, "the name of Greece strikes home to the hearts of men of education in Europe." [11] No one would attempt to deny that the Greeks left an imperishable legacy of literature and art to our European world, and the same is true in regard to philosophic speculation. After its first beginnings in Asia Minor, Greek philosophy pursued its course of development until it flowered in the two great philosophies of Plato and Aristotle, and later, through Neo-Platonism, exercised a great influence on the formation of Christian thought. Both in its character as the first period of European speculation and also for its intrinsic value, it cannot but be of interest to every student of philosophy. In Greek philosophy we watch problems come to light that have by no means lost their relevance for us, we find answers suggested that are not without value; and even though we may discern a certain *naïveté*, a certain over-confidence and precipitation, Greek philosophy remains one of the glories of European achievement. Moreover, if the philosophy of the Greeks must be of interest to every student of philosophy for its influence on subsequent speculation and for its own intrinsic value, still more should it be of interest to students of Scholastic philosophy, which owes so much to Plato and to Aristotle. And this philosophy of the Greeks was really their own achievement, the fruit of their vigour and freshness of mind, just as their literature and art were their own achievement. We must not allow the laudable desire of taking into account possible non-Greek influence to lead us to exaggerate the importance of that influence and to underestimate the originality of the Greek mind: "the truth is that we are far more likely to underrate the originality of the Greeks than to exaggerate it." [12] The tendency of the historian always to seek for "sources" is, of course, productive of much valuable critical investigation, and it would be folly to belittle it; but it remains true that the tendency can be pushed too far, even to lengths when criticism threatens to be no longer scientific. For instance, one must not assume *a priori* that every opinion of every thinker is borrowed from a predecessor: if this is assumed, then we should be logically compelled to assume the existence of some primeval Colossus or Superman, from whom all subsequent philosophic speculation is ultimately derived. Nor can we safely assume that, whenever two succeeding contemporary thinkers or bodies of thinkers hold similar doctrines, one must have borrowed from the other. If it is absurd, as it is, to suppose that if some Christian custom or rite is partially found in Asiatic Eastern religion, Christianity must have borrowed that custom or rite from Asia, so it is absurd to suppose that if Greek speculation contains some thought similar to that appearing in an Oriental philosophy, the latter must be the historical source of the former. After all, the human intellect is quite capable of interpreting similar experiences in a similar way, whether it be the intellect of a Greek or an Indian, without its being necessary to suppose that similarity of reaction is an irrefutable proof of borrowing. These remarks are not meant to depreciate historical criticism and research, but rather to point out that historical criticism must rest its conclusions on historical proofs and not deduce them from *a priori* assumptions, garnishing them with a pseudo-historical flavour. Legitimate historical criticism would not, as yet at least, seem to have seriously impaired the claim to originality made on behalf of the Greeks.

Roman philosophy, however, is but a meagre production compared with that of the Greeks, for the Romans depended in large part on the Greeks for their philosophic ideas, just as they depended on the Greeks in art and, to a great extent at least, in the field of literature. They had their own peculiar glory and achievements (we think at once of the creation of Roman Law and the achievements of Roman political genius), but their glory did not lie in the realm of philosophical speculation. Yet, though the dependence of Roman Schools of philosophy on Greek predecessors is undeniable, we cannot afford to neglect the philosophy of the Roman world, since it shows us the sort of ideas that became current among the more cultured members of the class that was Master of the European civilised world. The thought of the later Stoa, for example, the teaching of Seneca, Marcus Aurelius and Epictetus, affords in many respects an impressive and noble picture which can hardly fail to arouse admiration and esteem, even if at the same time we are conscious of much that is lacking. It is desirable too that the Christian student should know something of the best that paganism had to offer, and should acquaint himself with the various currents of thought in that Greco-Roman world in which the Revealed Religion was implanted and grew. It is to be regretted if students should be acquainted with the campaigns of Julius Caesar or Trajan, with the infamous careers of Caligula or Nero, and yet should be ignorant of the philosopher-Emperor, Marcus Aurelius, or the influence at Rome of the Greek Plotinus, who though not a Christian was a deeply religious man, and whose name was so dear to the first great figure of Christian philosophy, St. Augustine of Hippo.

Part One

PRE-SOCRATIC PHILOSOPHY

Chapter Two

THE CRADLE OF
WESTERN THOUGHT: IONIA

The birthplace of Greek philosophy was the sea-board of
Asia Minor and the early Greek philosophers were Ionians.
While Greece itself was in a state of comparative chaos or
barbarism, consequent on the Dorian invasions of the eleventh
century B.C., which submerged the old Aegean culture, Ionia
preserved the spirit of the older civilisation,[1] and it was to
the Ionian world that Homer belonged, even if the Homeric
poems enjoyed the patronage of the new Achaean aristocracy. While the Homeric poems cannot indeed be called a
philosophical work (though they are, of course, of great value
through their revelation of certain stages of the Greek outlook and way of life, while their educational influence on
Greeks of later times should not be underestimated), since
the isolated philosophical ideas that occur in the poems are
very far from being systematised (considerably less so than
in the poems of Hesiod, the epic writer of mainland Greece,
who portrays in his work his pessimistic view of history, his
conviction of the reign of law in the animal world and his
ethical passion for justice among men), it is significant that
the greatest poet of Greece and the first beginnings of systematic philosophy both belong to Ionia. But these two
great productions of Ionian genius, the poems of Homer and
the Ionian cosmology, did not merely follow on one another;
at least, whatever view one holds of the authorship, composition and date or dates of the Homeric poems, it is clear
enough that the society reflected in those poems was not

that of the period of the Ionian cosmology, but belonged to a more primitive era. Again, the society depicted by Hesiod, the later of the "two" great epic poets, is a far cry from that of the Greek *Polis,* for between the two had occurred the breakdown of the power of the noble aristocracy, a breakdown that made possible the free growth of city life in mainland Greece. Neither the heroic life depicted in the *Iliad* nor the domination of the landed nobility depicted in the poems of Hesiod was the setting in which Greek philosophy grew up: on the contrary, early Greek philosophy, though naturally the work of individuals, was also the product of the City and reflected to a certain extent the reign of law and the conception of law which the pre-Socratics systematically extended to the whole universe in their cosmologies. Thus in a sense there is a certain continuity between the Homeric conception of an ultimate law or destiny or will governing gods and men, the Hesiodic picture of the world and the poet's moral demands, and the early Ionian cosmology. When social life was settled, men could turn to rational reflection, and in the period of philosophy's childhood it was Nature as a whole which first occupied their attention. From the psychological standpoint this is only what one would expect.

Thus, although it is undeniable that Greek philosophy arose among a people whose civilisation went back to the pre-historic times of Greece, what we call early Greek philosophy was "early" only in relation to subsequent Greek philosophy and the flowering of Greek thought and culture on the mainland; in relation to the preceding centuries of Greek development it may be looked on rather as the fruit of a mature civilisation, marking the closing period of Ionian greatness on the one hand and ushering in on the other hand the splendour of Hellenic, particularly of Athenian, culture.[3]

We have represented early Greek philosophic thought as the ultimate product of the ancient Ionian civilisation; but it must be remembered that Ionia forms, as it were, the meeting-place of West and East, so that the question may be raised whether or not Greek philosophy was due to Oriental influences, whether, for instance, it was borrowed from Babylon or Egypt. This view has been maintained, but has had to be abandoned. The Greek philosophers and writers know nothing of it—even Herodotus, who was so eager to run his pet theory as to the Egyptian origins of Greek religion and civilization—and the Oriental-origin theory is due mainly to Alexandrian writers, from whom it was taken over by Christian apologists. The Egyptians of Hellenistic times, for instance, interpreted their myths according to the ideas of Greek philosophy, and then asserted that their myths were the origin of the Greek philosophy. But this is simply an instance of allegorising on the part of the Alexandrians: it has no more objective value than the Jewish notion that Plato drew his wisdom from the Old Testament. There would, of course, be difficulties in explaining *how* Egyptian thought could be transmitted to the Greeks (traders are not the sort of people we would expect to convey philosophic notions), but, as has been remarked by Burnet, it is practically a waste of time to inquire whether the philosophical ideas of this or that Eastern people could be communicated to the Greeks or not, unless we have first ascertained that the people in question really possessed a philosophy.[3] That the Egyptians had a philosophy to communicate has never been shown, and it is out of the question to suppose that Greek philosophy came from India or from China.[4]

But there is a further point to be considered. Greek philosophy was closely bound up with mathematics, and it has been maintained that the Greeks derived their mathematics from Egypt and their astronomy from Babylonia. Now, that Greek mathematics were influenced by Egypt and Greek astronomy by Babylon is more than probable: for one thing, Greek science and philosophy began to develop in that very region where interchange with the East was most to be expected. But that is not the same as saying that Greek scientific mathematics *derive* from Egypt or their astronomy from Babylon. Detailed arguments left aside, let it suffice to point out that Egyptian mathematics consisted of empirical, rough and ready methods of obtaining a practical result. Thus Egyptian geometry largely consisted of practical methods of marking out afresh the fields after the inundation of the river Nile. Scientific geometry was not developed by them, but it was developed by the Greeks. Similarly Babylonian astronomy was pursued with a view to divination: it was mainly astrology, but among the Greeks it became a scientific pursuit. So even if we grant that the practical gardener-mathematics of the Egyptians and the astronomical observations of Babylonian astrologers influenced the Greeks and supplied them with preliminary material, this admission is in no way prejudicial to the originality of the Greek genius. Science and Thought, as distinct from mere practical calculation and astrological lore, were the result of the Greek genius and were due neither to the Egyptians nor to the Babylonians.

The Greeks, then, stand as the uncontested original thinkers and scientists of Europe.[5] They first sought knowledge for its own sake, and pursued knowledge in a scientific, free and unprejudiced spirit. Moreover, owing to the character of Greek religion, they were free from any priestly class that might have strong traditions and unreasoned doctrines of their own, tenaciously held and imparted only to a few, which might hamper the development of free science. Hegel, in his history of philosophy, dismisses Indian philosophy rather curtly, on the ground that it is identical with Indian religion. While admitting the presence of philosophical *notions,* he maintains that these do not take the form of *thought,* but are couched in poetical and symbolic form, and have, like religion, the practical purpose of freeing men from the illusions and unhappiness of life rather than knowledge for its own sake. Without committing oneself to agreement with Hegel's view of Indian philosophy (which has been far more clearly presented to the Western world in its purely philosophic aspects since the time of Hegel), one can agree with him that Greek philosophy was from the first *thought* pursued in the spirit of free science. It may with some have tended to take the place of religion, both from the point of view of belief and conduct; yet this was due to the inadequacy of Greek religion rather than to any mythological or mystical character in Greek philosophy. (It is not meant, of course, to belittle the place and function of "Myth" in Greek thought, nor yet the tendency of philosophy at certain times to pass into religion, e.g. with Plotinus. Indeed as regards myth, "In the earlier cosmologies of the Greek physicists the mythical and the rational elements interpenetrate in an as yet undivided unity." So Professor Werner Jaeger in *Aristotle, Fundamentals of the History of His Development,* p. 377.)

Professor Zeller emphasises the impartiality of the Greeks as they regarded the world about them, which in combination with their sense of reality and power of abstraction, "enabled them at a very early date to recognise their religious ideas for what they actually were—creations of an artistic imagination." [6] (This, of course, would scarcely hold good for the Greek people at large—the non-philosophical majority.) From the moment when the proverbial wisdom of the Wise Men and the myths of the poets were succeeded by the half-scientific, half-philosophic reflections and investigations of the Ionian cosmologists, art may be said to have been succeeded (logically, at any rate) by philosophy, which was to reach a splendid culmination in Plato and Aristotle, and at length in Plotinus to reach up to the heights where philosophy is transcended, not in mythology, but in mysticism. Yet there was no abrupt transition from "myth" to philosophy; one might even say that the Hesiodic theogony, for example, found a successor in Ionian cosmogonic speculation, the myth-element retreating before growing rationalisation yet not disappearing. Indeed it is present in Greek philosophy even in post-Socratic times.

The splendid achievement of Greek thought was cradled in Ionia; and if Ionia was the cradle of Greek philosophy, Miletus was the cradle of Ionian philosophy. For it was at Miletus that Thales, the reputedly earliest Ionian philosopher, flourished. The Ionian philosophers were profoundly impressed with the fact of change, of birth and growth, decay and death. Spring and Autumn in the external world of nature, childhood and old age in the life of man, coming-into-being and passing-away—these were the obvious and inescapable facts of the universe. It is a great mistake to suppose that the Greeks were happy and careless children of the sun, who only wanted to lounge in the porticoes of the cities and gaze at the magnificent works of art or at the achievements of their athletes. They were very conscious of the dark side of our existence on this planet, for against the background of sun and joy they saw the uncertainty and insecurity of man's life, the certainty of death, the darkness of the future. "The best for man were not to have been born and not to have seen the light of the sun; but, if once born (the second best for him is) to pass through the gates of death as speedily as may be," declares Theognis,[7] reminding us of the words of Calderón (so dear to Schopenhauer), "*El mayor delito del hombre, Es haber nacido.*" And the words of Theognis are re-echoed in the words of Sophocles in the *Oedipus Coloneus*, "Not to have been born exceeds every reckoning" . . . μὴ φῦναι τὸν ἅπαντα νικᾷ λόγον.[8]

Moreover, although the Greeks certainly had their ideal of moderation, they were constantly being lured away from it by the will to power. The constant fighting of the Greek cities among themselves, even at the heyday of Greek culture, and even when it was to their obvious interest to unite together against a common foe, the constant uprisings within the cities, whether led by an ambitious oligarch or a democratic demagogue, the venality of so many public men in Greek political life—even when the safety and honour of their city was at stake—all manifest the will to power which was so strong in the Greek. The Greek admired efficiency, he admired the ideal of the strong man who knows what he wants and has the power to get it; his conception of ἀρετή was largely that of ability to achieve success. As Professor De Burgh remarks, "The Greek would have regarded Napoleon as a man of pre-eminent arête." [9] For a very frank, or rather blatant, acknowledgment of the unscrupulous will to power, we have only to read the report that Thucydides gives of the conference between the representatives of Athens and those of Melos. The Athenians declare, "But you and we should say what we really think, and aim only at what is possible, for we both alike know that into the discussion of human affairs the question of justice only enters where the pressure of necessity is equal, and that the powerful exact what they can, and the weak grant what they must." Similarly in the celebrated words, "For of the Gods we believe, and of men we know, that by a law of their nature wherever they can rule they will. This law was not made by us, and we are not the first who have acted upon it; we did but inherit it, and shall bequeath it to all time, and we know that you and all mankind, if you were as strong as we are, would do as we do." [10] We could hardly ask for a more unashamed avowal of the will to power, and Thucydides gives no indication that he disapproved of the Athenian conduct. It is to be recalled that when the Melians eventually had to surrender, the Athenians put to death all those who were of military age, enslaved the women and children, and colonised the island with their own settlers—and all this at the zenith of Athenian splendour and artistic achievement.

In close connection with the will to power stands the conception of ὕβρις. The man who goes too far, who endeavours to be and to have more than Fate destines for him, will inevitably incur divine jealousy and come to ruin. The man or the nation who is possessed by the unbridled lust for self-assertion is driven headlong into reckless self-confidence and so to destruction. Blind passion breeds self-confidence, and overweening self-confidence ends in ruin.

It is as well to realise this side of the Greek character: Plato's condemnation of the "Might is Right" theory becomes then all the more remarkable. While not agreeing, of course, with Nietzsche's valuations, we cannot but admire his perspicacity in seeing the relation between the Greek culture and the will to power. Not, of course, that the dark side of Greek culture is the only side—far from it. If the drive of the will to power is a fact, so is the Greek ideal of moderation and harmony a fact. We must realise that there are two sides to the Greek character and culture: there is the side of moderation, of art, of Apollo and the Olympian deities, and there is the side of excess, unbridled self-assertion, of Dionysian frenzy, as seen portrayed in the *Bacchae* of Euripides. As beneath the splendid achievements of Greek culture we see the abyss of slavery, so beneath the dream-world of Olympian religion and Olympian art we see the abyss of Dionysian frenzy, of pessimism and of all manner of lack of moderation. It may, after all, not be entirely fanciful to suppose, inspired by the thought of Nietzsche, that there can be seen in much of the Olympian religion a self-imposed check on the part of the Dionysian Greek. Driven on by the will to power to self-destruction, the Greek creates the Olympian dream-world, the gods of which watch over him with jealousy to see that he does not transgress the limits of human endeavour. So does he express his consciousness that the tumultuous forces in his soul would be ultimately ruinous to him. (This interpretation is not of course offered as an account of the origin of the Greek Olympian religion from the scientific viewpoint of the historian of religion: it is only meant to suggest psychological factors—provisions of "Nature," if you like—that may have been operative, even if unconsciously, in the soul of the Greek.)

To return from this digression. In spite of the melancholic side of the Greek, his perception of the constant process

of change, of transition from life to death and from death
to life, helped to lead him, in the person of the Ionian philosophers, to a beginning of philosophy; for these wise men
saw that, in spite of all the change and transition, there
must be something permanent. Why? Because the change
is from something into something else. There must be something which is primary, which persists, which takes various
forms and undergoes this process of change. Change cannot be merely a conflict of opposites; thoughtful men were
convinced that there was something behind these opposites, something that was primary. Ionian philosophy or cosmology is therefore mainly an attempt to decide what this
primitive element or *Urstoff*[11] of all things is, one philosopher
deciding for one element, another for another element. What
particular element each philosopher decided on as his
Urstoff is not so important as the fact that they had in
common this idea of Unity. The fact of change, of motion
in the Aristotelian sense, suggested to them the notion of
unity, though, as Aristotle says, they did not explain motion.

The Ionians differed as to the character of their *Urstoff*,
but they all held it to be material—Thales plumping for
water, Anaximenes for air, Heraclitus for fire. The antithesis
between spirit and matter had not yet been grasped; so that,
although they were *de facto* materialists—in that they
assigned a form of matter as the principle of unity and
primitive stuff of all things—they can scarcely be termed
materialists in our sense of the word. It is not as though
they conceived a clear distinction between spirit and matter, and then denied it; they were not fully conscious of the
distinction, or at least they did not realise its implications.

One might be tempted, therefore, to say that the Ionian
thinkers were not philosophers so much as primitive scientists, trying to account for the material and external world.
But it must be remembered that they did not stop short
at *sense*, but went beyond appearance to *thought*. Whether
water or air or fire be assigned as the *Urstoff*, it certainly
does not *appear* as such, i.e. as the ultimate element. In
order to arrive at the conception of any of these as the
ultimate element of all things it is necessary to go beyond
appearance and sense. And they did not arrive at their
conclusions through a scientific, experimental approach, but
by means of the speculative reason: the unity posited is indeed a material unity, but it is a unity posited by thought.

Moreover, it is abstract—abstracting, that is to say, from the data of appearance—even if materialist. Consequently we might perhaps call the Ionian cosmologies instances of *abstract materialism:* we can already discern in them the notion of unity in difference and of difference as entering into unity: and this is a philosophic notion. In addition the Ionian thinkers were convinced of the reign of law in the universe. In the life of the individual ὕβρις, the overstepping of what is right and proper for man, brings ruin in its train, the redressing of the balance; so, by extension to the universe, cosmic law reigns, the preservation of a balance and the prevention of chaos and anarchy. This conception of a law-governed universe, a universe that is no plaything of mere caprice or lawless spontaneity, no mere field for lawless and "egoistic" domination of one element over another, formed a basis for a scientific cosmology as opposed to fanciful mythology.

From another point of view, however, we may say that with the Ionians science and philosophy are not yet distinguished. The early Ionian thinkers or wise men pursued all sorts of scientific considerations, astronomical for instance, and these were not clearly separated from philosophy. They were Wise Men, who might make astronomical observations for the sake of navigation, try to find out the one primary element of the universe, plan out feats of engineering, etc., and all without making any clear distinction between their various activities. Only that mixture of history and geography, which was known as ἱστορίη, was separated off from the philosophico-scientific activities, and that not always very clearly. Yet as real philosophic notions and real speculative ability appear among them, as since they form a stage in the development of the classical Greek philosophy, they cannot be omitted from the history of philosophy as though they were mere children whose innocent babblings are unworthy of serious attention. The first beginnings of European philosophy cannot be a matter of indifference to the historian.

Chapter Three

THE PIONEERS:
EARLY IONIAN PHILOSOPHERS

1. Thales

The mixture of philosopher and practical scientist is seen
very clearly in the case of Thales of Miletus. Thales is said
to have predicted the eclipse of the sun mentioned by
Herodotus[1] as occurring at the close of the war between
the Lydians and the Medes. Now, according to the calculations of astronomers, an eclipse, which was probably visible
in Asia Minor, took place on May 28th, 585 B.C. So if the
story about Thales is true, and if the eclipse which he fore-
told is the eclipse of 585, then he must have flourished in
the early part of the sixth century B.C. He is said to have
died shortly before the fall of Sardis in 546/5 B.C. Among
other scientific activities ascribed to Thales are the construction of an almanac and the introduction of the Phoeni-
cian practice of steering a ship's course by the Little Bear.
Anecdotes narrated about him, which may be read in the
life of Thales by Diogenes Laërtius, e.g. that he fell into
a well or ditch while star-gazing, or that, foreseeing a scar-
city of olives, he made a corner in oil, are probably just
tales of the type easily fathered on a Sage or Wise Man.[2]

In the *Metaphysics* Aristotle asserts that according to
Thales the earth is superimposed upon water (apparently
regarding it as a flat floating disc). But the most important
point is that Thales declared the primary stuff of all things
to be water . . . indeed, that he raised the question of the
One at all. Aristotle conjectures that observation may have

led Thales to this conclusion, "getting the notion perhaps from seeing that the nutriment of all things is moist, and that heat itself is generated from the moist and kept alive by it (and that from which they come to be is a principle of all things). He got his notion from this fact, and from the fact that the seeds of all things have a moist nature, and water is the origin of the nature of moist things." [3] Aristotle also suggests, though with diffidence, to be sure, that Thales was influenced by the older theologies, wherein water—as the Styx of the poets—was the object of adjuration among the gods. However this may be, it is clear that the phenomenon of evaporation suggests that water may become mist or air, while the phenomenon of freezing might suggest that, if the process were carried further, water could become earth. In any case the importance of this early thinker lies in the fact that he raised the question, what is the ultimate nature of the world; and not in the answer that he actually gave to that question or in his reasons, be they what they may, for giving that answer.

Another statement attributed to Thales by Aristotle, that all things are full of gods, that the magnet has a soul because it moves iron,[4] cannot be interpreted with certainty. To declare that this statement asserts the existence of a world-soul, and then to identify this world-soul with God[5] or with the Platonic Demiurge[6]—as though the latter formed all things out of water—is to go too far in freedom of interpretation. The only certain and the only really important point about Thales' doctrine is that he conceived "things" as varying forms of one primary and ultimate element. That he assigns *water* as this element is his distinguishing historical characteristic, so to speak, but he earns his place as the First Greek philosopher from the fact that he first conceives the notion of Unity in Difference (even if he does not isolate the notion on to the logical plane), and, while holding fast to the idea of unity, endeavours to account for the evident diversity of the many. Philosophy naturally tries to understand the plurality that we experience, its existence and nature, and to understand in this connection means, for the philosopher, to discover an underlying unity or first principle. The complexity of the problem cannot be grasped until the radical distinction between matter and spirit has been clearly apprehended: before this has been apprehended (and indeed even after its apprehension, if, once "apprehended," it is then denied), *simpliste* solutions of the problem are bound to suggest themselves: reality will be conceived as a material unity (as in the thought of Thales) or as Idea (as in certain modern philosophies). Justice can be done to the complexity of the problem of the One and the Many only if the essential degrees of reality and the doctrine of the analogy of being are clearly understood and unambiguously maintained: otherwise the richness of the manifold will be sacrificed to a false and more or less arbitrarily conceived unity.

It is indeed possible that the remark concerning the magnet being alive, attributed by Aristotle to Thales, represents the lingering-on of a primitive animism, in which the concept of the anima-phantasma (the shadowy double of a man that is perceived in dreams) came to be extended to sub-human organic life, and even to the forces of the inorganic world; but, even if this is so, it is but a relic, since in Thales we see clearly the transition from myth to science and philosophy, and he retains his traditional character as initiator of Greek philosophy, ἀλλὰ Θαλῆς μὲν ὁ τῆς τοιαύτης ἀρχηγὸς φιλοσοφίας.[7]

2. *Anaximander*

Another philosopher of Miletus was Anaximander. He was apparently a younger man than Thales, for he is described by Theophrastus as an "associate" of Thales.[8] Like him, Anaximander busied himself with practical scientific pursuits, and is credited with having constructed a map—probably for the Milesian sailors on the Black Sea. Participating in political life, as so many other Greek philosophers, he led a colony to Apollonia.

Anaximander composed a prose-work on his philosophical theories. This was extant in the time of Theophrastus, and we are indebted to the latter for valuable information as to the thought of Anaximander. He sought, like Thales, for the primary and ultimate element of all things; but he decided that it could not be any one particular kind of matter, such as water, since water or the moist was itself one of the "opposites," the conflicts and encroachments of which had to be explained. If change, birth and death, growth and decay, are due to conflict, to the encroachment of one element at the expense of another, then—on the supposition that everything is in reality water—it is hard to see why the other elements have not long ago been absorbed in water. Anaximander therefore arrived at the idea, the primary element, the *Urstoff*, is indeterminate. It is more primitive than the opposites, being that out of which they come and that into which they pass away.[9]

This primary element (ἀρχή) was called by Anaximander —and, according to Theophrastus, he was the first so to call it—the material cause. "It is neither water nor any other of the so-called elements, but a nature different from them and infinite, from which arise all the heavens and worlds within them." It is τὸ ἄπειρον, the subtance without limits. "Eternal and ageless" it "encompasses all the worlds."[10]

The encroachments of one element on another are poetically represented as instances of injustice, the warm element committing an injustice in summer and the cold in winter. The determinate elements make reparation for their injustice by being absorbed again into the Indeterminate Boundless.[11] This is an instance of the extension of the conception of law from human life to the universe at large.

There is a plurality of co-existent worlds which are innumerable.[12] Each is perishable, but there seems to be an unlimited number of them in existence at the same time, the worlds coming into being through eternal motion. "And in addition there was an eternal motion in which the heavens came to be."[13] This eternal motion seems to have been an ἀπόκρισις or "separating off," a sort of sifting in a sieve, as we find in the Pythagorean doctrine represented in the *Timaeus* of Plato. Once things had been separated off, the world as we know it was formed by a vortex movement or δίνη—the heavier elements, earth and water, remaining in the centre of the vortex, fire going back to the circumference and air remaining in between. The earth is not a disc, but a short cylinder "like the drum of a pillar."[14]

Life comes from the sea, and by means of adaptation to environment the present forms of animals were evolved. Anaximander makes a clever guess as to the origin of man. "... he further says that in the beginning man was born from animals of another species, for while other animals quickly find nourishment for themselves, man alone needs a lengthy period of suckling, so that had he been originally as he is now, he could never have survived."[15] He does not explain—a perennial difficulty for evolutionists—how man survived in the transition stage.

The Doctrine of Anaximander shows an advance, then, on that of Thales. He proceeds beyond the assignation of any one determinate element as primary to the conception of an Indeterminate Infinite, out of which all things come. Moreover, he makes some attempt at least to answer the question *how* the world developed out of this primary element.

3. Anaximenes

The third philosopher of the Milesian School was Anaximenes. He must have been younger than Anaximander—at least Theophrastus says that he was an "associate" of Anaximander. He wrote a book, of which a small fragment has survived. According to Diogenes Laërtius, "he wrote in the pure unmixed Ionic dialect."

The doctrine of Anaximenes appears, at first sight at any rate, to be a decided retrogression from the stage reached by Anaximander, for Anaximenes, abandoning the theory of τὸ ἄπειρον, follows Thales in assigning a determinate element as the *Urstoff*. This determinate element is not water, but *Air*. This may have been suggested to him by the fact of breathing, for man lives so long as he breathes, and it might easily appear that air is the principle of life. In fact, Anaximenes draws a parallel between man and nature in general. "Just as our soul, being air, holds us together, so do breath and air encompass the whole world." [16] Air then is the *Urstoff* of the world, from which the things that are and have been and shall be, the gods and things divine, arose, while other things come from its offspring." [17]

But there is obviously a difficulty in explaining how all things came from air, and it is in his proffered solution to this difficulty that Anaximenes shows a trace of genius. In order to explain how concrete objects are formed from the primitive element, he introduces the notion of condensation and rarefaction. Air in itself is invisible, but it becomes visible in this process of condensation and rarefaction, becoming fire as it is dilated or rarefied; wind, cloud, water, earth and finally stones, as it is condensed. And indeed this notion of condensation and rarefaction suggests another reason why Anaximenes fixed on air as the

primary element. He thought that, when air becomes rarefied, it becomes warmer and so tends to fire; while when
it becomes condensed, it grows colder and tends towards
the solid. Air then stands midway between the circumam-
bient ring of flame and the cold, moist mass within it, and
Anaximenes fixes on air as a sort of half-way house. The
important point in his doctrine, however, may be said to
be his attempt to found all quality on quantity—for that
is what his theory of condensation and rarefaction amounts
to in modern terminology. (We are told that Anaximenes
pointed out that when we breathe with the mouth open,
the air is warm; while when we breathe with the mouth
shut, the air is cold—an experimental proof of his position.)[18]

As with Thales, the earth is conceived as flat. It floats
on the air like a leaf. In the words of Professor Burnet,
"Ionia was never able to accept the scientific view of the
earth, and even Democritus continued to believe it was
flat."[19] Anaximenes gave a curious explanation of the rain-
bow. It is due to the sun's rays falling on a thick cloud,
which they cannot penetrate. Zeller remarks that it is a
far cry from Iris, Homer's living messenger of the gods, to
this "scientific" explanation.[20]

With the fall of Miletus in 494, the Milesian School must
have come to an end. The Milesian doctrines as a whole
came to be known as the philosophy of Anaximenes, as
though in the eyes of the ancients he was the most important representative of the School. Doubtless his historical
position as the last of the School would be sufficient to
explain this, though his theory of condensation and rarefaction—the attempt to explain the properties of the concrete objects of the world by a reduction of quality to
quantity—was probably also largely responsible.

In general we may once more repeat that the main importance of the Ionians lies in the fact that they raised the
question as to the ultimate nature of things, rather than
in any particular answer which they gave to the question
raised. We may also point out that they all assume the
eternity of matter: the idea of an absolute beginning of this
material world does not enter into their heads. Indeed for
them *this* world is the only world. It would scarcely be correct, however to regard the Ionian cosmologists as dogmatic
materialists. The distinction between matter and spirit had
as yet not been conceived, and, until this happened, there

could hardly be materialists in our sense. They were materialists in the sense that they tried to explain the origin of all things out of some material element: but they were not materialists in the sense of deliberately denying a distinction between matter and spirit, for the very good reason that the distinction had not been so clearly conceived that its formal denial was possible.

It scarcely needs to be indicated that the Ionians were "dogmatists," in the sense that they did not raise the "critical problem." They assumed that we could know things as they are: they were filled with the *naïveté* of wonder and the joy of discovery.

Chapter Four

THE PYTHAGOREAN SOCIETY

It is important to realise that the Pythagoreans were not
merely a crowd of disciples of Pythagoras, more or less
independent and isolated from one another: they were members of a religious society or community, which was founded
by Pythagoras, a Samian, at Kroton in South Italy in the
second half of the sixth century B.C. Pythagoras himself
was an Ionian, and the earlier members of the School spoke
the Ionic dialect. The origins of the Pythagorean Society,
like the life of the founder, are shrouded in obscurity.
Iamblichus, in his life of Pythagoras, calls him "leader and
father of divine philosophy," "a god, a 'demon' (i.e. a super-
human being), or a divine man." But the Live of Pythagoras by Iamblichus, Porphyry and Diogenes Laërtius, can
hardly be said to afford us reliable testimony, and it is
doubtless right to call them romances.[1]

To found a school was probably not new in the Greek
world. Although it cannot be proved definitely, it is highly
probable that the early Milesian philosophers had what
amounted pretty well to Schools about them. But the Pythagorean School had a distinguishing characteristic, namely,
its ascetic and religious character. Towards the end of the
Ionian civilisation there took place a religious revival,
attempting to supply genuine religious elements, which
were catered for neither by the Olympian mythology nor
by the Milesian cosmology. Just as in the Roman Empire,
a society verging towards its decline, its pristine vigour
and freshness lost, we see a movement to scepticism on

the one hand and to "mystery religions" on the other hand, so at the close of the rich and commercial Ionian civilisation we find the same tendencies. The Pythagorean Society represents the spirit of this religious revival, which it combined with a strongly marked scientific spirit, this latter of course being the factor which justifies the inclusion of the Pythagoreans in a history of philosophy. There is certainly common ground between Orphicism and Pythagoreanism, though it is not altogether easy to determine the precise relations of the one to the other, and the degree of influence that the teaching of the Orphic sect may have had on the Pythagoreans. In Orphicism we certainly find an organisation in communities bound together by initiation and fidelity to a common way of life, as also the doctrine of the transmigration of souls—a doctrine conspicuous in Pythagorean teaching—and it is hard to think that Pythagoras was uninfluenced by the Orphic beliefs and practices, even if it is with Delos that Pythagoras is to be connected, rather than with the Thracian Dionysian religion.[2]

The view has been held that the Pythagorean communities were *political* communities, a view, however, that cannot be maintained, at least in the sense that they were essentially political communities—which they certainly were not. Pythagoras, it is true, had to leave Kroton for Metapontum on the instance of Cylon; but it seems that this can be explained without having to suppose any specifically political activities on the part of Pythagoras in favour of any particular party. The Pythagoreans did, however, obtain political control in Kroton and other cities of Magna Graecia, and Polybius tells us that their "lodges" were burnt down and they themselves subjected to persecution—perhaps about 440-430 B.C.,[3] though this fact does not necessarily mean that they were an essentially political rather than a religious society. Calvin ruled at Geneva, but he was not primarily a politician. Professor Stace remarks: "When the plain citizen of Crotona was told not to eat beans, and that under no circumstances could he eat his own dog, this was too much"[4] (though indeed it is not certain that Pythagoras prohibited beans or even all flesh as articles of food. Aristoxenus affirms the very opposite as regards the beans.[5] Burnet, who is inclined to accept the prohibitions as Pythagorean, nevertheless admits the possibility of Aristoxenus being right about the taboo on beans).[6] The Society revived after some years and continued its activities in Italy, notably at Tarentum, where in the first half of the fourth century B.C. Archytas won for himself a reputation. Philolaus and Eurytus also worked in that city.

As to the religious-ascetic ideas and practices of the Pythagoreans, these centred round the idea of purity and purification, the doctrine of the transmigration of souls naturally leading to the promotion of soul-culture. The practice of silence, the influence of music and the study of mathematics were all looked on as valuable aids in tending the soul. Yet some of their practices were of a purely external character. If Pythagoras really did forbid the eating of flesh-meat, this may easily have been due to, or at least connected with, the doctrine of metempsychosis; but such purely external rules as are quoted by Diogenes Laërtius as having been observed by the School can by no stretch of the imagination be called philosophical doctrines. For example, to abstain from beans, not to walk in the main street, not to stand upon the parings of your nails, to efface the traces of a pot in the ashes, not to sit down on a bushel, etc. And if this were all that the Pythagorean doctrines contained, they might be of interest to the historian of religion, but would hardly merit serious attention from the historian of philosophy. However, these external rules of observance by no means comprise all that the Pythagoreans had to offer.

(In discussing briefly the theories of the Pythagoreans, we cannot say how much was due to Pythagoras himself, and how much was due to later members of the School, e.g. to Philolaus. And Aristotle in the *Metaphysics* speaks of the Pythagoreans rather than of Pythagoras himself. So that if the phrase, "Pythagoras held . . ." is used, it should not be understood to refer necessarily to the founder of the School in person.)

In his life of Pythagoras, Diogenes Laërtius tells us of a poem of Xenophanes, in which the latter relates how Pythagoras, seeing somebody beating a dog, told him to stop, since he had recognised the voice of a friend in the yelping of a dog. Whether the tale be true or not, the ascription to Pythagoras of the doctrine of metempsychosis may be accepted. The religious revival had brought to fresh life the old idea of the power of the soul and its continued vigour after death—a contrast to the Homeric conception of the gibbering shades of the departed. In such a doctrine as that of the transmigration of souls, the consciousness of personal identity, self-consciousness, is not held in mind or is not regarded as bound up with soul, for in the words of Dr. Julius Stenzel: ". . . *die Seele wandert von Ichzustand zu Ichzustand, oder, was dasselbe ist, von Leib zu Leib; denn die Einsicht, dass zum Ich der Leib gehört, war dem philosophischen Instinkt der Griechen immer selbstverständlich.*" [7] The theory of the soul as the harmony of the body, which is proposed by Simmias in Plato's *Phaedo* and attacked by Plato, would hardly fit in with the Pythagorean view of the Soul as immortal and as undergoing transmigration; so the ascription of this view to the Pythagoreans (Macrobius refers expressly to Pythagoras and Philolaus) [8] is at least doubtful. Yet, as Dr. Praechter points out, it is not out of the question if the statement that the soul was harmony of the body, or *tout simple* a harmony, could be taken to mean that it was the principle of order and life in the body. This would not necessarily compromise the soul's immortality.[9]

(The similarity in several important points between Orphicism and Pythagoreanism may be due to an influence exerted by the former on the latter; but it is very hard to determine if there actually was any direct influence, and if there was, how far it extended. Orphicism was connected with the worship of Dionysus, a worship that came to Greece from Thrace or Scythia, and was alien to the spirit of the Olympian cult, even if its "enthusiastic" and "ecstatic" character found an echo in the soul of the Greek. But it is not the "enthusiastic" character of the Dionysian religion which connects Orphicism with Pythagoreanism; rather it is the fact that the Orphic initiates, who, be it noted, were organised in communities, were taught the doctrine of the transmigration of souls, so that for them it is the soul, and not the imprisoning body, which is the important part of man; in fact, the soul is the "real" man, and is not the mere shadow-image of the body, as it appears in Homer. Hence the importance of soul-training and soul-purification, which included the observance of such precepts as avoidance of flesh-meat. Orphicism was indeed a religion rather than a philosophy—though it tended towards Pantheism, as may be seen from the famous fragment Ζεὺς κεφαλή, Ζεὺς μέσσα, Διὸς δ' ἐκ πάντα τέτυκται [10];

but, in so far as it can be called a philosophy, it was a *way of life* and not mere cosmological speculation, and in this respect Pythagoreanism was certainly an inheritor of the Orphic spirit.)

To turn now to the difficult subject of the Pythagorean mathematico-metaphysical philosophy. Aristotle tells us in the *Metaphysics* that "the Pythagoreans, as they are called, devoted themselves to mathematics, they were the first to advance this study, and having been brought up in it they thought its principles were the principles of all things . . ." [11] They had the enthusiasm of the early students of an advancing science, and they were struck by the importance of number in the world. All things are numerable, and we can express many things numerically. Thus the relation between two related things may be expressed according to numerical proportion: order between a number of ordered subjects may be numerically expressed, and so on. But what seems to have struck them particularly was the discovery that the musical intervals between the notes on the lyre may be expressed numerically. Pitch may be said to depend on number, in so far as it depends on the lengths, and the intervals on the scale may be expressed by numerical ratios. [12] Just as musical harmony is dependent on number, so it might be thought that the harmony of the universe depends on number. The Milesian cosmologists spoke of a conflict of opposites in the universe, and the musical investigations of the Pythagoreans may easily have suggested to them the idea of a solution to the problem of the "conflict" through the concept of number. Aristotle says: "since they saw that the attributes and the ratios of the musical scales were expressible in numbers; since then all other things seemed in their whole nature to be modelled after numbers, and numbers seemed to be the first things in the whole of nature, and the whole heaven to be a musical scale and a number." [13]

Now Anaximander had produced everything from the Unlimited or Indeterminate, and Pythagoras combined with this notion that of the Limit, or τὸ πέρας, which gives form to the Unlimited. This is exemplified in music (in health too, where the limit is the "tempering," which results in the harmony that is health), in which proportion and harmony are arithmetically expressible. Transferring this to the world at large, the Pythagoreans spoke of the cosmical harmony. But, not content with stressing the important part played by numbers in the universe, they went further and declared that things *are* numbers.

This is clearly not an easy doctrine to understand, and it is a hard saying that all things are numbers. What did the Pythagoreans mean by this? First of all, what did they mean by numbers, or how did they think of numbers? This is an important question, for the answer to it suggests one reason why the Pythagoreans said that things are numbers. Now, Aristotle tells us that "(the Pythagoreans) hold that the elements of number are the even and the odd, and of these the former is unlimited and the latter limited; and the I proceeds from both of these (for it is both even and odd), and number from the I; and the whole heaven, as has been said, is numbers." [14] Whatever precise period of Pythagorean development Aristotle may be referring to, and whatever be the precise interpretation to be put on his remarks concerning the even and the odd, it seems clear that the Pythagoreans regarded numbers spatially. One is the point, two is the line, three is the surface, four is the solid.[15] To say then that all things are numbers, would mean that "all bodies consist of points or units in space, which when taken together constitute a number." [16] That the Pythagoreans regarded numbers in this way is indicated by the "tetraktys," a figure which they regarded as sacred.

This figure shows to the eye that ten is the sum of one, two, three and four; in other words, of the first four integers. Aristotle tells us that Eurytus used to represent numbers by pebbles, and it is in accord with such a method of representation that we get the "square" and the "oblong" numbers.[17] If we start with one and add odd numbers successively in the form of "gnomons," we get square numbers,

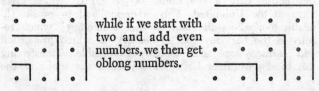

while if we start with two and add even numbers, we then get oblong numbers.

This use of figured numbers or connection of numbers with geometry clearly makes it easier to understand how the Pythagoreans regarded things as being numbers, and not merely as being numerable. They transferred their mathematical conceptions to the order of material reality. Thus "by the juxtaposition of several points a line is generated, not merely in the scientific imagination of the mathematician, but in external reality also; in the same way the surface is generated by the juxtaposition of several lines, and finally the body by the combination of several surfaces. Points, lines and surfaces are therefore the real units which compose all bodies in nature, and in this sense all bodies must be regarded as numbers. In fact, every material body is an expression of the number Four (τετρακτύς), since it results, as a fourth term, from three constituent elements (Points, Lines, Surfaces)." [18] But how far the identification of things with numbers is to be ascribed to the habit of representing numbers by geometrical patterns, and how far to an extension to all reality of Pythagorean discoveries in regard to music, it is extremely difficult to say. Burnet thinks that the original identification of things with numbers was due to an extension of the discovery that musical sounds can be reduced to numbers, and not to an identification of numbers with geometrical figures. [19] Yet if objects are regarded—as the Pythagoreans apparently regarded them—as sums of material quantitative points, and if, at the same time, numbers are regarded geometrically as sums of points, it is easy to see how the further step, that of identifying objects with numbers, could be taken. [20]

Aristotle, in the above-quoted passage, declares that the Pythagoreans held that "the elements of number are the even and the odd, and of these the former is unlimited and the latter limited." How do the limited and the unlimited come into the picture? For the Pythagoreans the limited cosmos or world is surrounded by the unlimited or boundless cosmos (air) which it "inhales." The objects of the limited cosmos are thus not pure limitation, but have an admixture of the unlimited. Now, the Pythagoreans, regarding numbers geometrically, considered that they also (composed of the even and the odd) are products of the limited and the unlimited. From this point of view too, then, it is but an easy step to the identification of numbers with things, the even being identified with the unlimited and the odd with the limited. A contributory explanation may be seen in the fact that the odd gnomons (cf. figures) conserve a fixed quadratic shape (limited), while the even gnomons present a continually changing rectangular shape (unlimited).[21]

When it came to assigning definite numbers to definite things, scope was naturally allowed for all manner of arbitrary caprice and fancy. For example, although we may be able to see more or less why justice should be declared to be four, it is not so easy to see why καιρός should be seven or animation six. Five is declared to be marriage, because five is the product of three—the first masculine number, and two—the first feminine number. However, in spite of all these fanciful elements the Pythagoreans made a real contribution to mathematics. A knowledge of "Pythagoras' Theorem" as a geometrical fact is shown in Sumerian computations: the Pythagoreans, however, as Proclus remarked,[22] transcended mere arithmetical and geometrical facts, and digested them into a deductive system, though this was at first, of course, of an elementary nature. "Summing up the Pythagorean geometry, we may say that it covered the bulk of Euclid's Books i, ii, iv, vi (and probably iii), with the qualification that the Pythagorean theory of proportion was inadequate in that it did not apply to incommensurable magnitudes."[23] The theory which did solve this last arose under Eudoxus in the Academy.

To the Pythagoreans, not only was the earth spherical,[24] but it is not the centre of the universe. The earth and the planets revolve—along with the sun—round the central fire or "hearth of the Universe" (which is identified with the number One). The world inhales air from the boundless mass outside it, and the air is spoken of as the Unlimited. We see here the influence of Anaximenes. (According to Aristotle—*De Caelo*, 293, a 25-7—the Pythagoreans did not deny geocentricism in order to explain phenomena, but from arbitrary reasons of their own.)

The Pythagoreans are of interest to us, not only because of their musical and mathematical investigations; not only because of their character as a religious society; not only because through their doctrine of transmigration of souls and their mathematical metaphysic—at least in so far as they did not "materialise" numbers[25]—they tended to break away from the *de facto* materialism of the Milesian cosmologists; but also because of their influence on Plato, who was doubtless influenced by their conception of the soul (he probably borrowed from them the doctrine of the tripartite nature of the soul) and its destiny. The Pythagoreans were certainly impressed by the importance of the soul and its right tendance, and this was one of the most cherished convictions of Plato, to which he clung all his life. Plato was also strongly influenced by the mathematical speculations of the Pythagoreans—even if it is difficult to determine the precise extent of his debt to them in this respect. And to say of the Pythagoreans that they were one of the determining influences in the formation of the thought of Plato, is to pay them no mean tribute.

Chapter Five

THE WORD OF HERACLITUS

Heraclitus was an Ephesian noble and flourished, according to Diogenes, about the 69th Olympiad, i.e. *c.* 504-501 B.C.; his dates cannot be accurately determined. The office of *Basileus* was hereditary in his family, but Heraclitus relinquished it in favour of his brother. He was, we gather, a melancholy man, of aloof and solitary temperament, who expressed his contempt for the common herd of citizens, as also for the eminent men of the past. "The Ephesians," he said of the citizens of his own city, "would do well to hang themselves, every grown man of them, and leave the city to beardless lads; for they have cast out Hermodorus, the best man among them, saying, "We will have none who is best among us; if there be any such, let him be so elsewhere and among others." [1] Again he comments: "In Priene lived Bias, son of Teutamas, who is of more account than the rest." (He said: "Most men are bad.") [2]

Heraclitus expresses his opinion of Homer in the saying: "Homer should be turned out of the lists and whipped, and Archilochus likewise." Similarily he observed: "The learning of many things does not teach understanding, otherwise it would have taught Hesiod and Pythagoras, and again Xenophanes and Hecataeus." As for Pythagoras, he "practised scientific inquiry beyond all other men, and making a selection of these writings, claimed for his own wisdom what was but a knowledge of many things and an imposture." [3]

Many of Heraclitus' sayings are pithy and pungent in

character, if somewhat amusing on occasion. For example: "Physicians who cut, burn, stab and rack the sick, demand a fee for it which they do not deserve to get"; "Man is called a baby by God, even as a child by man"; "Asses prefer straw to gold"; "Man's character is his fate." [4] In regard to Heraclitus' attitude to religion, he had little respect for the mysteries, and even declares that "The mysteries practised among men are unholy mysteries." [5] Moreover, his attitude towards God was pantheistic, in spite of the religious language he employed.

The style of Heraclitus seems to have been somewhat obscure for he gained in later time the nickname of ὁ σκοτεινός. This practice appears to have been not altogether unintentional: at least we find among the fragments sentences such as: "Nature loves to hide"; "The lord whose is the oracle by Delphi neither utters nor hides its meaning, but shows it by a sign." And of his own message to mankind he says: "Men are as unable to understand it when they hear it for the first time, as before they have heard it at all." [6] Burnet points out that Pindar and Aeschylus possess the same prophetic tone, and attributes it in part to the contemporary religious revival. [7]

Heraclitus is known to many for the famous saying attributed to him, though apparently not his own: "All things are in a state of flux, πάντα ῥεῖ." Indeed this is all that many people know about him. This statement does not represent the kernel of his philosophic thought, though it does indeed represent an important aspect of his doctrine. Is he not responsible for the saying: "You cannot step twice into the same river, for fresh waters are ever flowing in upon you"? [8] Moreover, Plato remarks that "Heraclitus says somewhere that all things pass and nought abides; and comparing things to the current of a river, he says you cannot step twice into the same stream." [9] And Aristotle describes Heraclitus' doctrine as affirming that "All things are in motion, nothing steadfastly is." [10] In this respect Heraclitus is a Pirandello in the ancient world, crying out that nothing is stable, nothing abides, proclaiming the unreality of "Reality."

It would be a mistake, however, to suppose that Heraclitus meant to teach that there is nothing which changes, for this is contradicted by the rest of his philosophy. [11] Nor is the proclamation of change even the most important and significant feature of his philosophy. Heraclitus lays stress

on his "Word," i.e. on his special message to mankind, and
he could scarcely feel himself justified in doing this if the
message amounted to no more than the truth that things
are constantly changing; a truth seen by the other Ionian
philosophers and hardly bearing the character of novelty.
No, Heraclitus' original contribution to philosophy is to be
found elsewhere: it consists in the conception of unity in
diversity, difference in unity. In the philosophy of Anaximander, as we have seen, the opposites are regarded as
encroaching on one another, and then as paying in turn the
penalty for this act of injustice. Anaximander regards the
war of the opposites as something disorderly, something
that ought not to be, something that mars the purity of the
One. Heraclitus, however, does not adopt this point of view.
For him the conflict of opposites, so far from being a blot
on the unity of the One, is essential to the being of the
One. In fact, the One only exists in the tension of opposites:
this tension is essential to the unity of the One.

That Reality is One for Heraclitus is shown clearly enough
by his saying: "It is wise to hearken, not to me, but to my
Word, and to confess that all things are one." [12] On the
other hand, that the conflict of opposites is essential to
the existence of the One is also shown clearly by such statements as: "We must know that war is common to all and
strife is justice, and that all things come into being and
pass away through strife," [13] and Homer was wrong in
saying: "Would that strife might perish from among gods
and men!" He did not see that he was praying for the
destruction of the universe, for, if his prayer were heard, all
things would pass away.[14] Again, Heraclitus says positively:
"Men do not know how what is at variance agrees with
itself. It is an attunement of opposite tensions, like that of
the bow and the lyre." [15]

For Heraclitus, then, Reality is One; but it is many at the
same time—and that not merely accidentally, but essentially.
It is essential to the being and existence of the One that it
should be one and many at the same time; that it should
be Identity in Difference. Hegel's assignment of Heraclitus'
philosophy to the category of Becoming is therefore based
on a misconception—and also errs by putting Parmenides
earlier than Heraclitus, for Parmenides was a critic as well
as a contemporary of Heraclitus, and must be the later
writer.[16] The philosophy of Heraclitus corresponds much

more to the idea of the concrete universal, the One existing in the many, Identity in Difference.

But what is the One-in-many? For Heraclitus, as for the Stoics of later times, who borrowed the notion from him, the essence of all things is Fire. Now, it might seem at first sight that Heraclitus is merely ringing the changes on the old Ionian theme—as though because Thales made Reality to be Water and Anaximenes Air, Heraclitus, simply in order to find something different from his predecessors, fixed on Fire. Naturally, the wish to find a different *Urstoff* may have operated to a certain extent, but there was something more in his choice of Fire than that: he had a positive reason, and a very good reason for fixing on Fire, a reason bound up with the central thought of his philosophy.

Sense-experience tells us that fire lives by feeding, by consuming and transforming into itself heterogeneous matter. Springing up, as it were, from a multitude of objects, it changes them into itself, and without this supply of material it would die down and cease to exist. The very existence of the fire depends on this "strife" and "tension." This is, of course, a sensual symbolism of a genuine philosophic notion, but it clearly bears a relation to that notion that water or air will not so easily bear. Thus Heraclitus' choice of Fire as the essential nature of Reality was not due simply to arbitrary caprice on his part, nor merely to the desire for novelty, to the necessity of differing from his predecessors, but was suggested by his main philosophic thought. "Fire," he says, "is want and surfeit"—it is, in other words, all things that are, but it is these things in a constant state of tension, of strife, of consuming, of kindling and of going out.[17] In the process of fire Heraclitus distinguished two paths—the upward and the downward paths. "He called change the upward and the downward path and said that the cosmos comes into being in virtue of this. When fire is condensed it becomes moist, and under compression it turns to water; water being congealed is turned to earth, and this he calls the downward path. And, again, the earth is itself lique-fied and from it water comes, and from that everything else; for he refers almost everything to the evaporation from the sea. This is the upward path." [18]

However, if it be maintained that all things are fire, and are consequently in a constant state of flux, it is clear that some explanation must be offered of what appears at least to be the stable nature of things in the world. The explanation offered by Heraclitus is in terms of measure: the world is "an ever-living Fire, with measures of it kindling and measures going out." [19] So if Fire takes from things, transforming into itself by kindling, it also gives as much as it takes. "All things are an exchange for Fire, and Fire for all things, even as wares for gold and gold for wares." [20] Thus, while the substance of each kind of matter is always changing, the aggregate quantity of that kind of matter remains the same.

But it is not only the relative stability of things that Heraclitus tries to explain, but also the varying preponderance of one kind of matter over another, as seen in day and night, summer and winter. We learn from Diogenes that Heraclitus explained the preponderance of different elements as due to "the different exhalations." Thus "the bright exhalation, when ignited in the circle of the sun, produced day; and the preponderance of the opposite exhalation produced night. The increase of warmth proceeding from the bright exhalation produced summer; and the preponderance of moisture from the dark exhalation produced winter." [21]

There is, as we have seen, constant strife in the universe, and there is also a relative stability of things, due to the different measures of Fire, kindling or going out in more or less equal proportions. And it is the fact of this measure, of the balance of the upward and downward paths, which constitutes what Heraclitus calls the "hidden attunement of the Universe," and which he declares is "better than the open." [22] "Men," says Heraclitus is an already-quoted fragment, "do not know how what is at variance agrees with itself. It is an attunement of opposite tensions, like that of the bow and the lyre." [23] The One, in short, is its differences, and the differences are themselves one, they are different aspects of the one. Neither of the aspects, neither the upward nor the downward path, can cease: if they were to cease, then the One itself would no longer exist. This inseparability of opposites, the essential character of the different moments of the One, comes out in such sayings as: "The way up and the way down is the same," and "It is death to souls to become water, and death to water to become earth. But water comes from earth, and from water, soul." [24] It leads, of course, to a certain relativism, as in the statements that "Good and ill are one"; "The sea is the purest and the impurest water. Fish can drink it and it is good for them: to men it is undrinkable and destructive"; "Swine wash in the mire, and barnyard fowls in the dust." [25] However, in the One all tensions are reconciled, all differences harmonised: "To God all things are fair and good and right, but men hold some things wrong and some right." [26] This is, of course, the inevitable conclusion of a pantheistic philosophy—that everything is justified *sub specie aeternitatis*.

Heraclitus speaks of the One as God, and as wise: "The wise is one only. It is unwilling and willing to be called by the name of Zeus." [27] God is the universal Reason (Λόγος), the universal law immanent in all things, binding all things into a unity and determining the constant change in the universe according to universal law. Man's reason is a moment in this universal Reason, or a contraction and canalisation of it, and man should therefore strive to attain to the viewpoint of reason and to live by reason, realising the unity of all things and the reign of unalterable law, being content with the necessary process of the universe and not rebelling against it, inasmuch as it is the expression of the all-comprehensive, all-ordering Λόγος or Law. Reason and consciousness in man—the fiery element—are the valuable element: when the pure fire leaves the body, the water and earth which are left behind are worthless, a thought which Heraclitus expresses in the saying: "Corpses are more fit to be cast out than dung." [28] A man's interest, then, is to preserve his soul in as dry a state as possible: "The dry is the wisest and best." [29] It may be pleasure to souls to become moist, but all the same "it is death to soul to become water." [30] Souls should strive to rise above the private worlds of the "sleeping" to the common world of the "waking," i.e. to the common world of thought and reason. This thought is of course the Word of Heraclitus. There is, then, one immanent law and Reason in the universe, of which human laws should be the embodiment, though at best they can be but its imperfect and relative embodiment. By stressing universal law and man's participation in Reason, Heraclitus helped to pave the way for the universalist ideals of Stoicism.

This conception of universal, all-ordering Reason appears in the system of the Stoics, who borrowed their cosmology from Heraclitus. But we are not entitled to suppose that Heraclitus regarded the One, Fire, as a *personal* God, any more than Thales or Anaximenes regarded Water or Air as a personal God: Heraclitus was a pantheist, just as the Stoics in later times were pantheists. It is, however, true that the conception of God as the immanent, ordering Principle of all things, together with the moral attitude of acceptance of events as the expression of divine Law, tends to produce a psychological attitude that is at variance with what would seem to be logically demanded by the theoretical identification of God with the cosmic unity. This discrepancy between psychological attitude and the strict demands of theory became very clear in the Stoic School, the members of which so often betray a mental attitude and employ language that would suggest a theistic conception of God, rather than the pantheistic conception logically demanded by the cosmological system—a discrepancy which was aggravated among the later Stoics especially, owing to their increasing concentration on ethical questions.

Did Heraclitus teach the doctrine of a universal conflagration recurring periodically? As the Stoics certainly held this doctrine, and as they borrowed from Heraclitus, the doctrine of the periodic and universal conflagration has been attributed to Heraclitus too; but, for the following reasons, it does not seem possible to accept this attribution. In the first place, Heraclitus, as we have seen, insisted on the fact that the tension or conflict of opposites is essential to the very existence of the One. Now, if all things were periodically to relapse into pure fire, the fire itself should logically cease to exist. In the second place, does not Heraclitus expressly say that the "sun will not go beyond his measures; otherwise the Erinyes, the handmaids of Justice, will find him out," [31] and "this world was ever, is now, and ever shall be an ever-living Fire, with measures of it kindling and measures going out"? In the third place, Plato contrasts Heraclitus and Empedocles on the ground that, according to Heraclitus the One is always Many, while, according to Empedocles, the One is many and one by turns.[32] When Professor Zeller says: "It is a contradiction which he, and probably Plato too, has not observed," he is making an unwarrantable supposition. Of course, if it were clear from certain evidence that Heraclitus actually did teach the doctrine of a periodic general conflagration, then we should indeed have to conclude that the contradiction involved was unobserved by both Heraclitus himself and by Plato; but as evidence goes to show that Heraclitus did not teach this doctrine, we cannot reasonably be called upon to attribute a mistake to Plato in this matter. Moreover, it was apparently the Stoics who first stated that Heraclitus maintained the doctrine of a general conflagration;[33] and even the Stoics are divided on the subject. Does not Plutarch make a character say; "I see the Stoic conflagration spreading over the poems of Hesiod, just as it does over the writings of Heraclitus and the verses of Orpheus"?[34]

What are we to say of the doctrine of Heraclitus, the notion of unity in difference? That there is a many, a plurality, is clear enough. But at the same time the intellect constantly strives to conceive a unity, a system, to obtain a comprehensive view to link things up; and this goal of thought corresponds to a real unity in things: things *are* interdependent. Even man, with his immortal soul, depends on the rest of creation. His body depends, in a very real sense, on the whole past history of the world and of the human race: he depends on the material universe for life —bodily life through air, food, drink, sunlight, etc.—for his intellectual life too, through sensation as the starting-point of knowledge. He depends also for his cultural life on the thought and culture, the civilisation and development of the past. But though man is right in seeking a unity, it would be wrong to assert unity to the detriment of plurality. Unity, the only unity that is worth having, is a unity in difference, identity in diversity, a unity, that is to say, not of poverty, but of richness. Every material thing is a unity in diversity (consisting of molecules, atoms, electrons, etc.), every living organism also—even God Himself, as we know by Revelation, is Unity in Distinction of Persons. In Christ there is unity in diversity—unity of Person in diversity of Natures. The union of the Beatific Vision is a union in distinction—otherwise it would lose its richness (apart of course, from the impossibility of a "simple" unity of identification between God and creature).

Can we look on the created universe as a unity? The universe is certainly not a substance: it comprises a plurality of substance. It is, however, a totality in our idea of it, and if the law of the conservation of energy be valid, then it is in a sense a physical totality. The universe, then, may to a certain degree be considered a unity in diversity; but we may perhaps go further and suggest with Heraclitus that the conflict of opposites—change—is necessary to the existence of the material universe.

(i) As far as inorganic matter is concerned, change—at the very least in the sense of locomotion—is necessarily involved, at any rate if modern theories of the composition of matter, the theory of light, etc., are to be accepted.

(ii) This, too, is clear, that if there is to be finite, materially-conditioned life, then change is essential. The life of a bodily organism must be sustained by respiration, assimilation, etc., all of which processes involve change, and so the "conflict of opposites." The preservation of specific life on the planet involves reproduction, and birth and death may well be termed opposites.

(iii) Would it be possible to have a material universe in which there was no conflict of opposites, absolutely no change at all? In the first place, there could be no life in such a universe, for embodied life, as we have seen involves change. But would it be possible to have a material universe—in which there was no life—that was entirely static, entirely without change and movement? If matter be regarded in terms of energy, it is very hard to see how there could be any such purely static material universe. But, prescinding from all physical theories, even if such a universe were physically possible, could it be rationally possible? We could at least discover no possible function for such a universe—without life, without development, without change, a sort of primitive chaos.

A purely material universe seems, then, to be inconceivable not only *a posteriori* but also *a priori*. The idea of a material universe, in which organic life is present, demands change. But change means diversity on the one hand, for there must be a *terminus a quo* and a *terminus ad quem* of the change, and stability on the other hand, for there must be *something which changes*. And so there will be identity in diversity.

We conclude, then, that Heraclitus of Ephesus conceived a genuine philosophic notion, even though he pursued the same way of sensual symbolism as his Ionian predecessors, and this notion of the One as essentially many can be clearly discerned beneath all the sensual symbolism. Heraclitus did not indeed rise to the conception of substantial thought, the νόησις νοήσεως of Aristotle, nor did he sufficiently account for the element of stability in the universe as Aristotle tried to do; but, as Hegel says, "if we wish to consider fate so just as always to preserve to posterity what is best, we must at least say of what we have of Heraclitus, that it is worthy of this preservation." [35]

Chapter Six

THE ONE OF
PARMENIDES AND MELISSUS

The reputed founder of the Eleatic School was Xenophanes. However, as there is no real evidence that he ever went to Elea in Southern Italy, it is unlikely that he is to be accounted anything more than a tutelary founder, a patron of the School. It is not difficult to see why he was adopted as a patron by the School that held fast to the idea of the motionless One, when we consider some of the sayings attributed to him. Xenophanes attacks the anthropomorphic Greek deities: "If oxen and horses or lions had hands, and could paint with their hands, and produce works of art as men do, horses would paint the forms of the gods like horses, and oxen like oxen, and make their bodies in the image of their several kinds":[1] and substitutes in their place, "One god, the greatest among Gods and men, neither in form like unto mortals, nor in thought," who "abideth ever in the self same place, moving not at all; nor doth it befit him to go about now hither now thither." [2] Aristotle tells us in the *Metaphysics* that Xenophanes, "referring to the whole world, said the One was god." [3] Most probably, then, he was a monist and not a monotheist, and this interpretation of his "theology" would certainly be more compatible with the Eleatic attitude towards him than a theistic interpretation. A really monotheistic theology may be a familiar enough notion to us, but in the Greece of the period it would have been something exceptional.

But whatever the opinions of Xenophanes may have been,

the real founder of the Eleatic School from a philosophical
and historical viewpoint was undoubtedly Parmenides, a
citizen of Elea. Parmenides seems to have been born towards
the close of the sixth century B.C., since round about 451-449
B.C., when 65 years old, he conversed with the young Socrates at Athens. He is said to have drawn up laws for his
native city of Elea, and Diogenes preserves a statement of
Sotion to the effect that Parmenides began by being a Pythagorean, but afterwards abandoned that philosophy in favour
of his own.[4]

Parmenides wrote in verse, most of the fragments we
possess being preserved by Simplicius in his commentary.
His doctrine in brief is to the effect that Being, the One, *is*,
and that Becoming, change, is illusion. For if anything
comes to be, then it comes either out of being or out of
not-being. If the former, then it already is—in which case
it does not come to be; if the latter, then it is nothing,
since out of nothing comes nothing. Becoming is, then,
illusion. Being simply *is* and Being is One, since plurality is
also illusion. Now, this doctrine is obviously not the type
of theory that rises immediately to the mind of the man
in the street, and so it is not surprising to find Parmenides
insisting on the radical distinction between the Way of Truth
and the Way of Belief or Opinion. It is very probable that
the Way of Opinion exposed in the second part of the poem,
represents the cosmology of the Pythagoreans; and since
the Pythagorean philosophy would itself scarcely occur to
the man who went *merely* by sense-knowledge, it should not
be maintained that Parmenides' distinction between the two
Ways has all the formal generality of Plato's later distinction
between Knowledge and Opinion, Thought and Sense. It is
rather the rejection of one definite philosophy in favour of
another definite philosophy. Yet it is true that Parmenides
rejects the Pythagorean philosophy—and, indeed, every philosophy that agrees with it on the point—because it admits
change and movement. Now change and movement are most
certainly phenomena which appear to the senses, so that in
rejecting change and movement, Parmenides is rejecting the
way of sense-appearance. It is, therefore, not incorrect to
say that Parmenides introduces the most important distinction
between Reason and Sense, Truth and Appearance. It is true,
of course, that even Thales recognised this distinction to a
certain extent, for his supposed truth, that all is Water, is

scarcely perceptible immediately to the senses: it needs reason, which passes beyond appearance, in order to be conceived. The central "truth" of Heraclitus is, again, a truth of reason and far exceeds the common opinion of men, who trust in everything to sense-appearance. It is also true that Heraclitus even makes the distinction partly explicit, for does he not distinguish between mere common sense and his Word? Yet it is Parmenides who first lays great and explicit stress on the distinction, and it is easy enough to understand why he does so, when we consider the conclusions to which he came. In the Platonic philosophy the distinction became of cardinal importance, as indeed it must be in all forms of idealism.

Yet though Parmenides enunciates a distinction which was to become a fundamental tenet of idealism, the temptation to speak of him as though he were himself an idealist is to be rejected. As we shall see, there is very good reason for supposing that in Parmenides' eyes the One is sensual and material, and to turn him into an objective idealist of the nineteenth-century type is to be guilty of an anachronism: it does not follow from the negation of change that the One is Idea. We may be called upon to follow the way of thought, but it does not follow that Parmenides regarded the One, at which we arrive by this way, as actually being Thought itself. If Parmenides had represented the One as self-subsistent Thought, Plato and Aristotle would hardly have failed to record the fact, and Socrates would not have found the first sober philosopher in Anaxagoras, with his concept of Mind or Nous. The truth really seems to be that though Parmenides does assert the distinction between Reason and Sense, he asserts it not to establish an idealist system, but to establish a system of Monistic Materialism, in which change and movement are dismissed as illusory. Only Reason can apprehend Reality, but the Reality which Reason apprehends is material. This is not idealism but materialism.

To turn now to the doctrine of Parmenides on the nature of the world. His first great assertion is that "It is." "It," i.e. Reality, Being, of whatever nature it may be, is, exists, and cannot not be. It is, and it is impossible for it not to be. Being can be spoken of and it can be the object of my thought. But that which I can think about and speak of can be, "for it is the same thing that can be thought and that can be." But if "It" *can* be, then it *is*. Why? Because if it could be and yet were not, then it would be nothing. Now, nothing cannot be the object of speech or thought, for to speak about nothing is not to speak, and to think about nothing is the same as not thinking at all. Besides, if it merely *could be*, then, paradoxically, it could never come to be, for it would have to come out of nothing, and out of nothing comes nothing and not something. Being, then, Reality, "It" was not first possible, i.e. nothing, and then existent: it was always existent—more accurately, "It is."

Why do we say "more accurately, It is?" For this reason: If something comes into being, it must arise either out of being or out of not-being. If it arises out of being, then there is no real arising, no coming-to-be; for if it comes out of being, it already is. If, however, it arises out of not-being, then not-being must be already something, in order for being to be able to arise out of it. But this is a contradiction. Being therefore, "It" arises neither out of being nor out of not-being: it never came into being, but simply *is*. And as this must apply to all being, nothing ever becomes. For if anything ever becomes, however trifling, the same difficulty always recurs: does it come out of being or out of not-being? If the former, then it already is; if the latter, then you fall into a contradiction, since not-being is nothing and cannot be the source of being. Change, therefore, becoming and movement are impossible. Accordingly "It is." "One path only is left for us to speak of, namely, that *It is*. In this path are very many tokens that what is, is uncreated and indestructible, for it is complete, immovable and without end." [5]

Why does Parmenides say that "It" is complete, i.e. one Reality, which cannot be added to? Because if it is not one but divided, then it must be divided by something other than itself. But Being cannot be divided by something other than itself, for besides being there is nothing. Nor can anything be added to it, since anything that was added to being would itself be being. Similarly, it is immovable and continuous, for all movement and change, forms of becoming, are excluded.

Now, of what nature is this "It," Being, according to Parmenides? That Parmenides regarded Being as material, seems to be clearly indicated by his assertion that Being, the One, is finite. Infinite for him must have meant indeterminate and indefinite, and Being, as the Real, cannot be indefinite or indeterminate, cannot change, cannot be conceived as expanding into empty space: it must be definite, determinate, complete. It is temporarily infinite, as having neither beginning nor end, but it is spatially finite. Moreover, it is equally real in all directions, and so is spherical in shape, "equally poised from the centre in every direction: for it cannot be greater or smaller in one place than in another." [6] Now, how could Parmenides possibly think of Being as spherical, unless he thought of it as material? It would seem, then, that Burnet is right when he aptly says: "Parmenides is not, as some have said, 'the father of idealism'; on the contrary, all materialism depends on his view of reality." [7] Professor Stace has to admit that "Parmenides, Melissus and the Eleatics generally did regard Being as, in some sense, material"; but he still tries to make out that Parmenides was an idealist in that he held the "cardinal thesis of idealism," "that the absolute reality, of which the world is a manifestation, consists in thought, in concepts." [8] It is perfectly true that the Being of Parmenides can be grasped only by thought, but so can the reality of Thales or Anaximenes be grasped only by thought, in concepts. But to equate "being grasped in thought" with "being thought" is surely a confusion.

As an historical fact, then, it would seem that Parmenides was a materialist and nothing else. However, that does not prevent there being an unreconciled contradiction in Parmenides' philosophy, as affirmed by Professor Stace, [9] so that, though a materialist, his thought contains also the germs of idealism, or would at any rate form the *point de départ* for idealism. On the one hand Parmenides asserted the unchangeability of Being, and, in so far as he conceived of Being as material, he asserted the indestructibility of matter. Empedocles and Democritus adopted this position and used it in their atomistic doctrine. But while Parmenides felt himself compelled to dismiss change and becoming as illusion, thus adopting the very opposite position to that of Heraclitus, Democritus could not reject what appears to be an inescapable fact of experience, which needs more explanation than a curt dismissal. Democritus, therefore, while adopting Parmenides' thesis that being can neither arise nor pass away—the indestructibility of matter—interpreted change as due to the aggregation and separation of indestructible particles of matter. On the other hand, it is an historical fact that Plato seized on the thesis of Parmenides concerning the unchangeability of Being, and identified the abiding being with the subsistent and objective Idea. To that extent, therefore, Parmenides may be called the father of idealism, in that the first great idealist adopted a cardinal tenet of Parmenides and interpreted it from an idealistic standpoint. Moreover, Plato made great use of Parmenides' distinction between the world of reason and the world of sense or appearance. But if in that historical sense Parmenides may rightly be described as the father of idealism, through his undoubted influence on Plato, it must be understood at the same time that Parmenides himself taught a materialistic doctrine, and that materialists like Democritus were his legitimate children.

Heraclitus, in his theory of the πάντα ῥεῖ, laid stress on *Becoming*. As we have seen, he did not assert Becoming to the total exclusion of Being, saying that there is becoming, but nothing which becomes. He affirmed the existence of the One—Fire, but held that change, becoming, tension, are essential to the existence of the One. Parmenides, on the other hand, asserted Being even to the exclusion of Becoming, affirming that change and movement are illusory. Sense tells us that there is change, but truth is to be sought, not in sense, but in reason and thought. We have, therefore, two tendencies exemplified in these two philosophers, the tendency to emphasise Becoming and the tendency to emphasise Being. Plato attempted a synthesis of the two, a combination of what is true in each. He adopts Parmenides' distinction between thought and sense, and declares that sense-objects, the objects of sense-perception, are not the objects of true knowledge, for they do not possess the necessary stability, being subject to the Heraclitean flux. The objects of true knowledge are stable and eternal, like the Being of Parmenides; but they are not material, like the Being of Parmenides. They are, on the contrary, ideal, subsistent and immaterial Forms, hierarchically arranged and culminating in the Form of the Good.

The synthesis may be said to have been worked out further by Aristotle. Being, in the sense of ultimate and immaterial Reality, God, is changeless, subsistent Thought, νόησις νοήσεως. As to material being, Aristotle agrees with Heraclitus that it is subject to change, and rejects the position of Parmenides; but Aristotle accounts better than

Heraclitus did for the relative stability in things by making Plato's Forms or Ideas concrete, formal principles in the objects of this world. Again, Aristotle solves the dilemma of Parmenides by emphasising the notion of potentiality. He points out that it is no contradiction to say that a thing is X actually but Y potentially. It *is* X, but is going to be Y in the future in virtue of a potentiality, which is not simply nothing, yet is not actual being. Being therefore arises, not out of not-being nor out of being precisely as being *actu*, but out of being considered as being *potentia*, δυνάμει. Of the second part of the poem of Parmenides, *The Way of Belief*, it is unnecessary to say anything, but it is as well to say a few words concerning Melissus, as he supplemented the thought of his master, Parmenides. Parmenides had declared that Being, the One, is spatially finite; but Melissus, the Samian disciple of Parmenides, would not accept this doctrine. If Being is finite, then beyond being there must be nothing: being must be bounded or limited by nothing. But if being is limited by nothing, it must be infinite and not finite. There cannot be a void outside being, "for what is empty is nothing. What is nothing cannot be." [10]

Aristotle tells us that the One of Melissus was conceived as material.[11] Now, Simplicius quotes a fragment to prove that Melissus did *not* look upon the One as corporeal, but as incorporeal. "Now, if it were to exist, it must needs to be one; but if it is one, it cannot have body; for if it had body, it would have parts, and would no longer be one." [12] The explanation seems to be indicated by the fact that Melissus is speaking of an hypothetical case. Burnet, following Zeller, points out the similarity of the fragment to an argument of Zeno, in which Zeno is saying that if the ultimate units of the Pythagoreans existed, then each would have parts and would not be one. We may suppose, therefore, that Melissus, too, is speaking of the doctrine of the Pythagoreans, is trying to disprove the existence of their ultimate units, and is not talking of the Parmenidean One at all.

Chapter Seven

THE DIALECTIC OF ZENO

Zeno is well known as the author of several ingenious arguments to prove the impossibility of motion, such as the riddle of Achilles and the tortoise; arguments which may tend to further the opinion that Zeno was no more than a clever riddler who delighted in using his wits in order to puzzle those who were less clever than himself. But in reality Zeno was not concerned simply to display his cleverness—though clever he undoubtedly was—but had a serious purpose in view. For the understanding of Zeno and the appreciation of his conundrums, it is therefore essential to grasp the character of this purpose, otherwise there is danger of altogether misapprehending his position and aim.

Zeno of Elea, born probably about 489 B.C., was a disciple of Parmenides, and it is from this point of view that he is to be understood. His arguments are not simply witty toys, but are calculated to prove the position of the Master. Parmenides had combated pluralism, and had declared change and motion to be illusion. Since plurality and motion seem to be such evident data of our sense-experience, this bold position was naturally such as to induce a certain amount of ridicule. Zeno, a firm adherent of the theory of Parmenides, endeavours to prove it, or at least to demonstrate that it is by no means ridiculous, by the expedient of showing that the pluralism of the Pythagoreans is involved in insoluble difficulties, and that change and motion are impossible even on their pluralistic hypothesis. The arguments of Zeno then are meant to refute the Pythagorean opponents of Par-

71

menides by a series of clever *reductiones ad absurdum.*
Plato makes this quite clear in the *Parmenides,* when he
indicates the purpose of Zeno's (lost) book. "The truth is
that these writings were meant to be some protection to the
arguments of Parmenides against those who attack him and
show the many ridiculous and contradictory results which
they suppose to follow from the affirmation of the one. My
writing is an answer to the partisans of the many and it
returns their attack with interest, with a view to showing
that the hypothesis of the many, if examined sufficiently in
detail, leads to even more ridiculous results than the hypothesis of the One." [1] And Proclus informs us that "Zeno composed forty proofs to demonstrate that being is one, thinking
it a good thing to come to the help of his master." [2]

1. Proofs against Pythagorean Pluralism

1. Let us suppose with the Pythagoreans that Reality is
made up of units. These units are either with magnitude or
without magnitude. If the former, then a line for example,
as made up of units possessed of magnitude, will be infinitely divisible, since, however far you divide, the units
will still have magnitude and so be divisible. But in this
case the line will be made up of an infinite number of
units, each of which is possessed of magnitude. The line,
then, must be infinitely great, as composed of an infinite
number of bodies. Everything in the world, then, must be
infinitely great, and *a fortiori* the world itself must be infinitely great. Suppose, on the other hand, that the units
are without magnitude. In this case the whole universe will
also be without magnitude, since, however many units you
add together, if none of them has any magnitude, then the
whole collection of them will also be without magnitude.
But if the universe is without any magnitude, it must be
infinitely small. Indeed, everything in the universe must be
infinitely small.

The Pythagoreans are thus faced with this dilemma. Either
everything in the universe is infinitely great, or everything
in the universe is infinitely small. The conclusion which
Zeno wishes us to draw from this argument is, of course,
that the supposition from which the dilemma flows is an
absurd supposition, namely, that the universe and everything
in it are composed of units. If the Pythagoreans think that

the hypothesis of the One is absurd and leads to ridiculous conclusions, it has now been shown that the contrary hypothesis, that of the many, is productive of equally ridiculous conclusions.[3]

2. If there is a many, then we ought to be able to say *how many* there are. At least, they should be numerable; if they are not numerable, how can they exist? On the other hand, they cannot possibly be numerable, but must be infinite. Why? Because between any two assigned units there will always be other units, just as a line is infinitely divisible. But it is absurd to say that the many are finite in number and infinite in number at the same time.[4]

3. Does a bushel of corn make a noise when it falls to the ground? Clearly. But what of a grain of corn, or the thousandth part of a grain of corn? It makes no noise. But the bushel of corn is composed only of the grains of corn or of the parts of the grains of corn. If, then, the parts make no sound when they fall, how can the whole make a sound, when the whole is composed only of the parts?[5]

2. Arguments against the Pythagorean Doctrine of Space

Parmenides denied the existence of the void or empty space, and Zeno tries to support this denial by reducing the opposite view to absurdity. Suppose for a moment that there is a space in which things are. If it is nothing, then things cannot be in it. If, however, it is something, it will itself be in space, and *that* space will itself be in space, and so on indefinitely. But this is an absurdity. Things, therefore, are not in space or in an empty void, and Parmenides was quite right to deny the existence of a void.[6]

3. Arguments Concerning Motion

The most celebrated arguments of Zeno are those concerning motion. It should be remembered that what Zeno is attempting to show is this: that motion, which Parmenides denied, is equally impossible on the pluralistic theory of the Pythagoreans.

1. Let us suppose that you want to cross a stadium or race-course. In order to do so, you would have to traverse an infinite number of points—on the Pythagorean hypothesis, that is to say. Moreover, you would have to travel the

distance in finite time, if you wanted to get to the other side at all. But how can you traverse an infinite number of points, and so an infinite distance, in a finite time? We must conclude that you *cannot* cross the stadium. Indeed, we must conclude that no object can traverse any distance whatsoever (for the same difficulty always recurs), and that all motion is consequently impossible.[7]

2. Let us suppose that Achilles and a tortoise are going to have a race. Since Achilles is a sportsman, he gives the tortoise a start. Now, by the time that Achilles has reached the place from which the tortoise started, the latter has again advanced to another point; and when Achilles reaches *that* point, then the tortoise will have advanced still another distance, even if very short. Thus Achilles is always coming nearer to the tortoise, but never actually overtakes it—and never *can* do so, on the supposition that a line is made up of an infinite number of points, for then Achilles would have to traverse an infinite distance. On the Pythagorean hypothesis, then, Achilles will never catch up the tortoise; and so, although they assert the reality of motion, they make it impossible on their own doctrine. For it follows that the slower moves as fast as the faster.[8]

3. Suppose a moving arrow. According to the Pythagorean theory the arrow should occupy a given position in space. But to occupy a given position in space is to be at rest. Therefore the flying arrow is at rest, which is a contradiction.[9]

4. The fourth argument of Zeno, which we know from Aristotle[10] is, as Sir David Ross says, "very difficult to follow, partly owing to use of ambiguous language by Aristotle, partly owing to doubts as to the readings." [11] We have to represent to ourselves three sets of bodies on a stadium or race-course. One set is stationary, the other two are moving in opposite directions to one another with equal velocity.

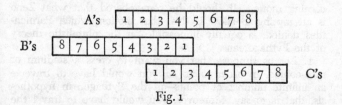

Fig. 1

The A's are stationary; the B's and C's are moving in opposite directions with the same velocity. They will come to occupy the following position:

A's | 1 | 2 | 3 | 4 | 5 | 6 | 7 | 8 |

B's | 8 | 7 | 6 | 5 | 4 | 3 | 2 | 1 |

C's | 1 | 2 | 3 | 4 | 5 | 6 | 7 | 8 |

Fig. 2

In attaining this second position the front of B1 has passed four of the A's, while the front of C1 has passed all the B's. If a unit of length is passed in a unit of time, then the front of B1 has taken half the time taken by the front of C1 in order to reach the position of Fig. 2. On the other hand the front of B1 has passed all the C's, just as the front of C1 has passed all the B's. The time of their passage must then be *equal*. We are left then with the absurd conclusion that the half of a certain time is equal to the whole of that time.

How are we to interpret these arguments of Zeno? It is important not to let oneself think: "These are mere sophistries on the part of Zeno. They are ingenious tricks, but they err by supposing that a line is composed of points and time of discrete moments." It may be that the solution of the riddles is to be found in showing that the line and time are continuous and not discrete; but, then, Zeno was not concerned to hold that they are discrete. On the contrary, he is concerned to show the absurd consequences which flow from supposing that they are discrete. Zeno, as a disciple of Parmenides, believed that motion is an illusion and is impossible, but in the foregoing arguments his aim is to prove that even on the pluralistic hypothesis motion is equally impossible, and that the assumption of its possibility leads to contradictory and absurd conclusions. Zeno's position was as follows: "The Real is a plenum, a complete continuum and motion is impossible. Our adversaries assert motion and try to explain it by an appeal to a pluralistic hypothesis. I propose to show that this hypothesis does nothing to explain motion, but only lands one in absurdities."

Zeno thus reduced the hypothesis of his adversaries to absurdity, and the real result of his dialectic was not so much to establish Parmenidean monism (which is exposed to insuperable objections), as to show the necessity of admitting the concept of continuous quantity.

The Eleatics, then, deny the reality of multiplicity and motion. There is one principle, Being, which is conceived of as material and motionless. They do not deny, of course, that we *sense* motion and multiplicity, but they declare that what we sense is illusion: it is mere appearance. True being is to be found, not by sense but by thought, and thought shows that there can be no plurality, no movement, no change.

The Eleatics thus attempt, as the earlier Greek philosophers attempted before them, to discover the one principle of the world. The world, however, as it presents itself to us, is clearly a pluralistic world. The question is, therefore, how to reconcile the one principle with the plurality and change which we find in the world, i.e. the problem of the One and the Many, which Heraclitus had tried to solve in a philosophy that professed to do justice to both elements through a doctrine of Unity in Diversity, Identity in Difference. The Pythagoreans asserted plurality to the practical exclusion of the One—there are many ones; the Eleatics asserted the One to the exclusion of the many. But if you cling to the plurality which is suggested by sense-experience, then you must also admit change; and if you admit change of one thing into another, you cannot avoid the recurring problem as to the character of the common element in the things which change. If, on the other hand, you start with the doctrine of the One, you must—unless you are going to adopt a one-sided position like that of the Eleatics, which cannot last—deduce plurality from the One, or at least show how the plurality which we observe in the world is consistent with the One. In other words, justice must be done to both factors—the One and the Many, Stability and Change. The one-sided doctrine of Parmenides was unacceptable, as also was the one-sided doctrine of the Pythagoreans. Yet the philosophy of Heraclitus was also unsatisfactory. Apart from the fact that it hardly accounted sufficiently for the stable element in things, it was bound up with materialistic monism. Ultimately it was bound to be suggested that the highest and truest being is immaterial. Meanwhile it is not surprising to find what Zeller calls "compromise-systems," trying to weld together the thought of their predecessors.

Note on "Pantheism" in Pre-Socratic Greek Philosophy

(i) If a Pantheist is a man who has a subjective religious attitude towards the universe, which latter he identifies with God, then the Pre-Socratics are scarcely to be called pantheists. That Heraclitus speaks of the One as Zeus is true, but it does not appear that he adopted any religious attitude towards the One—Fire.

(ii) If a pantheist is a man who, while denying a Transcendent Principle of the universe, makes the universe to be ultimately *Thought* (unlike the materialist, who makes it Matter alone), then the Pre-Socratics again scarcely merit the name of pantheists, for they conceive or speak of the One in material terms (though it is true that the spirit-matter distinction had not yet been so clearly conceived that they could deny it in the way that the modern materialistic monist denies it).

(iii) In any case the One, the universe, could not be identified with the Greek gods. It has been remarked (by Schelling) that there is no supernatural in Homer, for the Homeric god is part of nature. This remark has its application in the present question. The Greek god was finite and anthropomorphically conceived; he could not possibly be identified with the One, nor would it occur to anyone to do so literally. The *name* of a god might be sometimes transferred to the One, e.g. Zeus, but the one is not to be thought of as identified with the "actual" Zeus of legend and mythology. The suggestion may be that the One is the only "god" there is, and that the Olympian deities are anthropomorphic fables; but even then it seems very uncertain if the philosopher ever *worshipped* the One. Stoics might with justice be called pantheists; but, as far as the early Pre-Socratics are concerned, it seems decidedly preferable to call them monists, rather than pantheists.

Chapter Eight

EMPEDOCLES OF AKRAGAS

Empedocles was a citizen of Akragas, or Agrigentum, in Sicily. His dates cannot be fixed, but it appears that he visited the city of Thurii shortly after its foundation in 443-44 B.C. He took part in the politics of his native city, and seems to have been the leader of the democratic party there. Stories were later circulated about Empedocles' activities as magician and wonder-worker, and there is a story that he was expelled from the Pythagorean Order for "stealing discourses." [1] Apart from thaumaturgic activities, Empedocles contributed to the growth of medicine proper. The death of the philosopher has been made the subject of several entertaining fables, the best known being that he jumped into the crater of Etna in order to make people think that he had gone up to heaven and esteem him as a god. Unfortunately, he left one of his slippers on the brink of the volcano, and, as he used to wear slippers with brazen soles, it was easily recognised. [2] Diogenes, however, who recounts this story, also informs us that "Timaeus contradicts all these stories, saying expressly that he departed into Peloponnesus, and never returned at all, on which account the manner of his death is uncertain." [3] Empedocles, like Parmenides and unlike the other Greek philosophers, expressed his philosophical ideas in poetical writings, more or less extensive fragments of which have come down to us.

Empedocles does not so much produce a new philosophy, as endeavour to weld together and reconcile the thought of his predecessors. Parmenides had held that Being is, and

78

that being is material. Empedocles not only adopted this position, but also the fundamental thought of Parmenides, that being cannot arise or pass away, for being cannot arise from not-being, nor can being pass into not-being. Matter, then, is without beginning and without end; it is indestructible. "Fools!—for they have no far-reaching thoughts—who deem that what before was not comes into being, or that aught can perish and be utterly destroyed. For it cannot be that aught can arise from what in no way is, and it is impossible and unheard of that what *is* should perish, for it will always *be*, wherever one may keep putting it." [4] And again: "And in the All there is naught empty and naught too full," and "In the All there is naught empty. Whence, then, could aught come to increase it?" [5]

So far, then, Empedocles agrees with Parmenides. But on the other hand, change is a fact which cannot be denied, and the dismissal of change as illusory could not long be maintained. It remained, then, to find a way of reconciling the fact of the existence of change and motion with the principle of Parmenides, that Being—which, be it remembered, is material according to Parmenides—neither comes into being nor passes away. This reconciliation Empedocles tried to effect by means of the principle that objects as wholes begin to be and cease to be—as experience shows they do—but that they are composed of material particles, which are themselves indestructible. There is "only a mingling and interchange of what has been mingled. Substance (Φύσις) is but a name given to these things by men." [6]

Now, though Thales had believed all things to be ultimately water and Anaximenes air, they believed that one kind of matter can become another kind of matter, at least in the sense that, e.g., water becomes earth and air becomes fire. Empedocles, however, interpreting Parmenides' principle of the unchangeability of being in his own way, held that one kind of matter cannot become another kind of matter, but that there are fundamental and eternal kinds of matter or elements—earth, air, fire and water. The familiar classification of the four elements was therefore invented by Empedocles, though he speaks of them, not as elements but as "the roots of all." [7] Earth cannot become water, nor water, earth: the four kinds of matter are unchangeable and ultimate particles, which form the concrete objects of the world by their mingling. So objects come into being through the mingling of the elements, and they cease to be through the separation of the elements: but the elements themselves neither come into being nor pass away, but remain ever unchanged. Empedocles, therefore, saw the only possible way of reconciling the materialistic position of Parmenides with the evident fact of change, the way of postulating a multiplicity of ultimate material particles, and may thus be called a mediator between the system of Parmenides and the evidence of the senses.

Now the Ionian philosophers had failed to explain the process of Nature. If everything is composed of air, as Anaximenes thought, how do the objects of our experience come into being? What force is responsible for the cyclical process of Nature? Anaximenes assumed that air transforms itself into other kinds of matter through its own inherent power; but Empedocles saw that it is necessary to postulate active forces. These forces he found in Love and Hate, or Harmony and Discord. In spite of their names, however, the forces are conceived by Empedocles as physical and material forces, Love or Attraction bringing the particles of the four elements together and building up, Strife or Hate separating the particles and causing the cessation of the being of objects.

According to Empedocles the world-process is circular, in the sense that there are periodic world-cycles. At the commencement of a cycle the elements are all mixed up together—not separated out to form concrete objects as we know them—a general mixture of particles of earth, air, fire and water. In this primary stage of the process Love is the governing principle, and the whole is called a "blessed god." "Hate, however, is round about the sphere, and when Hate penetrates within the sphere the process of separation, the disuniting of the particles, is begun. Ultimately, the separation becomes complete: all the water particles are gathered together, all the fire particles, and so on. Hate reigns supreme, Love having been driven out. Yet Love in turn begins its work, and so causes gradual mingling and uniting of the various elements, this process going on until the element-particles are mixed up together as they were in the beginning. It is then the turn of Hate to start its operations anew. And so the process continues, without first beginning and without last end.[8]

As to the world as we know it, this stands at a stage

half-way between the primary sphere and the stage of total separation of the elements: Hate is gradually penetrating the sphere and driving out Love as it does so. As our earth began to be formed out of the sphere, air was the first element to be separated off; this was followed by fire, and then came earth. Water is squeezed out by the rapidity with which the world rotates. The primary sphere, i.e. primary in the cyclical process, not primary in an absolute sense, is described in what appear to us somewhat amusing terms. "There" (i.e. in the sphere) "are distinguished neither the swift limbs of the sun; no, nor the shaggy earth in its might, nor the sea—so fast was the god bound in the close covering of Harmony, spherical and round, rejoicing in his circular solitude." [9] The activity of Love and Strife is illustrated in various ways. "This" (i.e. the contest between them) "is manifest in the mass of mortal limbs. At one time all the limbs that are the body's portion are brought together by Love in blooming life's high season; at another, severed by cruel Strife, they wander each alone by the breakers of life's sea. It is the same with plants and the fish that make their homes in the waters, with the beasts that have their lairs on the hills and the seabirds that sail on wings." [10]

The doctrine of transmigration of souls is taught by Empedocles in the book of the Purifications. He even declares: "For I have already been in the past a boy and a girl, a shrub and a bird and a fish which lives in the sea." [11] It can scarcely be said, however, that this doctrine fits in well with the cosmological system of Empedocles, since, if all things are composed of material particles which separate at death, and if "the blood round the heart is the thought of men," [12] there is little room left for immortality. But Empedocles may not have realised the discrepancy between his philosophical and religious theories. (Among the latter are certainly some very Pythagorean-sounding prescriptions, such as: "Wretches, utter wretches, keep your hands from beans!") [13]

Aristotle remarks that Empedocles made no distinction between thought and perception. His actual theory of vision is given by Theophrastus, a theory used by Plato in the *Timaeus*. [14] In sense-perception there is a meeting between an element in us and a similar element outside us. All things are constantly giving off effluences, and when the pores of the sense-organs are the right size, then these effluences enter in and perception takes place. In the case of vision, for example, effluences come to the eyes from things; while, on the other hand, the fire from inside the eye (the eye is composed of fire and water, the fire being sheltered from the water by membranes provided with very small pores, which prevent water getting through, but allow fire to get out) goes out to meet the object, the two factors together producing sight.

In conclusion, we may remind ourselves that Empedocles tried to reconcile the thesis of Parmenides, that being can neither come to be nor pass away, with the evident fact of change by postulating ultimate particles of the four elements, the mingling of which forms the concrete objects of this world and the separation of which constitutes the passing-away of such objects. He failed, however, to explain how the material cyclic process of Nature takes place, but had recourse to mythological forces, Love and Hate. It was left to Anaxagoras to introduce the concept of Mind as the original cause of the world-process.

Chapter Nine

THE ADVANCE OF
ANAXAGORAS

Anaxagoras was born at Clazomenae in Asia Minor about 500 B.C., and, although a Greek, he was doubtless a Persian citizen, for Clazomenae had been reduced after the suppression of the Ionian Revolt; and it may even be said that he came to Athens in the Persian Army. If this is so, it would certainly explain why he came to Athens in the year of Salamis, 480/79 B.C. He was the first philosopher to settle in the city, which was later to become such a flourishing centre of philosophic study.[1]

From Plato[2] we learn that the young Pericles was a pupil of Anaxagoras, an association which afterwards got the philosopher into trouble, for after he had resided about thirty years in the city, Anaxagoras was brought to trial by the political opponents of Pericles, i.e. about 450 B.C. Diogenes tells us that the charges were those of impiety (he refers to Sotion) and Medism (referring to Satyros). As to the first charge, Plato relates, it was based on the fact that Anaxagoras taught that the sun is a red-hot stone and the moon is made of earth.[3] These charges were doubtless trumped up, mainly in order to get a hit at Pericles through Anaxagoras. (Pericles' other teacher, Damon, was ostracised.) Anaxagoras was condemned, but was got out of prison, probably by Pericles himself, and he retired to Ionia where he settled at Lampsacus, a colony of Miletus. Here he probably founded a school. The citizens erected a monument to his memory in the market-place (an altar dedicated to Mind and Truth), and the anniversary of his death was long observed as a holiday for school children, at his own request, it is said.

Anaxagoras expressed his philosophy in a book, but only fragments of this remain, and these appear to be confined to the first part of the work. We owe the preservation of the fragments we possess to Simplicius (A.D. sixth century).

Anaxagoras, like Empedocles, accepted the theory of Parmenides that Being neither comes into being nor passes away, but is unchangeable. "The Hellenes do not understand rightly coming into being and passing away, for nothing comes into being or passes away, but there is a mingling and a separation of things which are" (i.e. persist).[4] Both thinkers, then, are in agreement as to the indestructibility of matter, and both reconcile this theory with the evident fact of change by positing indestructible material particles, the mingling of which forms objects, the separation of which explains the passing away of objects. But Anaxagoras will not agree with Empedocles that the ultimate units are particles corresponding to the four elements—earth, air, fire and water. He teaches that everything which has parts qualitatively the same as the whole is ultimate and underived. Aristotle calls these wholes, which have qualitatively similar parts, τὰ ὁμοιομερῆ; τὸ ὁμοιομερὲς being opposed to τὸ ἀνομοιομερές. This distinction is not difficult to grasp if one takes an example. If we suppose that a piece of gold is cut in half, the halves are themselves gold. The parts are thus qualitatively the same as the whole, and the whole can be said to be ὁμοιομερές. If, however, a dog, a living organism, be cut in half, the halves are not themselves two dogs. The whole is in this case therefore ἀνομοιομερές. The general notion is thus clear, and it is unnecessary to confuse the issue by introducing considerations from modern scientific experiment. Some things have qualitatively similiar parts, and such things are ultimate and underived (as regards *kind*, that is to say, for no given conglomeration of particles is ultimate and underived). "How can hair come from what is not hair, or flesh from what is not flesh?" asks Anaxagoras.[5] But it does not follow that everything which seems to be ὁμοιομερές is really so. Thus it is related by Aristotle that Anaxagoras did not hold Empedocles' elements—earth, air, fire and water—to be really ultimate; on the contrary, they are mixtures composed of many qualitatively different particles.[6]

In the beginning, particles—there is no indivisible particle, according to Anaxagoras—of all kinds were mingled together. "All things were together, infinite both in number and in smallness; for the small too was infinite. And, when all things were together, none of them could be distinguished for their smallness." [7] "All things are in the whole." The objects of experience arise, when ultimate particles have been so brought together that in the resulting object particles of a certain kind predominate. Thus in the original mixture particles of gold were scattered about and mixed with all sorts of other particles; but when particles of gold have been so brought together—with other particles—that the resultant visible object consists predominantly of gold-particles, we have the gold of our experience. Why do we say "with other particles"? Because in concrete objects of experience there are, according to Anaxagoras, particles of *all* things; yet they are combined in such a way that one kind of particle predominates and from this fact the whole object gets its denomination. Anaxagoras held the doctrine that "in everything there is a portion of everything," [8] apparently because he did not see how he could otherwise explain the fact of change. For instance, if grass becomes flesh, there must have been particles of flesh in the grass (for how can "flesh" come "from what is not flesh"?), while on the other hand in the grass the grass-particles must predominate. Grass, therefore, consists predominantly of grass, but it also contains other kinds of particles, for "in everything there is a portion of everything," and "the things that are in one world are not divided nor cut off from one another with a hatchet, neither the warm from the cold nor the cold from the warm." [9] In this way Anaxagoras sought to maintain the Parmenidean doctrine concerning being, while at the same time adopting a realist attitude towards change, not dismissing it as an illusion of the senses but accepting it as a fact, and then trying to reconcile it with the Eleatic theory of being. Later on Aristotle would attempt to solve the difficulties raised by the doctrine of Parmenides in regard to change by means of his distinction between potency and act.

Burnet does not think that Anaxagoras considered, as the Epicureans supposed him to, "that there must be minute particles in bread and water which were like the particles of blood, flesh and bones." [10] In his opinion it was of the opposites, the warm and the cold, the dry and the moist, that everything contained a portion according to Anaxagoras. Burnet's view has certainly much to support it. We have already seen the fragment in which Anaxagoras declares that "the things that are in one world are not cut off from one another with a hatchet, neither the warm from the cold, nor the cold from the warm." Moreover, since according to Anaxagoras, there are no indivisible particles, there cannot be any ultimate particles in the sense of what cannot be further divided. But it would not seem to follow necessarily from the indivisibility of the particles that, in the philosopher's opinion, there were no ultimate *kinds* which could not be qualitatively resolved. And does not Anaxagoras explicitly ask how hair can come from what is not hair? In addition to this we read in fragment 4 of the mixture of all things—"of the moist and the dry, and the warm and the cold, and the bright and the dark, and of much earth that was in it, and a multitude of innumerable seeds in no way like each other. For none of the other things either is like any other. And these things being so, we must hold that all things are in the whole." This fragment scarcely gives the impression that the "opposites" stand in any peculiar position of privilege. While admitting, therefore, that Burnet's view has much to be said for it, we prefer the interpretation already given in the text.[11]

So far Anaxagoras' philosophy is a variant from Empedocles' interpretation and adaptation of Parmenides, and offers no particularly valuable features. But when we come to the question of the power or force that is responsible for the forming of things out of the first mass, we arrive at the peculiar contribution of Anaxagoras to philosophy. Empedocles had attributed motion in the universe to the two physical forces of Love and Strife, but Anaxagoras introduces instead the principle of Nous or Mind. "With Anaxagoras a light, if still a weak one, begins to dawn, because the understanding is now recognized as the principle." [12] "Nous," says Anaxagoras, "has power over all things that have life, both greater and smaller. And Nous had power over the whole revolution, so that it began to revolve at the start. . . . And Nous set in order all things that were to be, and all things that were and are now and that will be, and this revolution in which now revolve the stars and the sun and the moon and the air and the aether which are separated off. And the revolution itself caused the separating off, and the dense is separated off from the rare, the warm from the cold, the bright from the dark, and the dry from the moist. And there are many portions in many things. But no thing is altogether separated off from anything else except Nous. And all Nous is alike, both the greater and the smaller; but nothing else is like anything else, but each single thing is and was most manifestly those things of which there are most in it." [13]

Nous "is infinite and self-ruled, and is mixed with nothing, but is alone, itself by itself." [14] How then did Anaxagoras conceive of Nous? He calls it "the finest of all things and the purest, and it has all knowledge about everything and the greatest power . . ." He also speaks of Nous being "there where everything else is, in the surrounding mass." [15] The philosopher thus speaks of Nous or Mind in material terms as being "the thinnest of all things," and as occupying space. On the strength of this Burnet declares that Anaxagoras never rose above the conception of a corporeal principle. He made Nous purer than other material things, but never reached the idea of an immaterial or incorporeal thing. Zeller will not allow this, and Stace points out how "all philosophy labours under the difficulty of having to express non-sensuous thought in language which has been evolved for the purpose of expressing sensuous ideas." [16] If we speak of a mind as "clear" or as someone's mind as being "greater" than that of another, we are not on that account to be called materialists. That Anaxagoras conceived of Nous as occupying space is not sufficient proof that he would have declared Nous to be corporeal, had he ever conceived the notion of a sharp distinction between mind and matter. The non-spatiality of the mind is a later conception. Probably the most satisfactory interpretation is that Anaxagoras, in his concept of the spiritual, did not succeed in grasping clearly the radical difference between the spiritual and the corporeal. But that is not the same as saying that he was a *dogmatic* materialist. On the contrary, he first introduces a spiritual and intellectual principle, though he fails to understand fully the essential difference between that principle and the matter which it forms or sets in motion.

Nous is present in all living things, men, animals and plants, and is the same in all. Differences between these objects are due, then, not to essential differences between their souls, but to differences between their bodies, which facilitate or handicap the fuller working of Nous. (Anaxagoras, however, does not explain the human consciousness of independent selfhood.)

Nous is not to be thought of as *creating* matter. Matter is eternal, and the function of Nous seems to be to set the rotatory movement or vortex going in part of the mixed mass, the action of the vortex itself, as it spreads, accounting for the subsequent motion. Thus Aristotle, who says in the *Metaphysics* that Anaxagoras "stood out like a sober man from the random talkers that had preceded him," [17] also says that "Anaxagoras uses Mind as a *deus ex machina* to account for the formation of the world; and whenever he is at a loss to explain why anything necessarily is, he drags it in. But in other cases he makes anything rather than Mind the cause." [18] We can easily understand, then, the disappointment of Socrates who, thinking that he had come upon an entirely new approach when he discovered Anaxagoras, found "my extravagant expectations were all dashed to the ground when I went on and found that the man made no use of Mind at all. He ascribed no causal power whatever to it in the ordering of things, but to airs, and aethers, and waters, and a host of other strange things." [19] Nevertheless, though he failed to make full use of the principle, Anaxagoras must be credited with the introduction into Greek philosophy of a principle possessed of the greatest importance, that was to bear splendid fruit in the future.

Chapter Ten

THE ATOMISTS

The founder of the Atomist School was Leucippus of Miletus. It has been maintained that Leucippus never existed,[1] but Aristotle and Theophrastus make him to be the founder of the Atomist philosophy, and we can hardly suppose that they were mistaken. It is not possible to fix his dates, but Theophrastus declares that Leucippus had been a member of the School of Parmenides, and we read in Diogenes' *Life of Leucippus* that he was a disciple of Zeno (οὗτος ἤκουσε Ζήνωνος). It appears that the *Great Diakosmos,* subsequently incorporated in the works of Democritus of Abdera, was really the work of Leucippus, and no doubt Burnet is quite right when he compares the Democritean *corpus* with the Hippocritean, and remarks that in neither case can we distinguish the authors of the various component treatises.[2] The whole *corpus* is the work of a School, and it is most unlikely that we shall ever be in a position to assign each work to its respective author. In treating of the Atomist philosophy, therefore, we cannot pretend to distinguish between what is due to Leucippus and what is due to Democritus. But since Democritus is of considerably later date and cannot with historical accuracy be classed among the Pre-Socratics, we will leave to a later chapter his doctrine of sense-perception, by which he attempted to answer Protagoras, and his theory of human conduct. Some historians of philosophy, indeed, treat of Democritus' views on these points when dealing with the Atomist philosophy in the section devoted to the Pre-Socratics, but in view of the undoubtedly later date of Democritus, it seems preferable to follow Burnet in this matter.

The Atomist philosophy is really the logical development of the philosophy of Empedocles. The latter had tried to reconcile the Parmenidean principle of the denial of the passage of being into not-being or vice versa, with the evident fact of change by postulating four elements which, mixed together in various proportions, form the objects of our experience. He did not, however, really work out his doctrine of particles, nor did he carry the quantitative explanation of qualitative differences to its logical conclusion. The philosophy of Empedocles formed a transitional stage to the explanation of all qualitative differences by a mechanical juxtaposition of material particles in various patterns. Moreover, Empedocles' forces—Love and Strife—were metaphorical powers, which would have to be eliminated in a thorough-going mechanical philosophy. The final step to complete mechanism was attempted by the Atomists.

According to Leucippus and Democritus there are an infinite number of indivisible units, which are called atoms. These are imperceptible, since they are too small to be perceived by the senses. The atoms differ in size and shape, but have no quality save that of solidity or impenetrability. Infinite in number, they move in the void. (Parmenides had denied the reality of space. The Pythagoreans had admitted a void to keep their units apart, but they identified it with the atmospheric air, which Empedocles showed to be corporeal. Leucippus, however, affirmed at the same time the non-reality of space and its existence, meaning by non-reality, non-corporeity. This position is expressed by saying that "what is not" is just as much real as "what is." Space, then, or the void, is not corporeal, but it is as real as body.) The later Epicureans held that the atoms all move downwards in the void through the force of *weight*, probably influenced by Aristotle's idea of absolute weight and lightness. (Aristotle says that none of his predecessors had held this notion.) Now Aëtius expressly says that while Democritus ascribed size and shape to the atoms, he did not ascribe to them weight, but that Epicurus added weight in order to account for the movement of the atoms.[3] Cicero relates the same, and also declares that according to Democritus there was no "top" or "bottom" or "middle" in the void.[4] If this is what Democritus held, then he was of course quite right, for there is no absolute up or down; but how in this case did he conceive the motion of the atoms? In the *De Anima*[5] Aristotle attributes to Democritus a comparison between the motions of the atoms of the soul and the motes in a sunbeam, which dart hither and thither in all directions, even when there is no wind. It may be that this was also the Democritean view of the original motion of the atoms.

However, in whatever way the atoms originally moved in the void, at some point of time collisions between atoms occurred, those of irregular shape becoming entangled with one another and forming groups of atoms. In this way the vortex (Anaxagoras) is set up, and a world is in process of formation. Whereas Anaxagoras thought that the larger bodies would be driven farthest from the centre, Leucippus said the opposite, believing, wrongly that in an eddy of wind or water the larger bodies tend towards the centre. Another effect of the movement in the void is that atoms which are alike in size and shape are brought together as a sieve brings together the grains of millet, wheat and barley, or the waves of the sea heap up together long stones with long and round with round. In this way are formed the four "elements"—fire, air, earth and water. Thus innumerable worlds arise from the collisions among the infinite atoms moving in the void.

It is at once noticeable that neither Empedocles' forces, Love and Strife, nor the Nous of Anaxagoras appear in the Atomist philosophy: Leucippus evidently did not consider any moving force to be a necessary hypothesis. In the beginning existed atoms in the void, and that was all: from that beginning arose the world of our experience, and no external Power or moving Force is assumed as a necessary cause for the primal motion. Apparently the early cosmologists did not think of motion as requiring any explanation, and in the Atomist philosophy the eternal movement of the atoms is regarded as self-sufficient. Leucippus speaks of everything happening ἐκ λόγου καὶ ὑπ' ἀνάγκης[6] and this might at first sight appear inconsistent with his doctrine of the unexplained original movement of the atoms and of the collisions of the atoms. The latter, however, occur necessarily owing to the configuration of the atoms and their irregular movements, while the former, as a self-sufficient fact, did not require further explanation. To us,

indeed, it may well seem strange to deny chance and yet
to posit an eternal unexplained motion—Aristotle blames the
Atomists for not explaining the source of motion and the
kind of motion[7]—but we ought not to conclude that Leucippus meant to ascribe the motion of the atoms to *chance:*
to him the eternal motion and the continuation of motion
required no explanation. In our opinion, the mind boggles
at such a theory and cannot rest content with Leucippus'
ultimate; but it is an interesting historical fact, that he
himself was content with this ultimate and sought no "First
Unmoved Mover."

It is to be noted that the atoms of Leucippus and Democritus are the Pythagorean monads endowed with the properties of Parmenidean being—for each is as the Parmenidean
One. And inasmuch as the elements arise from the various
arrangements and positions of the atoms, they may be likened to the Pythagorean "numbers," if the latter are to be
regarded as patterns or "figurate numbers." This can be the
only sense to be attached to Aristotle's dictum that "Leucippus and Democritus virtually make all things number too
and produce them from numbers." [8]

In his detailed scheme of the world, Leucippus was somewhat reactionary, rejecting the Pythagorean view of the
spherical character of the earth and returning, like Anaxagoras, to the view of Anaximenes, that the earth is like a
tambourine floating in the air. But, though the details of
the Atomist cosmology do not indicate any new advance,
Leucippus and Democritus are noteworthy for having carried previous tendencies to their logical conclusion, producing a purely mechanical account and explanation of reality.
The attempt to give a complete explanation of the world in
terms of mechanical materialism has, as we all know, reap-
peared in a much more thorough form in the modern era
under the influence of physical science, but the brilliant
hypothesis of Leucippus and Democritus was by no means
the last word in Greek philosophy: subsequent Greek philosophers were to see that the richness of the world cannot
in all its spheres be reduced to the mechanical interplay
of atoms.

Chapter Eleven

PRE-SOCRATIC PHILOSOPHY

1. It is often said that Greek philosophy centres round the problem of the One and the Many. Already in the very earliest stages of Greek philosophy we find the notion of unity: things change into one another—therefore there must be some common substratum, some ultimate principle, some unity underlying diversity. Thales declares that water is that common principle, Anaximenes air, Heraclitus fire: they choose different principles, but they all three believe in one ultimate principle. But although the fact of change—what Aristotle called "substantial" change—may have suggested to the early Cosmologists the notion of an underlying unity in the universe, it would be a mistake to reduce this notion to a conclusion of physical science. As far as strict scientific proof goes, they had not sufficient data to warrant their assertion of unity, still less to warrant the assertion of any particular ultimate principle, whether water, fire or air. The fact is, that the early Cosmologists leapt beyond the data to the intuition of universal unity: they possessed what we might call the power of metaphysical intuition, and this constitutes their glory and their claim to a place in the history of philosophy. If Thales had contented himself with saying that out of water earth is evolved, "we should," as Nietzsche observes, "only have a scientific hypothesis: a false one, though nevertheless difficult to refute." But Thales went beyond a mere scientific hypothesis: he reached out to a metaphysical doctrine, expressed in the metaphysical doctrine, that *Everything is One.*

93

Let me quote Nietzsche again. "Greek philosophy seems to begin with a preposterous fancy, with the proposition that *water* is the origin and mother-womb of all things. Is it really necessary to stop there and become serious? Yes, and for three reasons: Firstly, because the proposition does enunciate something about the origin of things; secondly, because it does so without figure and fable; thirdly and lastly, because in it is contained, although only in the chrysalis state, the idea—Everything is one. The first-mentioned reason leaves Thales still in the company of religious and superstitious people; the second, however, takes him out of this company and shows him to us as a natural philosopher; but by virtue of the third, Thales becomes the first Greek philosopher." [1] This holds true of the other early Cosmologists; men like Anaximenes and Heraclitus also took wing and flew above and beyond what could be verified by mere empirical observation. At the same time they were not content with any mythological assumption, for they sought a real principle of unity, the ultimate substrate of change: what they asserted, they asserted in all seriousness. They had the notion of a world that was a whole, a system, of a world governed by law. Their assertions were dictated by reason or thought, not by mere imagination or mythology; and so they deserve to count as philosophers, the first philosophers of Europe.

2. But though the early Cosmologists were inspired by the idea of cosmic unity, they were faced by the fact of the Many, of multiplicity, of diversity, and they had to attempt the theoretical reconciliation of this evident plurality with the postulated unity—in other words, they had to account for the world as we know it. While Anaximenes, for example, had recourse to the principle of condensation and rarefaction, Parmenides, in the grip of his great theory that Being is one and changeless, roundly denied the facts of change and motion and multiplicity as illusions of the senses. Empedocles postulated four ultimate elements, out of which all things are built up under the action of Love and Strife, and Anaxagoras maintained the ultimate character of the atomic theory and the quantitative explanation of qualitative difference, thus doing justice to plurality, to the many, while tending to relinquish the earlier vision of unity, in spite of the fact that each atom represents the Parmenidean One.

We may say, therefore, that while the Pre-Socratics struggled with the problem of the One and the Many, they did not succeed in solving it. The Heraclitean philosophy contains, indeed, the profound notion of unity in diversity, but it is bound up with an over-assertion of Becoming and the difficulties consequent on the doctrine of Fire. The Pre-Socratics accordingly failed to solve the problem, and it was taken up again by Plato and Aristotle, who brought to bear on it their outstanding talent and genius.

3. But if the problem of the One and the Many continued to exercise Greek philosophy in the Post-Socratic period, and received much more satisfactory solutions at the hands of Plato and Aristotle, it is obvious that we cannot characterise Pre-Socratic philosophy by reference to that problem: we require some other note of characterisation and distinction. Where is it to be found? We may say that Pre-Socratic philosophy centres round the external world, the Object, the not-self. Man, the Subject, the self, is of course not excluded from consideration, but the interest in the not-self is predominant. This can be seen from the question which the successive Pre-Socratic thinkers set themselves to answer: "Of what is the world ultimately composed?" In their answers to this question the early Ionian philosophers certainly went beyond what the empirical data warranted, but, as already remarked, they tackled the question in a philosophic spirit and not in the spirit of weavers of mythological fancies. They had not differentiated between physical science and philosophy, and combined "scientific" observations of a purely practical character with philosophic speculations; but it must be remembered that a differentiation between physical science and philosophy was hardly possible at that early stage—men wanted to know something more about the world, and it was but natural that scientific questions and philosophical questions should be mingled together. Since they were concerned with the *ultimate* nature of the world, their theories rank as philosophical; but since they had not yet formed any clear distinction between spirit and matter, and since their question was largely prompted by the fact of material change, their answer was couched for the most part in terms and concepts taken from matter. They found the ultimate "stuff" of the universe to be some kind of matter—naturally enough—whether the water of Thales, the Indeterminate of Anaximander, the air of Anaximenes, the fire of Heraclitus, or the atoms of Leucippus, and so a large part of their subject-matter would be claimed

by physical scientists of to-day as belonging to their province.

The early Greek philosophers are then rightly called Cosmologists, for they were concerned with the nature of the Cosmos, the object of our knowledge, and man himself is considered in his objective aspect, as one item in the Cosmos, rather than in his subjective aspect, as the subject of knowledge or as the morally willing and acting subject. In their consideration of the Cosmos, they did not reach any final conclusion accounting for all the factors involved; and this apparent bankruptcy of Cosmology, together with other causes to be considered presently, naturally led to a swing-over of interest from Object to Subject, from the Cosmos to Man himself. This change of interest, as exemplified in the Sophists, we will consider in the following section of this book.

4. Although it is true that Pre-Socratic philosophy centres round the Cosmos, the external world, and that this cosmological interest is the distinguishing mark of Pre-Socratic as contrasted with Socratic philosophy, it must also be remarked that one problem at any rate connected with man as the knowing subject was raised in Pre-Socratic philosophy, that of the relation between sense-experience and reason. Thus Parmenides, starting with the notion of the One, and finding himself unable to explain coming-to-be and passing-away— which are given in sense-experience—set aside the evidence of the senses as illusion, and proclaimed the sole validity of reason, which alone is able to attain the Real and Abiding. But the problem was not treated in any full or adequate manner, and when Parmenides denied the validity of sense-perception, he did so because of a metaphysical doctrine or assumption, rather than from any prolonged consideration of the nature of sense-perception and the nature of non-sensuous thought.

5. Since the early Greek thinkers may justly be termed philosophers, and since they proceeded largely by way of action and reaction, or thesis and antithesis (e.g. Heraclitus over-emphasising Becoming and Parmenides over-stressing Being), it was only to be expected that the germs of later philosophical tendencies and Schools would already be discernible in Pre-Socratic philosophy. Thus in the Parmenidean doctrine of the One, when coupled with the exaltation of Reason at the expense of sense-perception, we can see the germs of later idealism; while in the introduction of Nous

by Anaxagoras—however restricted his actual use of Nous may have been—we may see the germs of later philosophical theism; and in the atomism of Leucippus and Democritus we may see an anticipation of later materialistic and mechanistic philosophies which would endeavor to explain all quality by quantity and to reduce everything in the universe to matter and its products.

6. From what has been said, it should be clear that Pre-Socratic philosophy is not simply a pre-philosophic stage which can be discounted in a study of Greek thought—so that we should be justified in starting immediately with Socrates and Plato. The Pre-Socratic philosophy is *not* a pre-philosophic stage, but is the first stage of Greek philosophy: it may not be pure and unmixed philosophy, but it is philosophy, and it deserves to be studied for the sake of its own intrinsic interest as the first Greek attempt to attain a rational understanding of the world. Moreover, it is not a self-contained unit, shut off from succeeding philosophic thought in a watertight compartment; rather is it preparatory to the succeeding period, for in it we see problems raised which were to occupy the greatest of Greek philosophers. Greek thought develops, and though we can hardly over-estimate the native genius of men like Plato and Aristotle, it would be wrong to imagine that they were uninfluenced by the past. Plato was profoundly influenced by Pre-Socratic thought, by the Heraclitean, Eleatic and Pythagorean systems; Aristotle regarded his philosophy as the heir and crown of the past; and both thinkers took up philosophic problems from the hands of their predecessors, giving, it is true, original solutions, but at the same time tackling the problems in their historic setting. It would be absurd, therefore, to start a history of Greek philosophy with a discussion of Socrates and Plato without any discussion of preceding thought, for we cannot understand Socrates or Plato—or Aristotle either—without a knowledge of the past.

We must now turn to the next phase of Greek philosophy, which may be considered the antithesis to the preceding period of Cosmological speculation—the Sophistic and Socratic period.

Part Two

THE SOCRATIC PERIOD

Chapter Twelve

THE SOPHISTS

The earlier Greek philosophers had been chiefly interested in the Object, trying to determine the ultimate principle of all things. Their success, however, did not equal their philosophic sincerity, and the successive hypotheses that they advanced easily led to a certain scepticism as to the possibility of attaining any certain knowledge concerning the ultimate nature of the world. Add to this that doctrines such as those of Heraclitus and Parmenides would naturally result in a sceptical attitude in regard to the validity of sense-perception. If being is static and the perception of movement is an illusion, or if, on the other hand, all is in a state of constant change and there is no real principle of stability, our sense-perception is untrustworthy, and so the very foundations of Cosmology are undermined. The systems of philosophy hitherto proposed excluded one another: there was naturally truth to be found in the opposing theories, but no philosopher had yet arisen of sufficient stature to reconcile the antitheses in a higher synthesis, in which error should be purged away and justice done to the truth contained in rival doctrines. The result was bound to be a certain mistrust of cosmologies. And, indeed, a swing-over to the Subject as point of consideration was necessary if real advance was to be made. It was Plato's consideration of thought that made possible a truer theory in which justice should be done to the facts of both stability and mutability; but the reaction from Object to Subject, which made possible the advance, first appears among the Sophists, and was

largely an effect of the bankruptcy of the older Greek philosophy. In face of the dialectic of Zeno, it might well appear
doubtful if advance in the study of cosmology was really
possible.

Another factor besides the scepticism consequent on the
former Greek philosophy, which directed attention to the
Subject, was the growing reflection on the phenomena of
culture and civilisation, due in large part to extended acquaintance on the part of the Greeks with foreign peoples.
Not only did they know something of the civilisations of
Persia, Babylon and Egypt, but they had also come into
contact with people of a much less advanced stage, such as
the Scythians and Thracians. This being so, it was but natural
that a highly intelligent people like the Greeks should begin
to ask themselves questions; e.g. Are the various national
and local ways of life, religious and ethical codes, merely
conventions or not? Was Hellenic culture, as contrasted with
non-Hellenic or barbarian cultures, a matter of νόμος, man-
made and mutable, existing νόμῳ, or did it rest on Nature,
existing Φύσει? Was it a sacred ordinance, having divine
sanction, or could it be changed, modified, adapted, developed? Professor Zeller points out in this connection how
Protagoras, most gifted of the Sophists, came from Abdera,
"an advanced outpost of Ionic culture in the land of the
Thracian barbarian." [1]

Sophism,[2] then, differed from the older Greek philosophy
in regard to the matter with which it dealt, namely, man
and the civilisation and customs of man: it treated of the
microcosm rather than the macrocosm. Man was becoming
self-conscious: as Sophocles says, "Miracles in the world are
many, there is no greater miracle than man." [3] But Sophism
also differed from previous Greek philosophy in its *method*.
Although the method of the older Greek philosophy by no
means excluded empirical observation, yet it was character-
istically deductive. When a philosopher had settled on his
general principle of the world, its ultimate constituent principle, it then remained to explain particular phenomena in
accordance with that theory. The Sophist, however, sought to
amass a wide store of particular observations and facts; they
were Encyclopaedists, Polymaths. Then from these accumulated facts they proceeded to draw conclusions, partly theoretical, partly practical. Thus from the store of facts they
accumulated concerning differences of opinion and belief,

they might draw the conclusion that it is impossible to have any certain knowledge. Or from their knowledge of various nations and ways of life, they might form a theory as to the origin of civilisation or the beginning of language. Or again they might draw practical conclusions, e.g. that society would be most efficiently organised if it were organised in this or that manner. The method of Sophism, then, was "empirico-inductive." [4]

It is to be remembered, however, that the practical conclusions of the Sophists were not meant to establish objective norms, founded on necessary truth. And this fact points to another difference between Sophism and the older Greek philosophy, namely, difference of end. The latter was concerned with objective truth: the Cosmologists wanted to find out the objective truth about the world, they were in the main disinterested seekers after truth. The Sophists, on the other hand, were not primarily intent on objective truth: their end was practical and not speculative. And so the Sophists became instruments of instruction and training in the Greek cities, aiming at teaching the art and control of life. It has been remarked that while a band of disciples was more or less accidental for the Pre-Socratic philosophers —since their primary aim was *finding out* the truth—it was essential for the Sophists, since they aimed at *teaching*.

In Greece, after the Persian Wars, political life was naturally intensified, and this was particularly the case in democratic Athens. The free citizen played some part, at any rate, in political life, and if he wanted to get on he obviously had to have some kind of training. The old education was insufficient for the man who wished to make his way in the State; the old aristocratic ideal was, whether intrinsically superior to the new ideals or not, incapable of meeting the demands made on leaders in the developing democracy: something more was needed, and this need was met by the Sophists. Plutarch says that the Sophists put a theoretical training in the place of the older practical training, which was largely an affair of family tradition, connection with prominent statesmen, practical and experiential training by actual participation in political life. What was now required was courses of instruction, and the Sophists gave such courses in the cities. They were itinerant professors who travelled about from city to city, thus gathering a valuable store of knowledge and experience, and they gave instruction on various themes—grammar, the interpretation of poets, the philosophy of mythology and religion, and so on. But, above all, they professed to teach the art of *Rhetoric,* which was absolutely necessary for political life. In the Greek city-state, above all at Athens, no one could hope to make his mark as a politician unless he could speak, and speak well. The Sophists professed to teach him to do so, training him in the chief expression of political "virtue," the virtue of the new aristocracy of intellect and ability. There was, of course, nothing wrong in this in itself, but the obvious consequence—that the art of rhetoric might be used to "get across" a notion or policy which was not disinterested or might be definitely harmful to the city or merely calculated to promote the politician's career—helped to bring the Sophists into bad repute. This was particularly the case with regard to their teaching of Eristic. If a man wanted to make money in the Greek democracy, it had to be done mainly by lawsuits, and the Sophists professed to teach the right way of winning these lawsuits. But clearly that might easily mean in practice the art of teaching men how to make the unjust appear the just cause. Such a procedure was obviously very different from the procedure of the old truth-seeking attitude of the philosophers, and helps to explain the treatment meted out to the Sophists at the hands of Plato.

The Sophists carried on their work of instruction by the education of the young and by giving popular lectures in the cities; but as they were itinerant professors, men of wide experience and representative of a, as yet, somewhat sceptical and superficial reaction, the idea became current that they gathered together the young men from their homes and then pulled to pieces before them the traditional ethical code and religious beliefs. Accordingly the strict adherents of tradition regarded the Sophists with some suspicion, though the young were their enthusiastic supporters. Not that the levelling-out tendencies of the Sophists were all weakening to Greek life: their breadth of view generally made them advocates of Panhellenism, a doctrine sorely needed in the Greece of the city-state. But it was their sceptical tendencies that attracted most attention, especially as they did not put anything really new and stable in place of the old convictions which they tended to unsettle. To this should be added the fact that they took payment for the instruction which they imparted. This practice, however legitimate in itself, was at variance with the practice of the older Greek philosophers, and did not agree with the Greek opinion of what was fitting. It was abhorrent to Plato, while Xenophon says that the Sophists speak and write to deceive for their gain, and they give no help to anyone.[5]

From what has been said, it is clear that Sophism does not deserve any sweeping condemnation. By turning the attention of thinkers to man himself, the thinking and willing subject, it served as a transition stage to the great Platonic-Aristotelian achievement. In affording a means of training and instruction, it fulfilled a necessary task in the political life of Greece, while its Panhellenistic tendencies certainly stand to its credit. And even its sceptical and relativist tendencies, which were, after all, largely the result of the breakdown of the older philosophy on the one hand, and of a wider experience of human life on the other, at least contributed to the raising of problems, even if Sophism itself was unable to solve these problems. It is not fanciful to discern the influence of Sophism in the Greek drama, e.g. in Sophocles' hymn to human achievement in the *Antigone* and in the theoretical discussions contained in plays of Euripides, and in the works of the Greek historians, e.g. in the celebrated Melian dialogue in the pages of Thucydides. The term Σοφιστής took some time to acquire its disparaging connotation. The name is applied by Herodotus to Solon and Pythagoras, by Androtion to the Seven Wise Men and to Socrates, by Lysias to Plato. Moreover, the older Sophists won for themselves general respect and esteem, and, as historians have pointed out, were not infrequently selected as "ambassadors" of their respective cities, a fact which hardly points to their being or being regarded as charlatans. It was only secondarily that the term "Sophist" acquired an unsavoury flavour—as in Plato; and in later times the term seems to have reacquired a good sense, being applied to the professors of rhetoric and prose writers of the Empire, without the significance of quibbler or cheat. "It is particularly through the opposition to Socrates and Plato that the Sophists have come into such disrepute that the word now usually signifies that, by false reasoning, some truth is either refuted and made dubious, or something false is proved and made plausible."[6]

On the other hand, the relativism of the Sophists, their encouragement of Eristic, their lack of stable norms, their acceptance of payment, and the hair-splitting tendencies of certain later Sophists, justify to a great extent the disparaging signification of the term. For Plato, they are "shopkeepers with spiritual wares";[7] and when Socrates is represented in the *Protagoras*[8] as asking Hippocrates, who wanted to receive instruction from Protagoras, "Wouldn't you be ashamed to show yourself to the Greeks as a Sophist?", Hippocrates answers: "Yes, truly, Socrates, if I am to say what I think." We must, however, remember that Plato tends to bring out the bad side of the Sophists, largely because he had Socrates before his eyes, who had developed what was good in Sophism beyond all comparison with the achievements of the Sophists themselves.

Chapter Thirteen

SOME INDIVIDUAL SOPHISTS

1. Protagoras

Protagoras was born, according to most authors, about 481 B.C., a native of Abdera in Thrace,[1] and seems to have come to Athens about the middle of the century. He enjoyed the favour of Pericles, and we are told that he was entrusted by that statesman with the task of drawing up a constitution for the Panhellenic colony of Thurii, which was founded in 444 B.C. He was again in Athens at the outbreak of the Peloponnesian War in 431 and during the plague in 430, which carried off two of Pericles' sons. Diogenes Laërtius relates the story that Protagoras was indicted for blasphemy because of his book on the gods, but that he escaped from the city before trial and was drowned on the crossing to Sicily, his book being burnt in the market-place. This would have taken place at the time of the oligarchic revolt of the Four Hundred in 411 B.C. Burnet is inclined to regard the story as dubious, and holds that if the indictment did take place, then it must have taken place before 411. Professor Taylor agrees with Burnet in rejecting the prosecution story, but he does so because he also agrees with Burnet in accepting a much earlier date for the birth of Protagoras, namely 500 B.C. The two writers rely on Plato's representation of Protagoras in the dialogue of that name as an elderly man, at least approaching 65, in about the year 435. Plato "must have known whether Protagoras really belonged to the generation before Socrates, and could have no motive for misrepresentation on such a point."[2] If this is correct,

then we ought also to accept the statement in the *Meno*
that Protagoras died in high repute.

The best-known statement of Protagoras is that contained
in his work, Ἀλήθεια ἢ Καταβάλλοντες (λόγοι), to the
effect that "man is the measure of all things, of those that
are that they are, of those that are not that they are not." [3]
There has been a considerable controversy as to the interpretation which should be put on this famous saying, some
writers maintaining the view that by "man" Protagoras does
not mean the individual man, but man in the specific sense.
If this were so, then the meaning of the dictum would not
be that "what appears to you to be true is true for you,
and what appears to me to be true is true for me," but
rather that the community or group or the whole human
species is the criterion and standard of truth. Controversy has
also turned round the question whether things—Χρήματα—
should be understood exclusively of the objects of sense-
perception or should be extended to cover the field of values
as well.

This is a difficult question and it cannot be discussed at
length here, but the present writer is not prepared to disregard the testimony of Plato in the *Theaetetus*, where
the Protagorean dictum, developed it is true, as Plato himself admits, is certainly interpreted in the individualistic
sense in regard to sense-perception.[4] Socrates observes that
when the same wind is blowing, one of us may feel chilly
and the other not, or one may feel slightly chilly and the
other quite cold, and asks if we should agree with Protagoras
that the wind is cold to the one who feels chilly and not to
the other. It is quite clear that in this passage Protagoras is
interpreted as referring to the individual man, and not at all
to man in the specific sense. Moreover, it is to be noted
that the Sophist is not depicted as saying that the wind
merely *appears* chilly to the one and not to the other. Thus
if I have come in from a run in the rain on a cold day,
and say that the water is warm; while you, coming from a
warm room, feel the same water as cold, Protagoras would
remark that neither of us is mistaken—the water *is* warm in
reference to my sense-organ, and *is* cold in reference to your
sense-organ. (When it was objected to the Sophist that geometrical propositions are constant for all, Protagoras replied
that in actual concrete reality there are no geometrical lines
or circles, so that the difficulty does not arise.[5])

Against this interpretation appeal is made to the *Protagoras* of Plato, where Protagoras is not depicted as applying the dictum in an individualistic sense to ethical values. But even granting that Protagoras must be made consistent with himself, it is surely not necessary to suppose that what is true of the objects of sense-perception is *ipso facto* true of ethical values. It may be pointed out that Protagoras declares that man is the measure of πάντων χρημάτων (*all* things), so that if the individualistic interpretation be accepted in regard to the objects of sense-perception, it should also be extended to ethical values and judgments, and that, conversely, if it is not accepted in regard to ethical values and judgments, it should not be accepted in regard to the objects of sense-perception: in other words, we are forced to choose between the *Theaetetus* and *Protagoras*, relying on the one and rejecting the other. But in the first place it is not certain that πάντων χρημάτων is meant to include ethical values, and in the second place it might be well that the objects of the special senses are of such character that they *cannot* become the subject of true and universal knowledge, while on the other hand ethical values are of such a kind that they *can* become the subject of true and universal knowledge. This was the view of Plato himself, who connected the Protagorean saying with the Heraclitan doctrine of flux, and held that true and certain knowledge can only be had of the supersensible. We are not trying to make out that Protagoras held the Platonic view on ethical values, which he did not, but to point out that sense-perception and intuition of values do not *necessarily* stand or fall together in relation to certain knowledge and truth for all.

What, then, was Protagoras' actual teaching in regard to ethical judgments and values? In the *Theaetetus* he is depicted as saying both that ethical judgments are relative ("For I hold that whatever practices seem right and laudable to any particular State are so for that State, so long as it holds by them") and that the wise man should attempt to substitute sound practices for unsound.[6] In other words, there is no question of one ethical view being true and another false, but there is question of one view being "sounder," i.e. more useful or expedient, than another. "In this way it is true both that some men are wiser than others and that no one thinks falsely." (A man who thinks that there is no absolute truth, is hardly entitled to declare abso-

lutely that "no one thinks falsely.") Now, in the *Protagoras*,
Plato depicts the Sophist as maintaining that αἰδώς and
δίκη, have been bestowed on *all* men by the gods, "because cities could not exist if, as in the case of other arts,
few men only were partakers of them." Is this at variance
with what is said in the *Theaetus*? It would appear that
what Protagoras means is this: that Law in general is
founded on certain ethical tendencies implanted in all men,
but that the individual varieties of Law, as found in particular States, are relative, the law of one State, without
being "truer" than that of another State, being perhaps
"sounder" in the sense of more useful or expedient. The State
or city-community would be the determiner of law in this
case and not the individual, but the relative character of
concrete ethical judgments and concrete determinations of
Nomos would be maintained. As an upholder of tradition
and social convention, Protagoras stresses the importance
of education, of imbibing the ethical traditions of the State,
while admitting that the wise man may lead the State to
"better" laws. As far as the individual citizen is concerned,
he should cleave to tradition, to the accepted code of the
community—and that all the more because no one "way" is
truer than another. αἰδώς and δίκη incline him to this,
and if he has no share in these gifts of the gods and refuses
to hearken to the State, the State must get rid of him.
While at first sight, therefore, the "relativistic" doctrine of
Protagoras might seem intentionally revolutionary, it turns
out to be used in support of tradition and authority. No
one code is "truer" than another, therefore do not set up
your private judgment against the law of the State. Moreover, through his conception of αἰδώς and δίκη Protagoras
gives at least some hints of the unwritten or natural law,
and in this respect contributed to the broadening of the
Greek outlook.

In a work, Περὶ θεῶν, Protagoras said: "With regard to
the gods, I cannot feel sure either that they are or that they
are not, nor what they are like in figure; for there are many
things that hinder sure knowledge, the obscurity of the
subject and the shortness of human life." [7] This is the only
fragment of the work that we possess. Such a sentence might
seem to lend colour to the picture of Protagoras as a sceptical and destructive thinker, who turned his critical powers
against all established tradition in ethics and religion; but

such a view does not agree with the impression of Protagoras which we receive from Plato's dialogue of that name, and would doubtless be mistaken. Just as the moral to be drawn from the relativity of particular codes of law is that the individual should submit himself to the traditional education, so the moral to be drawn from our uncertainty concerning the gods and their nature is that we should abide by the religion of the city. If we cannot be certain of absolute truth, why throw overboard the religion that we inherit from our fathers? Moreover, Protagoras' attitude is not so extraordinary or destructive as the adherents of a dogmatic religion might naturally suppose, since, as Burnet remarks, Greek religion did not consist "in theological affirmations or negations" but in worship.[8] The effect of the Sophists, it is true, would have been to weaken men's trust in tradition, but it would appear that Protagoras personally was conservative in temper and had no intention of educating revolutionaries; on the contrary, he professed to educate the good citizen. There are ethical tendencies in all men, but these can develop only in the organised community: if a man is to be a good citizen, therefore, he must absorb the whole social tradition of the community of which he is a member. The social tradition is not absolute truth, but it is the norm for a good citizen.

From the relativistic theory it follows that on every subject more than one opinion is possible, and Protagoras seems to have developed this point in his Ἀντιλογίαι. The dialectician and rhetorician will practise himself in the art of developing different opinions and arguments, and he will shine most brightly when he succeeds τὸν ἥττω λόγον κρείττω ποιεῖν. The enemies of the Sophists interpreted this in the sense of making the *morally worse* cause to prevail,[9] but it does not necessarily possess this morally destructive sense. A lawyer, for example, who pleaded with success the just cause of a client who was too weak to protect himself or the justice of whose cause it was difficult to substantiate, might be said to be making the "weaker argument" prevail, though he would be doing nothing immoral. In the hands of unscrupulous rhetoricians and devotees of eristic, the maxim easily acquired an unsavoury flavour, but there is no reason to father on Protagoras himself a desire to promote unscrupulous dealing. Still, it cannot be denied that the doctrine of relativism, when linked up with the practice of dialectic and eristic, very naturally produces a desire to succeed, without much regard for truth or justice.

Protagoras was a pioneer in the study and science of grammar. He is said to have classified the different kinds of sentence[10] and to have distinguished terminologically the genders of nouns.[11] In an amusing passage of the *Clouds* Aristophanes depicts the Sophist as coining the feminine 'αλεκτρύαινα from the masculine 'αλεκτρυών (cock).[12]

2. *Prodicus*

Prodicus came from the island of Ceos in the Aegean. The inhabitants of this island were said to be pessimistically inclined, and Prodicus was credited with the tendencies of his countrymen, for in the pseudo-Platonic dialogue *Axiochus* he is credited with holding that death is desirable in order to escape the evils of life. Fear of death is irrational, since death concerns neither the living nor the dead—the first, because they are still living, the second, because they are not living any more.[13] The authenticity of this quotation is not easy to establish.

Prodicus is perhaps chiefly remarkable for his theory on the origin of religion. He held that in the beginning men worshipped as gods the sun, moon, rivers, lakes, fruits, etc.—in other words, the things which were useful to them and gave them food. And he gives as an example the cult of the Nile in Egypt. This primitive stage was followed by another, in which the inventors of various arts—agriculture, viniculture, metal work, and so on—were worshipped as the gods Demeter, Dionysus, Hephaestus, etc. On this view of religion prayer would, he thought, be superfluous, and he seems to have got into trouble with the authorities at Athens.[14] Prodicus, like Protagoras, was noted for linguistic studies,[15] and he wrote a treatise on synonyms. He seems to have been very pedantic in his forms of expression.[16]

(Professor Zeller says:[17] "Although Plato usually treats him with irony, it nevertheless speaks well for him that Socrates occasionally recommended pupils to him [*Theaet.*, 151b], and that his native city repeatedly entrusted him with diplomatic mission [*Hipp. Maj.*, 282 c]." As a matter of fact, Zeller seems to have missed the point in the *Theaetetus* passage, since the young men that Socrates has sent to Prodicus are those who, he has found, have not been "pregnant" with thoughts when in his company. He has accordingly sent them off to Prodicus, in whose company they have ceased to be "barren.")

3. Hippias

Hippias of Elis was a younger contemporary of Protagoras and was celebrated particularly for his versatility, being acquainted with mathematics, astronomy, grammar and rhetoric, rhythmics and harmony, history and literature and mythology—in short, he was a true Polymath. Not only that, but when present at a certain Olympiad, he boasted that he had made all his own clothes. His list of the Olympic victors laid the foundation for the later Greek system of dating by means of the Olympiads (first introduced by the historian Timaeus).[18] Plato, in the *Protagoras*, makes him say that "law being the tyrant of men, forces them to do many things contrary to nature."[19] The point seems to be that the law of the city-state is often narrow and tyrannical and at variance with the natural laws (ἄγραφοι νόμοι).

4. Gorgias

Gorgias of Leontini, in Sicily, lived from about 483 to 375 B.C., and in the year 427 he came to Athens as ambassador of Leontini, in order to ask for help against Syracuse. On his travels he did what he could to spread the spirit of Panhellenism.

Gorgias seems to have been at first a pupil of Empedocles, and to have busied himself with questions of natural science, and may have written a book on Optics. He was led, however, to scepticism by the dialectic of Zeno and published a work entitled *On Not-being or Nature* (Περὶ τοῦ μὴ ὄντος ἢ περὶ Φύσεως), the chief ideas of which can be gathered from Sextus Empiricus and from the pseudo-Aristotelian writing *On Melissus, Xenophanes and Gorgias*. From these accounts of the contents of Gorgias' work it is clear that he reacted to the Eleatic dialectic somewhat differently to Protagoras, since while the latter might be said to hold that everything is true, Gorgias maintained the very opposite. According to Gorgias, (i) Nothing exists, for if there were anything, then it would have either to be eternal or to have come into being. But it cannot have come into being, for neither out of Being nor out of Not-being can anything come to be. Nor can it be eternal, for if it were eternal, then it would have to be infinite. But the infinite is impossible for the following reason. It could not be in another, nor could it be in itself, therefore it would be nowhere. But what is nowhere, is nothing. (ii) If there were anything, then it could not be known. For if there is knowledge of being, then what is thought must be, and Not-being could not be thought at all. In which case there could be no error, which is absurd. (iii) Even if there were knowledge of being, this knowledge could not be imparted. Every sign is different from the thing signified; e.g. how could we impart knowledge of colours by word, since the ear hears tones and not colours? And how could the same representation of being be in the two persons at once, since they are different from one another?[20]

While some have regarded these astonishing ideas as expressing a seriously meant philosophical Nihilism, others have thought that the doctrine constitutes a joke on the part of Gorgias, or, rather, that the great rhetorician wanted to show that rhetoric or the skilful use of words was able to make plausible even the most absurd hypothesis. (*Sic* H. Gomperz.) But this latter view hardly agrees with the fact that Isocrates sets Gorgias' opinions besides those of Zeno and Melissus, nor with the writing Πρὸς τὰ Γοργίου, which treats Gorgias' opinions as worth a philosophical criticism.[21] In any case a treatise on Nature would scarcely be the place for such rhetorical *tours de force*. On the other hand, it is difficult to suppose that Gorgias held in all seriousness that nothing exists. It may be that he wished to employ the Eleatic dialectic in order to reduce the Eleatic philosophy to absurdity.[22] Afterwards, renouncing philosophy, he devoted himself to rhetoric.

Rhetorical art was regarded by Gorgias as the mastery of the art of persuasion, and this necessarily led him to a study of practical psychology. He deliberately practised the art of suggestion (ψυχαγωγία), which could be used both for practical ends, good and bad, and for artistic purposes. In connection with the latter Gorgias developed the art of justifiable deception (δικαία 'απάτη), calling a tragedy "a deception which is better to cause than not to cause; to succumb to it shows greater powers of artistic appreciation than not to." [23] Gorgias' comparison of the effects of tragedy to those of purgatives reminds us of Aristotle's much-discussed doctrine of the κάθαρσις.

The fact that Plato places the might-is-right doctrine in the mouth of Callicles,[24] while another disciple, Lycophron, asserted that nobility is a sham and that all men are equal, and that the law is a contract by which right is mutually guaranteed,[25] while yet another disciple demanded the liberation of slaves in the name of natural law,[26] we may ascribe with Zeller to Gorgias' renunciation of philosophy, which led him to decline to answer questions of truth and morality.[27]

Other Sophists whom one may briefly mention are Thrasymachus of Chalcedon, who is presented in the *Republic* as the brutal champion of the rights of the stronger,[28] and Antiphon of Athens, who asserts the equality of all men and denounces the distinction between nobles and commons, Greeks and barbarians, as itself a barbarism. He made education to be the most important thing in life, and created the literary *genre* of Τέχνη ἀλυπίας λόγοι παραμυθητικοί, declaring that he could free anyone from sorrow by oral means.[29]

5. Sophism

In conclusion I may observe again that there is no reason for ascribing to the great Sophists the intention of overthrowing religion and morality; men like Protagoras and Gorgias had no such end in view. Indeed, the great Sophists favoured the conception of a "natural law," and tended to broaden the outlook of the ordinary Greek citizen; they were an educative force in Hellas. At the same time it is true that "in a certain sense every opinion is true, according to Protagoras; every opinion is false, according to Gorgias." [30] This tendency to deny the absolute and objective character of truth easily leads to the consequence that, instead of trying to *convince* anyone, the Sophist will try to *persuade* him or talk him over. Indeed, in the hands of lesser men Sophism soon acquired an unpleasant connotation—that of "Sophistry." While one can only respect the cosmopolitanism and broad outlook of an Antiphon of Athens, one can only condemn the "Might-is-Right" theory of a Thrasymachus on the one hand and the hair-splitting and quibbling of a

Dionysodorus on the other. The great Sophists, as we have said, were an educative force in Hellas; but one of the chief factors in the Greek education which they fostered was rhetoric, and rhetoric had its obvious dangers, inasmuch as the orator might easily tend to pay more attention to the rhetorical presentation of a subject than to the subject itself. Moreover, by questioning the absolute foundations of traditional institutions, beliefs and ways of life, Sophism tended to foster a relativistic attitude, though the evil latent in Sophism lay not so much in the fact that it raised problems, as in the fact that it could not offer any satisfactory intellectual solution to the problems it raised. Against this relativism Socrates and Plato reacted, endeavouring to establish the sure foundation of true knowledge and ethical judgments.

Chapter Fourteen

SOCRATES

1. Early Life of Socrates

The death of Socrates fell in the year 399 B.C., and as Plato
tells us that Socrates was seventy years old or a little more
at the time of his death, he must have been born about
470 B.C.[1] He was the son of Sophroniscus and Phaenarete
of the Antiochid tribe and the *deme* of Alopecae. Some
have said that his father was a worker in stone,[2] but A. E.
Taylor thinks, with Burnet, that the story was a misunder-
standing which arose from a playful reference in the *Euthyphro* to Daedalus as the ancestor of Socrates.[3] In any case,
Socrates does not seem to have himself followed his father's
trade, if it was his father's trade, and the group of Graces
on the Akropolis, which were later shown as the work of
Socrates, are attributed by archaeologists to an earlier sculp-
tor.[4] Socrates cannot, however, have come from a very
poor family, as we find him later serving as a fully-armed
hoplite, and he must have been left sufficient patrimony to
enable him to undertake such a service. Phaenarete, Socrates'
mother, is described in the *Theaetetus*[5] as a midwife, but
even if she was, this should not be taken to imply that she
was a professional midwife in the modern sense, as Taylor
points out.[6] Socrates' early life thus fell in the great flowering
of Athenian splendour. The Persians had been defeated at
Plataea in 479 and Aeschylus had produced the *Persae* in
472: Sophocles and Euripides were still boys.[7] Moreover,
Athens had already laid the foundation of her maritime
empire.

In Plato's *Symposium* Alcibiades describes Socrates as

looking like a satyr or Silenus,[8] and Aristophanes said that
he strutted like a waterfowl and ridiculed his habit of
rolling his eyes.[9] But we also know that he was possessed
of particular robustness of body and powers of endurance.
As a man he wore the same garment winter and summer,
and continued his habit of going barefoot, even on a winter
campaign. Although very abstemious in food and drink, he
could drink a great deal without being any the worse for
it. From his youth upwards he was the recipient of pro-
hibitory messages or warnings from his mysterious "voice"
or "sign" or *daimon*. The *Symposium* tells us of his prolonged fits of abstraction, one lasting the whole of a day and
night—and that on a military campaign. Professor Taylor
would like to interpret these abstractions as ecstasies or rapts,
but it would seem more likely that they were prolonged fits
of abstraction due to intense mental concentration on some
problem, a phenomenon not unknown in the case of some
other thinkers, even if not on so large a scale. The very
length of the "ecstasy" mentioned in the *Symposium* would
seem to militate against its being a real rapture in the
mystico-religious sense,[10] though such a prolonged fit of
abstraction would also be exceptional.

When Socrates was in his early twenties, thought, as we
have seen, tended to turn away from the cosmological speculations of the Ionians towards man himself, but it seems
certain that Socrates began by studying the cosmological
theories of East and West in the philosophies of Archelaus,
Diogenes of Apollonia, Empedocles and others. Theophrastus
asserts that Socrates was actually a member of the School
of Archelaus, the successor of Anaxagoras at Athens.[11] In
any case Socrates certainly suffered a disappointment
through Anaxagoras. Perplexed by the disagreement of the
various philosophical theories, Socrates received a sudden
light from the passage where Anaxagoras spoke of Mind as
being the cause of all natural law and order. Delighted
with the passage, Socrates began to study Anaxagoras, in
the hope that the latter would explain how Mind works in
the universe, ordering all things for the best. What he
actually found was that Anaxagoras introduced Mind merely
in order to get the vortex-movement going. This disappointment set Socrates on his own line of investigation, abandoning the Natural Philosophy which seemed to lead nowhere,
save to confusion and opposite opinions.[12]

A. E. Taylor conjectures that on Archelaus' death, Socrates was to all intents and purposes his successor.[13] He tries to support this contention with the aid of Aristophanes' play, *The Clouds*, where Socrates and his associates of the notion-factory or Φροντιστήριον are represented as addicted to the natural sciences and as holding the air-doctrine of Diogenes of Apollonia.[14] Socrates' disclaimer, therefore, that he ever took "pupils" [15] would, if Taylor's conjecture be correct, mean that he had taken no paying pupils. He had had ἑταῖροι, but had never had μαθηταί. Against this it may be urged that in the *Apology* Socrates expressly declares: "But the simple truth is, O Athenians, that I have nothing to do with physical speculations." [16] It is true that at the time when Socrates was depicted as speaking in the *Apology* he had long ago given up cosmological speculation, and that his words do not necessarily imply that he *never* engaged in such speculations; indeed, we know for a fact that he *did;* but it seems to the present writer that the whole tone of the passage militates against the idea that Socrates was ever the professed head of a School dedicated to this kind of speculation. What is said in the *Apology* certainly does not prove, in the strict sense, that Socrates was not the head of such a School before his "conversion," but it would seem that the natural interpretation is that he never occupied such a position.

The "conversion" of Socrates, which brought about the definite change to Socrates the ironic moral philosopher, seems to have been due to the famous incident of the Delphic Oracle. Chaerephon, a devoted friend of Socrates, asked the Oracle if there was any man living who was wiser than Socrates, and received the answer "No." This set Socrates thinking, and he came to the conclusion that the god meant that he was the wisest man because he recognised his own ignorance. He then came to conceive of his mission as being to seek for the stable and certain truth, true wisdom, and to enlist the aid of any man who would consent to listen to him.[17] However strange the story of the Oracle may appear, it most probably really happened, since it is unlikely that Plato would have put a mere invention into the mouth of Socrates in a dialogue which obviously purports to give an historical account of the trial of the philosopher, especially as the *Apology* is of early date, and many who knew the facts were still living.

Socrates' marriage with Xanthippe is best known for the stories about her shrewish character, which may or may not be true. Certainly they are scarcely borne out by the picture of Socrates' wife given in the *Phaedo*. The marriage probably took place some time in the first ten years of the Peloponnesian War. In this war Socrates distinguished himself for bravery at the siege of Potidaea, 431/30, and again at the defeat of the Athenians by the Boeotians in 424. He was also present at the action outside Amphipolis in 422.[18]

2. *Problem of Socrates*

The problem of Socrates is the problem of ascertaining exactly what his philosophical teaching was. The character of the sources at our disposal—Xenophon's Socratic works (*Memorabilia* and *Symposium*), Plato's dialogues, various statements of Aristotle, Aristophanes' *Clouds*—make this a difficult problem. For instance, were one to rely on Xenophon alone, one would have the impression of a man whose chief interest was to make good men and citizens, but who did not concern himself with problems of logic and metaphysics—a popular ethical teacher. If, on the other hand, one were to found one's conception of Socrates on the Platonic dialogues taken as a whole, one would receive the impression of a metaphysician of the highest order, a man who did not content himself with questions of daily conduct, but laid the foundations of a transcendental philosophy, distinguished by its doctrine of a metaphysical world of Forms. Statements of Aristotle, on the other hand (if given their natural interpretation), give us to understand that while Socrates was not uninterested in theory, he did not himself teach the doctrine of subsistent Forms or Ideas, which is characteristic of Platonism.

The common view has been that though Xenophon's portrayal is too "ordinary" and "trivial," mainly owing to Xenophon's lack of philosophical ability and interest (it has indeed been held, though it seems unlikely, that Xenophon deliberately tried to make Socrates appear more "ordinary" than he actually was and than he knew him to be, for apologetic purposes), we cannot reject the testimony of Aristotle, and are accordingly forced to conclude that Plato, except in the early Socratic works, e.g. the *Apology*, put his own doctrines into the mouth of Socrates. This view has the great advantage that the Xenophontic and the Platonic Socrates are not placed in glaring opposition and inconsistency (for the shortcomings of Xenophon's picture can be explained as a result of Xenophon's own character and predominant interests), while the clear testimony of Aristotle is not thrown overboard. In this way a more or less consistent picture of Socrates is evolved, and no unjustified violence (so the upholders of the theory would maintain) is done to any of the sources.

This view has, however, been challenged. Karl Joel, for example, basing his conception of Socrates on the testimony of Aristotle, maintains that Socrates was an intellectualist or rationalist, representing the Attic type, and that the Xenophontic Socrates, a *Willensethiker*, representing the Spartan type, is unhistorical. According to Joel, therefore, Xenophon gave a Doric colouring to Socrates and misrepresented him.[19]

Döring, on the contrary, maintained that we must look to Xenophon in order to obtain our historical picture of Socrates. Aristotle's testimony simply comprises the summary judgment of the Old Academy on Socrates' philosophical importance, while Plato used Socrates as a peg on which to hang his own philosophical doctrines.[20] Another view has been propagated in this country by Burnet and Taylor. According to them the historic Socrates is the *Platonic* Socrates.[21] Plato no doubt elaborated the thought of Socrates, but, all the same, philosophical teaching which is put into his mouth in the dialogues substantially represents the actual teaching of Socrates. If this were correct, then Socrates would himself have been responsible for the metaphysical theory of Forms or Ideas, and the statement of Aristotle (that Socrates did not "separate" the Forms) must be either rejected, as due to ignorance, or explained away. It is most unlikely, say Burnet and Taylor, that Plato would have put his own theories into the mouth of Socrates if the latter had never held them, when people who had actually known Socrates and knew what he really taught, were still living. They point out, moreover, that in some of the later dialogues of Plato, Socrates no longer plays a leading part, while in the *Laws* he is left out altogether—the inference being that where Socrates *does* play the leading part, it is his own ideas, and not simply Plato's, that he is giving, while in the later dialogues Plato is developing independent views (independent of Socrates at least), and so Socrates is allowed to drop into the background. This last argument is undoubtedly a strong one, as is also the fact that in an "early" dialogue, such as the *Phaedo*, which deals with the death of Socrates, the theory of Forms occupies a prominent place. But, if the Platonic Socrates is the historic Socrates, we ought logically to say that in the *Timaeus*, for example, Plato is putting into the mouth of the chief speaker opinions for which he, Plato, did not take the responsibility, since, if Socrates does not stand for Plato himself, there is no compelling reason why Timaeus should do so either. A. E. Taylor indeed does not hesitate to adopt this extreme, if consistent, position; but not only is it *prima facie* extremely unlikely that we can thus free Plato from responsibility for most of what he says in the dialogues, but also, as regards the *Timaeus*, if Taylor's opinion is true, how are we to explain that this remarkable fact first became manifest in the twentieth century A.D.? [22] Again, the consistent maintenance of the Burnet-Taylor view of the Platonic Socrates involves the ascription to Socrates of elaborations, refinements and explanations of the Ideal Theory which it is most improbable that the historic Socrates really evolved, and which would lead to a complete ignoring of the testimony of Aristotle.

It is true that much of the criticism levelled against the Ideal Theory by Aristotle in the *Metaphysics* is directed against the mathematical form of the theory maintained by Plato in his lectures at the Academy, and that in certain particulars there is a curious neglect of what Plato says in the dialogues, a fact which might appear to indicate that Aristotle only recognised as Platonic the unpublished theory developed in the Academy; but it certainly would not be adequate to say that there was a complete dichotomy between the version of the theory that Aristotle gives (whether fairly or unfairly) and the evolving theory of the dialogues. Moreover, the very fact that the theory undergoes evolution, modification and refinement in the dialogues would imply that it represents, in part at least, Plato's own reflections on his position. Later writers of Antiquity certainly believed that we can look to the dialogues for Plato's own philosophy, though they differ concerning the relation of the dialogues to the teaching of Socrates, the earlier among them believing that Plato introduced much of his own thought into the dialogues. Syrianus contradicts Aristotle, but Professor Field observes that his reasons appear to be "his own sense of what was fitting in the relation of teacher and disciple." [23]

An argument in favour of the Burnet-Taylor hypothesis is constituted by the passage in the second Letter, where Plato affirms that what he has said in writing is nothing but Socrates "beautified and rejuvenated." [24] In the first place, however, the genuineness of the passage, or even of the whole letter, is not certain, while in the second place it could be perfectly well explained as meaning that the dialogues give what Plato considered the metaphysical super-structure legitimately elaborated by himself on the basis of what Socrates actually said. (Field suggests that it might refer to the application of the Socratic method and spirit to "modern" problems.) For no one would be so foolish as to maintain that the dialogues contain nothing of the historic Socrates. It is obvious that the early dialogues would naturally take as their point of departure the teaching of the historic Socrates, and if Plato worked out the epistemological and ontological theories of succeeding dialogues through reflection on this teaching, he might legitimately regard the results attained as a justifiable development and application of Socrates' teaching and method. His words in the Letter would gain in point from his conviction that while the Ideal Theory as elaborated in the dialogues might, without undue violence, be regarded as a continuation and development of the Socratic teaching, this would not be equally true of the mathematical form of the theory given in the Academy.

It would, of course, be ridiculous to suggest that a view sponsored by such scholars as Professor Taylor and Professor Burnet could be lightly dismissed, and to make any such suggestion is very far from the mind of the present writer; but in a general book on Greek philosophy it is impossible to treat of the question at any considerable length or to give the Burnet-Taylor theory the full and detailed consideration that it deserves. I must, however, express my agreement with what Mr. Hackforth, for example, has said[25] concerning the lack of justification for ignoring the testimony of Aristotle that Socrates did not separate the Forms. Aristotle had been for twenty years in the Academy and interested as he was in the history of philosophy, can scarcely have neglected to ascertain the origin of such an important Platonic doctrine as the theory of Forms. Add to this the fact that the extant fragments of the Dialogues of Aeschines give us no reason to differ from the view of Aristotle, and Aeschines was said to have given the most accurate portrait of Socrates. For these reasons it seems best to accept the testimony of Aristotle, and, while admitting that the Xenophontic Socrates is not the complete Socrates, to maintain the traditional view, that Plato did put his own theories into the mouth of the Master whom he so much reverenced. The short account of Socrates' philosophical activity now to be given is therefore based on the traditional view. Those who maintain the theory of Burnet and Taylor would, of course, say that violence is thereby done to Plato; but is the situation bettered by doing violence to Aristotle? If the latter had not enjoyed personal intercourse with Plato and his disciples over a long space of time, we might have allowed the possibility of a mistake on his part; but in view of his twenty years in the Academy this mistake would appear to be ruled out of court. However it is unlikely that we shall ever obtain absolute certainty as to the historically accurate picture of Socrates, and it would be most unwise to dismiss all conceptions save one's own as unworthy of consideration. One can only state one's reasons for accepting one picture of Socrates rather than another, and leave it at that.

(Use has been made of Xenophon in the following short account of Socrates' teaching: we cannot believe that Xenophon was either a nincompoop or a liar. It is perfectly true that while it is difficult—sometimes, no doubt, impossible—to distinguish between Plato and Socrates, "it is almost as hard to distinguish between Socrates and Xenophon. For the *Memorabilia* is as much a work of art as any Platonic dialogue, though the manner is as different as was Xenophon from Plato." [26] But, as Mr. Lindsay points out, Xenophon wrote much besides the *Memorabilia*, and consideration of his writings in general may often show us what is Xenophon, even if it does not always show us what is Socrates. The *Memorabilia* gives us the impression that Socrates made on Xenophon, and we believe that it is in the main trustworthy, even if it is always as well to remember the old scholastic adage, *Quidquid recipitur, secundum modum recipientis recipitur.*)

3. Philosophical Activity of Socrates

1. Aristotle declares that there are two improvements in science which we might justly ascribe to Socrates—his employment of "inductive arguments and universal definitions" (τοὺς τ' ἐπακτικοὺς λόγους καὶ τὸ ὁρίζεσθαι καθόλου).[27] The last remark should be understood in connection with the following statement, that "Socrates did not make the universals or the definitions exist apart; his successor, however, gave them separate existence, and this was the kind of thing they called Ideas."

Socrates was therefore concerned with universal definitions, i.e. with the attaining of fixed concepts. The Sophists propounded relativistic doctrines, rejecting the necessarily and universally valid. Socrates, however, was struck by the fact that the universal concept remains the same: particular instances may vary, but the definition stands fast. This idea can be made clear by an example. The Aristotelian definition of man is "rational animal." Now, individual men vary in their gifts: some are possessed of great intellectual gifts, others not. Some guide their lives according to reason: others surrender without thought to instinct and passing impulse. Some men do not enjoy the unhampered use of their reason, whether because they are asleep or because they are "mentally defective." But all animals who possess the gift of reason—whether they are actually using it or not, whether they can use it freely or are prevented by some organic defect—are men: the definition of man is fulfilled in them, and this definition remains constant, holding good for all. If "man," then "rational animal"; if "rational animal," then "man." We cannot now discuss the precise status or objective reference of our generic and specific notions: we simply want to illustrate the contrast between the particular and the universal, and to point out the constant character of the definition. Some thinkers have maintained that the universal concept is purely subjective, but it is very difficult to see how we could form such universal notions, and why we should be compelled to form them, unless there was a foundation for them in fact. We shall have to return later to the question of the objective reference and metaphysical status of universals: let it suffice at present to point out that the universal concept or definition presents us with something constant and abiding

that stands out, through its possession of these characteristics, from the world of perishing particulars. Even if all
men were blotted out of existence, the definition of man as
"rational animal" would remain constant. Again, we may
speak of a piece of gold as being "true gold," implying that
the definition of gold, the standard or universal criterion,
is realised in this piece of gold. Similarly we speak of things
as being more or less beautiful, implying that they approach
the standard of Beauty in a greater or less degree, a standard which does not vary or change like the beautiful objects
of our experience, but remains constant and "rules," as it
were, all particular beautiful objects. Of course, we might
be mistaken in supposing that we knew the standard of
Beauty, but in speaking of objects as more or less beautiful
we imply that there *is* a standard. To take a final illustration. Mathematicians speak of and define the line, the circle,
etc. Now, the perfect line and the perfect circle are not
found among the objects of our experience: there are at
best only approximations to the definitions of the line or
the circle. There is a contrast, therefore, between the imperfect and changeable objects of our everyday experience on
the one hand and the universal concept or definition on
the other hand. It is easy to see, then, how Socrates was
led to attach such importance to the universal definition.
With a predominant interest in ethical conduct, he saw
that the definition affords a sure rock on which men could
stand amidst the sea of the Sophist relativistic doctrines.
According to a relativistic ethic, justice, for example, varies
from city to city, community to community: we can never
say that justice is this or that, and that this definition
holds good for all States, but only that justice in Athens is
this and in Thrace that. But if we can once attain to a universal definition of justice, which expresses the innermost
nature of justice and holds good for all men, then we have
something sure to go upon, and we can judge not only
individual actions, but also the moral codes of different
States, in so far as they embody or recede from the universal
definition of justice.

2. To Socrates, says Aristotle, may rightly be ascribed
"inductive arguments." Now, just as it is a mistake to suppose that in occupying himself with "universal definitions"
Socrates was concerned to discuss the metaphysical status
of the universal, so it would be a mistake to suppose that

in occupying himself with "inductive arguments" Socrates was concerned with problems of logic. Aristotle, looking back on Socrates' actual practice and method, sums it up in logical terms; but that should not be taken to imply that Socrates developed an explicit theory of Induction from the standpoint of a logician.

What was Socrates' practical method? It took the form of "dialectic" or conversation. He would get into conversation with someone and try to elicit from him his ideas on some subject. For instance, he might profess his ignorance of what courage really is, and ask the other man if he had any light on the subject. Or Socrates would lead the conversation in that direction, and when the other man had used the world "courage," Socrates would ask him what courage is, professing his own ignorance and desire to learn. His companion had used the word, therefore he must know what it meant. When some definition or description had been given him, Socrates would profess his great satisfaction, but would intimate that there were one or two little difficulties which he would like to see cleared up. Accordingly he asked questions, letting the other man do most of the talking, but keeping the course of the conversation under his control, and so would expose the inadequacy of the proposed definition of courage. The other would fall back on a fresh or modified definition, and so the process would go on, with or without final success.

The dialectic, therefore, proceeded from less adequate definitions to a more adequate definition, or from consideration of particular examples to a universal definition. Sometimes indeed no definite result would be arrived at;[28] but in any case the aim was the same, to attain a true and universal definition; and as the argument proceeded from the particular to the universal, or from the less perfect to the more perfect, it may truly be said to be a process of induction. Xenophon mentions some of the ethical phenomena which Socrates sought to investigate, and the nature of which he hoped to enshrine in definitions—e.g. piety and impiety, just and unjust, courage and cowardice.[29] (The early dialogues of Plato deal with the same ethical values— the *Euthyphron* with piety (no result); the *Charmides* with temperance (no result); the *Lysis* with friendship (no result.) The investigation is, for instance, concerning the nature of injustice. Examples are brought forward—to deceive, to injure, to enslave, and so on. It is then pointed out that it is only when these things are done to friends that they are unjust. But the difficulty arises that if one, for example, steals a friend's sword when he is in a passing state of despair and wishes to commit suicide, no injustice is committed. Nor is it unjust on a father's part if he employs deception in order to induce his sick son to take the medicine which will heal him. It appears, therefore, that actions are unjust only when they are performed *against friends with the intention of harming them.*[30]

3. This dialectic might, of course, prove somewhat irritating or even disconcerting or humiliating to those whose ignorance was exposed and whose cocksureness was broken down—and it may have tickled the fancy of the young men who congregated round Socrates to hear their elders being "put in the sack"—but the aim of Socrates was not to humiliate or to disconcert. His aim was to discover the truth, not as matter of pure speculation, but with a view to the good life: in order to act well, one must know what the good life is. His "irony," then, his profession of ignorance, was sincere; he did not know, but he wanted to find out, and he wanted to induce others to reflect for themselves and to give real thought to the supremely important work of caring for their souls. Socrates was deeply convinced of the value of the soul, in the sense of the thinking and willing subject, and he saw clearly the importance of knowledge, of true wisdom, if the soul is to be properly tended. What are the true values of human life which have to be realised in conduct? Socrates called his method "midwifery," not merely by way of playful allusion to his mother, but to express his intention of getting others to produce true ideas in their minds, with a view to right action. This being so, it is easy to understand why Socrates gave so much attention to definition. He was not being pedantic, he was convinced that a clear knowledge of the truth is essential for the right control of life. He wanted to give birth to true ideas in the clear form of definition, not for a speculative but for a practical end. Hence his preoccupation with ethics.

4. I have said that Socrates' interest was predominantly ethical. Aristotle says quite clearly that Socrates "was busying himself about ethical matters." [31] And again, "Socrates occupied himself with the excellences of character, and in connection with them became the first to raise the problem

of universal definitions." [32] This statement of Aristotle is certainly borne out by the picture of Socrates given by Xenophon.

Plato in the *Apology* relates the profession of Socrates at his trial, that he went where he could do the greatest good to anyone, seeking "to persuade every man among you that he must look to himself, and seek virtue and wisdom before he looks to his private interests, and look to the State before he looks to the interests of the State; and that this should be the order which he observes in all his actions." [33] This was the "mission" of Socrates, which he regarded as having been imposed upon him by the god of Delphi, to stimulate men to care for their noblest possession, their soul, through the acquisition of wisdom and virtue. He was no mere pedantic logician, no mere destructive critic, but a man with a mission. If he criticised and exposed superficial views and easygoing assumptions, this was due not to a frivolous desire to display his own superior dialectical acumen, but to a desire to promote the good of his interlocutors and to learn himself.

Of course it is not to be expected in a member of a Greek City state that an ethical interest should be completely severed from a political interest, for the Greek was essentially a citizen and he had to lead the good life within the framework of the city. Thus Xenophon relates that Socrates inquired τί πόλις, τί πολιτικός, τί ἀρχὴ ἀνθρώπων, τί ἀρχηγὸς ἀνθρώπων, and we have seen Socrates' statement in the *Apology* about looking to the State itself before looking to the interests of the State. [34] But, as the last remark implies, and as is clear from Socrates' life, he was not concerned with party politics as such, but with political life in its ethical aspect. It was of the greatest importance for the Greek who wished to lead the good life to realise what the State is and what being a citizen means, for we cannot care for the State unless we know the nature of the State and what a good State is. Knowledge is sought as a means to ethical action.

5. This last statement deserves some development, since the Socratic theory as to the relation between knowledge and virtue is characteristic of the Socratic ethic. According to Socrates knowledge and virtue are one, in the sense that the wise man, he who *knows* what is right, will also *do* what is right. In other words, no one does evil knowingly

and of set purpose; no one chooses the evil *as such*.

This "ethical intellectualism" seems at first sight to be in blatant contradiction with the facts of everyday life. Are we not conscious that we ourselves sometimes deliberately do what we know to be wrong, and are we not convinced that other people act sometimes in the same way? When we speak of a man as being responsible for a bad action, are we not thinking of him as having done that act with knowledge of its badness? If we have reason to suppose that he was not culpably ignorant of its badness, we do not hold him to be morally responsible. We are therefore inclined to agree with Aristotle, when he criticises the identification of knowledge and virtue on the ground that Socrates forgot the irrational parts of the soul and did not take sufficient notice of the fact of moral weakness, which leads a man to do what he knows to be wrong.[35]

It has been suggested that, as Socrates was himself singularly free from the influence of the passions in regard to moral conduct, he tended to attribute the same condition to others, concluding that failure to do what is right is due to ignorance rather than to moral weakness. It has also been suggested that when Socrates identified virtue with knowledge or wisdom he had in mind not any sort of knowledge but a real personal conviction. Thus Professor Stace points out that people may go to church and say that they believe the goods of this world to be worth nothing, whereas they *act* as if they were the only goods they valued. This is not the sort of knowledge Socrates had in mind: he meant a real personal conviction.[36]

All this may well be true, but it is important to bear in mind what Socrates meant by "right." According to Socrates that action is right which serves man's true utility, in the sense of promoting his true happiness (εὐδαιμονία). Everyone seeks his own good as a matter of course. Now, it is not every kind of action, however pleasant it may appear at the time, which promotes man's true happiness. For instance, it might be pleasant to a man to get drunk constantly, especially if he is suffering from some overwhelming sorrow. But it is not to the true good of man. Besides injuring his health, it tends to enslave him to a habit, and it goes counter to the exercise of man's highest possession, that which differentiates him from the brute—his reason. If a man constantly gets drunk, believing this to be his true good, then he errs from ignorance, not realising what his true good is. Socrates would hold that if he knew that it was to his own true good and conducive to his happiness *not* to get drunk, then he would not get drunk. Of course we would remark with Aristotle that a man might well know that to contract a habit of drunkenness is not conducive to his ultimate happiness, and yet still contract the habit. This is doubtless true; it does not seem that Aristotle's criticism can be gainsaid; but at this point we might observe (with Stace) that if the man had a *real personal conviction* of the evil of the habit of drunkenness, he would not contract it. This does not dispose of Aristotle's objection, but it helps us to understand how Socrates could say what he did. And, as a matter of fact, is there not a good deal in what Socrates says, when viewed from the psychological standpoint? A man might know, intellectually, that to get drunk is not conducive to his ultimate happiness and dignity as a man, but when the impulse comes upon him, he may turn his attention away from this knowledge and fix it on the state of intoxication as seen against the background of his unhappy life, until this state and its desirability engage all his attention and take on the character of a true good. When the exhilaration has worn off, he recalls to mind the evil of drunkeness and admits: "Yes, I did wrong, knowing it to be wrong." But the fact remains, that at the moment when he surrendered to the impulse, that knowledge had slipped from the field of his mental attention, even if culpably.

Of course, we must not suppose that the utilitarian standpoint of Socrates envisages the following of whatever is pleasurable. The wise man realises that it is more advantageous to be self-controlled, than to have no self-control; to be just, rather than to be unjust; courageous, rather than cowardly—"advantageous" meaning what is conducive to true health and harmony of soul. Socrates certainly considered that pleasure is a good, but he thought that true pleasure and lasting happiness attend the moral rather than the immoral man, and that happiness does not consist in having a great abundance of external goods.

While we cannot accept the over-intellectualist attitude of Socrates, and agree with Aristotle that ἀκρασία or moral weakness is a fact which Socrates tended to overlook, we willingly pay tribute to the ethic of Socrates. For a rational ethic must be founded on human nature and the good of human nature as such. Thus when Hippias allowed ἄγραφοι νόμοι, but excepted from their number laws which varied from State to State, remarking that the prohibition of sexual intercourse between parents and children is not a universal prohibition. Socrates rightly answered that racial inferiority which results from such intercourse justifies the prohibition.[37] This is tantamount to appealing to what we would call "Natural Law," which is an expression of man's nature and conduces to its harmonious development. Such an ethic is indeed *insufficient*, since the Natural Law cannot acquire a morally binding force, obligatory in conscience—at least in the sense of our modern conception of "Duty"—unless it has a metaphysical basis and is grounded in a transcendental Source, God, Whose Will for man is expressed in the Natural Law; but, although insufficient, it enshrines a most important and valuable truth which is essential to the development of a rational moral philosophy. "Duties" are not simply senseless or arbitrary commands or prohibitions, but are to be seen in relation to human nature as such: the Moral Law expresses man's true good. Greek ethics were predominantly eudaemonological in character (cf. Aristotle's ethical system), and though, we believe, they need to be completed by Theism, and seen against the background of Theism, in order to attain their true development, they remain, even in their incomplete state, a perennial glory of Greek philosophy. Human nature is constant and so ethical values are constant, and it is Socrates' undying fame that he realised the constancy of these values and sought to fix them in universal definitions which could be taken as a guide and norm in human conduct.[38]

6. From the identification of wisdom and virtue follows the unity of virtue. There is really only one virtue, insight into what is truly good for man, what really conduces to his soul's health and harmony. A more important consequence, however, is the teachability of virtue. The Sophists, of course, professed to teach the art of virtue, but Socrates differed from them, not only in the fact that he declared himself to be a learner, but also in the fact that his ethical inquiries were directed to the discovery of universal and constant moral norms. But though Socrates' method was dialectic and not lecturing, it necessarily follows from his identification of virtue with knowledge that virtue can be

taught. We would make a distinction: intellectual knowledge of what virtue is can be imparted by instruction, but not virtue itself. However, if wisdom as real personal conviction is stressed, then *if* such wisdom can be taught, perhaps virtue could be taught too. The chief point to remark is that "teaching" for Socrates did not mean mere notional instruction, but rather leading a man to a real insight. Yet although such considerations undoubtedly render Socrates' doctrine of the teachability of virtue more intelligible, it remains true that in this doctrine the over-intellectualism of his ethic is again apparent. He insisted that as, e.g., the doctor is the man who has learnt medicine, so the just man is he who has learnt what is just.

7. This intellectualism was not likely to make Socrates particularly favourable to democracy as practised at Athens. If the doctor is the man who has learnt medicine, and if no sick man would entrust himself to the care of one who had no knowledge of medicine, it is unreasonable to choose public officials by lot or even by vote of the inexperienced multitude.[39] True rulers are those who know how to rule. If we would not appoint as pilot of a vessel a man devoid of all knowledge of the pilot's art and of the route to be traversed, why appoint as ruler of the State one who has no knowledge of ruling and who does not know what is to the good of the State?

8. In regard to religion, Socrates seems to have spoken generally of "gods" in the plural and to have meant thereby the traditional Greek deities; but one can discern a tendency towards a purer conception of Deity. Thus, according to Socrates, the knowledge of the gods is not limited, they are everywhere present and know all that is said and done. As they know best what is good, man should simply pray for the good and not for particular objects like gold.[40] Occasionally belief in one God comes to the fore,[41] but it does not appear that Socrates ever paid much attention to the question of monotheism or polytheism. (Even Plato and Aristotle find a place for the Greek gods.)

Socrates suggested that as man's body is composed of materials gathered from the material world, so man's reason is a part of the universal Reason or Mind of the world.[42] This notion was to be developed by others, as was also his teaching on teleology, anthropocentric in character. Not only are sense-organs given to man in order to enable him to exercise the corresponding senses, but anthropocentric teleology is extended to cosmic phenomena. Thus the gods give us the light without which we cannot see, and Providence is displayed in the gifts of food made to man by the earth. The sun does not approach so near the earth as to wither up or to scorch man, nor is it set so far away that he cannot be warmed thereby. These and suchlike considerations are natural in a man who studied in the School of the Cosmologists and was disappointed at the little use that Anaxagoras made of his principle of Mind; but Socrates was not a Cosmologist or a Theologian, and though he may be called "the real founder of Teleology in the consideration of the world," [43] he was, as we have seen, primarily interested in human conduct.[44]

9. The picture that Aristophanes gives of Socrates in the *Clouds* need not detain us.[45] Socrates had been a pupil of the old philosophers, and he had admittedly been influenced by the teaching of Anaxagoras. As to the "Sophistic" flavouring imparted to his character in the *Clouds*, it is to be remembered that Socrates like the Sophists, concentrated his attention on the Subject, on man himself. He was a public and familiar figure, known to all the audience for his dialectical activity, and to some he undoubtedly seemed to be "rationalistic," critically destructive and anti-traditionalist in tendency. Even if it were to be assumed that Aristophanes himself realised the difference that existed between Socrates and the Sophists—which is not at all clear—it would not necessarily follow that he would express this realisation before a public audience. And Aristophanes is known to have been a traditionalist and an opponent of the Sophists.

4. Trial and Death of Socrates

In 406 B.C. Socrates showed his moral courage by refusing to agree to the demand that the eight commanders who were to be impeached for their negligence at Arginusae should be tried together, this being contrary to the law and calculated to evoke a hasty sentence. He was at this time a member of the Committee of the πρυτάνεις or Committee of the Senate. His moral courage was again shown when he refused, at the demand of the Thirty in 404/3, to take part in the arrest of Leon of Salamis, whom the Oligarchs intended to murder, that they might confiscate his property.

They wished to incriminate as many prominent citizens as possible in their doings, doubtless with a view to the eventual day of reckoning. Socrates, however, simply refused to take any part in their crimes, and would probably have paid for his refusal with his life, had not the Thirty fallen.

In the year 400/399 Socrates was brought to trial by the leaders of the restored democracy. Anytus, the politician who remained in the background, instigated Meletus to carry on the prosecution. The indictment before the court of the King Archon is recorded as follows:[46] "Meletus, son of Miletus, of the deme of Pitthus, indicts Socrates, son of Sophroniscus, of the deme of Alopecae, on his oath, to the following effect. Socrates is guilty (i) of not worshipping the gods whom the State worships, but introducing new and unfamiliar religious practices; (ii) and, further, of corrupting the young. The prosecutor demands the death penalty."

The first charge was never explicitly defined, the reason seeming to be that the prosecutor was relying on the jury's recollection of the reputation of the old Ionian cosmologists and perhaps of the profanation of the mysteries in 415, in which Alcibiades had been involved. But no reference could be made to the profanation in view of the Amnesty of 404/3, of which Anytus had himself been the chief promoter. The second charge, that of corrupting the young, is really a charge of infusing into the young a spirit of criticism in regard to the Athenian Democracy. At the back of it all was doubtless the thought that Socrates was responsible for having "educated Alcibiades and Critias—Alcibiades, who had for a time gone over to Sparta and who led Athens into such straits, Critias, who was the most violent of the Oligarchs. This again could not be explicitly mentioned because of the Amnesty of 404/3, but the audience would have grasped easily enough what was meant. That is why Aeschines could say, some fifty years later: "You put Socrates the Sophist to death, because he was shown to have educated Critias." [47]

The accusers no doubt supposed that Socrates would go into voluntary exile without awaiting trial, but he did not. He remained for trial in 399 and defended himself in court. In the trial Socrates might have made much of his military service and of his defiance of Critias in the time of the Oligarchy, but he merely brought the facts in, coupling them with his defiance of the democracy in the matter of the trial of the commanders. He was condemned to death by a majority of either 60 or 6 votes by a jury of 500 or 501.[48] It then rested with Socrates to propose an alternative penalty, and it was obviously the wisest course to propose a sufficiently substantial penalty. Thus if Socrates had proposed exile, this alternative to the death penalty would doubtless have been accepted. Socrates, however, proposed as his proper "reward" free meals in the Pryntaneum, after which he consented to propose a small fine—and all this without any attempt to influence the jury, as was usual, by bringing a weeping wife and children into court. The jury was annoyed at Socrates' cavalier behaviour, and he was sentenced to death by a larger majority than the one that had found him guilty.[49] The execution had to be delayed for about a month, to await the return of the "sacred boat" from Delos (in memory of Theseus' deliverance of the city from the tribute of seven boys and girls imposed by Minos of Knossos), and there was plenty of time to arrange an escape, which the friends of Socrates did in fact arrange. Socrates refused to avail himself of their kind offers, on the ground that such a course would be contrary to his principles. Socrates' last day on earth is recounted by Plato in the *Phaedo,* a day that was spent by Socrates in discoursing on the immortality of the soul with his Theban friends, Cebes and Simmias.[50] After he had drunk the hemlock and lay dying, his last words were: "Crito, we owe a cock to Aesculapius; pay it, therefore, and do not neglect it." When the poison reached his heart there was a convulsive movement and he died, "and Crito, perceiving it, closed his mouth and eyes. This, Echecrates, was the end of our friend, a man, we should say, who was the best of all his time that we have known, and moreover, the most wise and just." [51]

Chapter Fifteen

MINOR SOCRATIC SCHOOLS

The term "Minor Socratic Schools" should not be taken to indicate that Socrates founded any definite School. He hoped, no doubt, that others would be found to carry on his work of stimulating men's minds, but he did not gather round him a band of disciples to whom he left a patrimony of definite doctrine. But various thinkers, who had been disciples of Socrates to a greater or less extent, emphasised one or other point in his teaching, combining it also with elements culled from other sources. Hence Dr. Praechter calls them *Die einseitigen Sokratiker,* not in the sense that these thinkers only *reproduced* certain sides of Socrates' teaching, but in the sense that each of them was a *continuation* of Socratic thought in a particular direction, while at the same time they modified what they took from earlier philosophising, in order to harmonise it with the Socratic legacy.[1] In some ways, then, the use of a common name, Minor Socratic Schools, is unfortunate, but it may be used, if it is understood that the connection of some of these thinkers with Socrates is but slender.

1. The School of Megara

Euclid of Megara (not to be confused with the mathematician) seems to have been one of the earliest disciples of Socrates, as—if the story be genuine—he continued his association with Socrates in spite of the prohibition (of 431/2) of Megarian citizens entering Athens, coming into the city at dusk dressed as a woman.² He was present at the death of Socrates in 400/399, and after that event Plato and other Socratics took refuge with Euclid at Megara.

Euclid seems to have been early acquainted with the doctrine of the Eleatics, which he so modified under the influence of the Socratic ethic as to conceive of the One as the Good. He also regarded virtue as a unity. According to Diogenes Laërtius, Euclid asserted that the One is known by many names, identifying the One with God and with Reason.³ The existence of a principle contrary to the Good he naturally denied, as that principle would be multiplicity, which is illusory on the Eleatic view. We may say that he remained an adherent of the Eleatic tradition, in spite of the Socratic influence that he underwent.

The Megaric philosophy, particularly under the influence of Eubulides, developed into an Eristic which concocted various ingenious arguments, designed to disprove a position through a *reductio ad absurdum*. For example, the famous difficulty: "One grain of corn is not a heap: add a grain and there is yet no heap: when does the heap begin?" was designed to show that plurality is impossible, as Zeno wanted to show that motion was impossible. Another conundrum is that ascribed by some to Diodorus Cronus, another Megaric: "That which you have not lost, you still have; but you have not lost horns; therefore you still have horns." Or again: "Electra knows her brother, Orestes. But Electra does not know Orestes (who stands before her, disguised). Therefore Electra does not know what she knows." ⁴

Another philosopher of the Megaric School, Diodorus Cronus (mentioned above), identified the actual and the possible: only the actual is possible. His argument was as follows: The possible cannot become the impossible. Now, if of two contradictories one has actually come to pass, the other is impossible. Therefore, if it had been possible before, the impossible would have come out of the possible. Therefore it was not possible before, and only the actual is possible; (e.g. "The world exists," and "The world does not exist," are contradictory propositions. But the world actually exists. Therefore it is impossible that the world does not exist. But if it were ever possible that the world should not exist a possibility has turned into an impossibility. This cannot be so. Therefore it was never possible that the world should not exist.) This proposition has been taken up in recent times by Professor Nicolai Hartmann of Berlin, who has identified the actual with the possible on the ground that what actually happens depends on the totality of given conditions, and—given those conditions—nothing else could have happened.[5]

A noted adherent of the School was Stilpo of Megara, who taught at Athens about 320, but was afterwards banished. He applied himself chiefly to ethics, developing the point of self-sufficiency in a theory of "apathy." When asked what he had lost in the plundering of Megara, he replied that he had not seen anyone carrying off wisdom or knowledge.[6] Zeno (the Stoic) was a pupil of Stilpo.

2. The Elean-Eretrian School

This School was named after Phaedo of Elis (the Phaedo of Plato's Dialogue) and Menedemus of Eretria. Phaedo of Elis seems to have resembled the Megarians in his use of dialectic, while Menedemus was chiefly interested in ethics, holding the unity of virtue and knowledge.

3. The Early Cynic School

The Cynics, or disciples of the dog, may have got their name from their unconventional mode of life or from the fact that Antisthenes, the founder of the School, taught in the gymnasium known as the *Kynosarges*. Perhaps both factors had something to do with the nickname.

Antisthenes (c. 445-c. 365) was born of an Athenian father and of a Thracian slave mother.[7] This might explain why he taught in the *Kynosarges*, which was reserved for those who were not of pure Athenian blood. The Gymnasium was dedicated to Heracles, and the Cynics took the hero as a sort of tutelary god or patron. One of Antisthenes' works was named after Heracles.[8]

At first a pupil of Gorgias, Antisthenes afterwards became an adherent of Socrates, to whom he was devoted. But what he chiefly admired in Socrates was the latter's independence of character, which led him to act in accordance with his convictions, no matter what the cost. Neglecting the fact that Socrates had been independent of earthly riches and the applause of men only in order to obtain the greater good of true wisdom, Antisthenes set up this independence and self-sufficiency as an ideal or end in itself. Virtue in his eyes was simply independence of all earthly possessions and pleasures: in fact, it was a negative concept —renunciation, self-sufficiency. Thus the negative side of Socrates' life was changed by Antisthenes into a positive goal or end. Similarly, Socrates' insistence on ethical knowledge was exaggerated by Antisthenes into a positive contempt for scientific learning and art. Virtue, he said, is sufficient by itself for happiness: nothing else is required—and virtue is the absence of desire, freedom from wants, and complete independence. Socrates, of course, had been independent of the opinion of others simply because he possessed deep convictions and principles, the surrender of which, to satisfy popular opinion, he regarded as treason to the Truth. He did not, however, set out to flout popular opinion or public convictions simply for the sake of doing so, as the Cynics, particularly Diogenes, seem to have done. The philosophy of the Cynics was thus an exaggeration of one side of Socrates' life and attitude, and that a negative one or at least one consequent on a much more positive side. Socrates was ready to disobey the Oligarchy at the risk of his life, rather than commit an act of injustice; but he would not have lived in a tub like Diogenes merely to flaunt his disregard for the ways of men.

Antisthenes was strongly opposed to the theory of Ideas, and maintained that there are only individuals. He is said to have remarked: "O Plato, I see a horse, but I do not see horseness." [9] To each thing only its own name should be applied: e.g. we can say "Man is man" or "The good is good," but not "The man is good." No predicate should be attributed to a subject other than the subject itself.[10] With this goes the doctrine that we can only predicate of an individual its own individual nature; one cannot predicate of it membership of a class. Hence the denial of the theory of Ideas. Another logical theory of Antisthenes was that of the impossibility of self-contradiction. For if a man says different things, he is speaking of different objects.[11]

Virtue is wisdom, but this wisdom consists principally in "seeing through" the values of the majority of mankind. Riches, passions, etc., are not really good, nor are suffering, poverty, contempt, really evil: independence is the true good. Virtue, then, is wisdom and it is teachable, though there is no need of long reasoning and reflection in order to learn it. Armed with this virtue, the wise man cannot be touched by any so-called evil of life, even by slavery. He stands beyond laws and conventions, at least those of the State that does not recognise true virtue. The ideal state or condition of life in which all would live in independence and freedom from desire, is of course incompatible with wars.[12]

Socrates had, indeed, placed himself in opposition on occasion to the authority of the Government, but he was so convinced of the rightness of the State's authority as such and of the Law, that he would not take advantage of the opportunity presented to him of escape from prison, but preferred to suffer death in accordance with the Law. Antisthenes, however, with his usual one-sided exaggeration denounced the historic and traditional State and its Law. In addition he renounced the traditional religion. There is only one God; the Greek pantheon is only a convention. Virtue is the only service of God: temples, prayers, sacrifices, etc., are condemned. "By convention there are many gods, but by nature only one." [13] On the other hand, Antisthenes interpreted the Homeric myths allegorically, trying to get moral applications and lessons out of them.

Diogenes of Sinope (d. c. 324 B.C.) thought that Antisthenes had not lived up to his own theories and called him a "trumpet which hears nothing but itself." [14] Banished from his country, Diogenes spent most of his life in Athens, though he died in Corinth. He called himself the "Dog," and held up the life of animals as a model for mankind. His task was the "recoining of values," [15] and to the civilisation of the Hellenic world he opposed the life of animals and of the barbaric peoples.

We are told that he advocated community of wives and children and free love, while in the political sphere he declared himself a citizen of the world.[16] Not content with Antisthenes' "indifference" to the external goods of civilisation, Diogenes advocated a positive asceticism in order to attain freedom. Connected therewith is his deliberate flouting of convention, doing in public what it is generally considered should be done in private—and even what should not be done in private.

Disciples of Diogenes were Monimus, Onesicritus, Philiscus, Crates of Thebes. The latter presented his considerable fortune to the city, and took up the Cynic life of mendicancy, followed by his wife Hipparchia.[17]

4. The Cyrenaic School

Aristippus of Cyrene, founder of the Cyrenaic School, was born about 435 B.C. From 416 he was in Athens, from 399 in Aegina, from 389/388 with Plato at the court of the elder Dionysius, and then again after 356 in Athens. But these dates and order of events cannot be regarded as beyond dispute, to say the least of it.[18] It has even been suggested that Aristippus never founded the Cyrenaic "School" at all, but was confused with his grandson, a later Aristippus. But in view of the statements of Diog. Laërt., Sotion and Panaetius (cf. D.L., 2, 84 f.), it does not seem possible to accept the statement of Sosicrates and others (D.L.) that Aristippus wrote nothing at all, while the passage in Eusebius' *Praeparatio Evangelica* (14, 18, 31) can be explained without having to suppose that Aristippus never laid a foundation for the Cyrenaic philosophy.

In Cyrene Aristippus seems to have become acquainted with the teaching of Protagoras, while afterwards at Athens he was in relation with Socrates. The Sophist may have been largely responsible for Aristippus' doctrine, that it is our sensations alone that give us certain knowledge:[19] of things in themselves they can give us no certain information, nor about the sensations of others. Subjective sensations, then, must be the basis for practical conduct. But if my individual sensations form the norm for my practical conduct, then, thought Aristippus, it follows as a matter of course that the end of conduct is to obtain pleasurable sensations.

Aristippus declared that sensation consists in movement. When the movement is gentle, the sensation is pleasurable; when it is rough, there is pain; when movement is imperceptible or when there is no movement at all, there is neither pleasure nor pain. The rough movement cannot be the ethical end. Yet it cannot consist in the mere absence of pleasure or pain, i.e. be a purely negative end. The ethical end must, therefore, be pleasure, a positive end.[20] Socrates had indeed declared that virtue is the one path to happiness, and he held out happiness as a motive for the practice of virtue, but he did not maintain that pleasure is the end of life. Aristippus, however, seized on the one side of the Socratic teaching and disregarded all the rest.

Pleasure, then, according to Aristippus, is the end of life. But what kind of pleasure? Later on for Epicurus it would be rather painlessness, negative pleasure, that is the end of life; but for Aristippus it was positive and present pleasure. Thus it came about that the Cyrenaics valued bodily pleasure above intellectual pleasure, as being more intense and powerful. And it would follow from their theory of knowledge that the quality of the pleasure does not come into account. The consequential following-out of this principle would obviously lead to sensual excesses; but, as a matter of fact, the Cyrenaics, no doubt adopting the hedonistic elements in Socrates' doctrine, declared that the wise man will, in his choice of pleasure, take cognisance of the future. He will, therefore, avoid unrestrained excess, which would lead to pain, and he will avoid indulgence that would occasion punishment from the State or public condemnation. The wise man, therefore, needs judgment in order to enable him to evaluate the different pleasures of life. Moreover, the wise man in his enjoyments will preserve a certain measure of independence. If he allows himself to be enslaved, then to that extent he cannot be enjoying pleasure, but rather is he in pain. Again, the wise man, in order to preserve cheerfulness and contentment, will limit his desires. Hence the saying attributed to Aristippus, ἔχω (Λαΐδα), καὶ οὐκ ἔχομαι ἐπεὶ τὸ κρατεῖν καὶ μὴ ἡττᾶσθαι ἡδονῶν ἄριστον, οὐ τὸ μὴ χρῆσθαι.[21]

This contradiction in the teaching of Aristippus between the principle of the pleasure of the moment and the principle of judgment, led to a divergence of views—or an emphasis on different sides of his doctrine—among his disciples. Thus *Theodorus the Atheist* declared indeed that judgment and justness are goods (the latter only because of the external advantages of a just life), and that individual acts of gratification are indifferent, the contentment of the mind being true happiness or pleasure, but he asserted too that the wise man will not give his life for his country and that he would steal, commit adultery, etc., if circumstances allowed it. He also denied the existence of any god at all.[22] *Hegesias* also demanded indifference towards individual acts of gratification, but he was so convinced of the miseries of life and of the impossibility of attaining happiness, that he emphasised a negative concept of the end of life, namely, absence of pain and sorrow.[23] Cicero and other sources tell us that Hegesias' lectures at Alexandria led to so many suicides on the part of his hearers, that Ptolemy Lagi forbade their continuance![24] *Anniceris*, on the other hand, stressed the positive side of Cyrenaicism, making positive pleasure and, indeed, individual acts of gratification the end of life. But he limited the logical conclusions of such a view by giving great weight to love of family and country, friendship and gratitude, which afford pleasure even when they demand sacrifice.[25] In the value he placed on friendship he differed from Theodorus, who declared (D.L.) that the wise are sufficient for themselves and have no need of friends.

Diogenes Laërtius clearly implies that these philosophers had their own peculiar disciples: for example, he speaks of "Hegesiakoi," though he also classes them together as "Cyrenaics." Thus, while Aristippus the Cyrenaic laid the foundation of the "Cyrenaic" or pleasure-philosophy (*v. sup.*), he can hardly be said to have founded a closely-knit philosophical School, comprising Theodorus, Hegesias, Anniceris, etc., as members. These philosophers were part-heirs of Aristippus the elder, and represent a philosophical tendency rather than a School in the strict sense.

Chapter Sixteen

DEMOCRITUS OF ABDERA

This would seem to be the right place to say something of the epistemological and ethical theories of Democritus of Abdera. Democritus was a disciple of Leucippus and, together with his Master, belongs to the Atomist School; but his peculiar interest for us lies in the fact that he gave attention to the problem of knowledge raised by Protagoras and to the problem of conduct which relativistic doctrines of the Sophists had rendered acute. Nowhere named by Plato, Democritus is frequently mentioned by Aristotle. He was head of a School at Abdera, and was still alive when Plato founded the Academy. The reports of his journeys to Egypt and Athens cannot be accepted with certainty.[1] He wrote copiously, but his writings have not been preserved.

1. The account of sensation given by Democritus was a mechanical one. Empedocles had spoken of "effluences" from objects which reach the eye, for example. The Atomists make these effluences to be atoms, images (δείκελα, εἴδωλα), which objects are constantly shedding. These images enter through the organs of sense, which are just passages (πόροι) and impinge on the soul, which is itself composed of atoms. The images, passing through the air, are subject to distortion by the air; and this is the reason why objects very far off may not be seen at all. Differences of colour were explained by differences of smoothness or roughness in the images, and hearing was given a like explanation, the stream of atoms flowing from the sounding body causing motion in the air between the body and the ear. Taste, smell and touch were all explained in the same way. (Secondary quali-

ties would, therefore, not be objective.) We also obtain knowledge of the gods through such εἴδωλα; but gods denote for Democritus higher beings who are not immortal, though they live longer than men. They are δύσφθαρτα but not ἄφθαρτα. Strictly speaking, of course, the Atomist system would not admit of God, but only of atoms and the void.[2]

Now, Protagoras the Sophist, a fellow-citizen of Democritus, declared all sensation to be equally true for the sentient subject: thus an object might be truly sweet for X, truly bitter for Y. Democritus, however, declared that all the sensations of the special senses are false, for there is nothing real corresponding to them outside the subject. "Νόμῳ there is sweet, νόμῳ there is bitter; νόμῳ there is warm and νόμῳ there is cold; νόμῳ there is colour. But ἐτεῇ there are atoms and the void."[3] In other words, our sensations are purely subjective, though they are caused by something external and objective—the atoms, namely—which, however, cannot be apprehended by the special senses. "By the senses we in truth know nothing sure, but only something that changes according to the disposition of the body and of the things that enter into it or resist it."[4] The special senses, then, give us no information about reality. Secondary qualities, at least, are not objective. "There are two forms of knowledge (γνώμη), the trueborn (γνησίη) and the bastard (σκοτίη). To the bastard belong all these: sight, hearing, smell, taste, touch. The trueborn is quite apart from these."[5] However, as the soul is composed of atoms, and as all knowledge is caused by the immediate contact with the subject of atoms coming from the outside, it is evident that the "trueborn" knowledge is on the same footing as the "bastard," in the sense that there is no absolute separation between sense and thought. Democritus saw this, and he comments: "Poor Mind, it is from us" (i.e. from the senses), "thou hast got the proofs to throw us with. Thy throw is a fall."[6]

2. Democritus' theory of conduct, so far as we can judge from the fragments, did not stand in scientific connection with his atomism. It is dominated by the idea of happiness or εὐδαιμονίη, which consists in εὐθυμίη or εὐεστώ. Democritus wrote a treatise on cheerfulness (Περὶ εὐθυμίης), which was used by Seneca and Plutarch. He considers that happiness is the end of conduct, and that pleasures and

pain determine happiness; but "happiness dwelleth not in herds nor in gold; the soul is the dwelling-place of the 'daimon.'"[7] "The best thing for a man is to pass his life so as to have as much joy and as little trouble as may be."[8] However, just as sense-knowledge is not true knowledge, so the pleasures of sense are not true pleasures. "The good and the true are the same for all men, but the pleasant is different for different people."[9] We have to strive after well-being (εὐεστώ) or cheerfulness (εὐθυμίη), which is a state of soul, and the attainment of which requires a weighing, judging and distinguishing of various pleasures. We should be guided by the principle of "symmetry" or of "harmony." By the use of this principle we may attain to calm of body—health, and calm of soul—cheerfulness. This calm or tranquillity is to be found chiefly in the goods of the soul. "He who chooses the goods of the soul, chooses the more divine; he who chooses the goods of the tabernacle (σκῆνος), chooses the human."[10]

3. It appears that Democritus exercised an influence on later writers through a theory of the evolution of culture.[11] Civilisation arose from need (χρεία) and prosecution of the advantageous or useful (συμφέρον), while man owes his arts to the imitation of nature, learning spinning from the spider, house-building from the swallow, song from the birds, etc. Democritus also (unlike Epicurus) emphasised the importance of the State and of political life, declaring that men should consider State affairs more important than anything else and see to it that they are well managed. But that his ethical ideas postulated freedom, whereas his atomism involved determinism, apparently did not occur to Democritus in the form of a problem.

4. It is clear from what has been said that Democritus, in carrying on the cosmological speculation of the older philosophers (in his philosophic atomism he was a follower of Leucippus), was hardly a man of his period—the Socratic period. His theories concerning perception, however, and the conduct of life, are of greater interest, as showing at least that Democritus realised that some answer was required to the difficulties raised by Protagoras. But, although he saw that some answer was required, he was personally unable to give any satisfactory solution. For an incomparably more adequate attempt to deal with epistemological and ethical problems, we have to turn to Plato.

Part Three

PLATO

Chapter Seventeen

LIFE OF PLATO

Plato, one of the greatest philosophers of the world, was born at Athens (or Aegina), most probably in the year 428/7 B.C., of a distinguished Athenian family. His father was named Ariston and his mother Perictione, sister of Charmides and niece of Critias, who both figured in the Oligarchy of 404/3. He is said to have been originally called Aristocles, and to have been given the name Plato only later, on account of his robust figure,[1] though the truth of Diogenes' report may well be doubted. His two brothers, Adeimantus and Glaucon, appear in the *Republic*, and he had a sister named Potone. After the death of Ariston, Perictione married Pyrilampes, and their son Antiphon (Plato's half-brother) appears in the *Parmenides*. No doubt Plato was brought up in the home of his stepfather; but although he was of aristocratic descent and brought up in an aristocratic household, it must be remembered that Pyrilampes was a friend of Pericles, and that Plato must have been educated in the traditions of the Periclean régime. (Pericles died in 429/8.) It has been pointed out by various authors that Plato's later bias against democracy can hardly have been due, at any rate solely, to his upbringing, but was induced by the influence of Socrates and still more by the treatment which Socrates received at the hands of the democracy. On the other hand, it would seem possible that Plato's distrust of democracy dated from a period very much earlier than that of the death of Socrates. During the later course of the Peloponnesian War (it is highly

151

probable that Plato fought at Arginusae in 406) it can hardly have failed to strike Plato that the democracy lacked a truly capable and responsible leader, and that what leaders there were were easily spoiled by the necessity of pleasing the populace. Plato's final abstention from home politics no doubt dates from the trial and condemnation of his Master; but the formulation of his conviction that the ship of State needs a firm pilot to guide her, and that he must be one who *knows* the right course to follow, and who is prepared to act conscientiously in accordance with that knowledge, can hardly fail to have been laid during the years when Athenian power was passing to its eclipse.

According to a report of Diogenes Laërtius, Plato "applied himself to the study of painting, and wrote poems, dithyrambics at first, and afterwards lyric poems and tragedies." [2] How far this is true, we cannot say; but Plato lived in the flourishing period of Athenian culture, and must have received a cultured education. Aristotle informs us that Plato had been acquainted in his youth with Cratylus, the Heraclitean philosopher.[3] From him Plato would have learnt that the world of sense-perception is a world of flux, and so not the right subject-matter for true and certain knowledge. That true and certain knowledge is attainable on the conceptual level, he would have learnt from Socrates, with whom he must have been acquainted from early years. Diogenes Laërtius indeed asserted that Plato "became a pupil of Socrates" when twenty years old,[4] but as Charmides, Plato's uncle, had made the acquaintance of Socrates in 431,[5] Plato must have known Socrates at least before he was twenty. In any case we have no reason for supposing that Plato became a "disciple" of Socrates, in the sense of devoting himself wholly and professedly to philosophy, since he tells us himself that he originally intended to embark on a political career—as was natural in a young man of his antecedents.[6] His relatives in the Oligarchy of 403-4 urged Plato to enter upon political life under their patronage; but when the Oligarchy started to pursue a policy of violence and attempted to implicate Socrates in their crimes, Plato became disgusted with them. Yet the democrats were no better, since it was they who put Socrates to death, and Plato accordingly abandoned the idea of a political career.

Plato was present at the trial of Socrates, and he was one

of the friends who urged Socrates to increase his proposed
fine from one to thirty *minae,* offering to stand security;[7]
but he was absent from the death-scene of his friend in
consequence of an illness.[8] After the death of Socrates,
Plato withdraw to Megara and took shelter with the philosopher Euclid, but in all probability he soon returned to
Athens. He is said by the biographers to have travelled to
Cyrene, Italy and Egypt, but it is uncertain what truth
there is in these stories. For instance, Plato himself says
nothing of any visit to Egypt. It may be that his knowledge
of Egyptian mathematics, and even of the games of the
children, indicate an actual journey to Egypt; on the other
hand, the story of the journey may have been built up as
a mere conclusion from what Plato has to say about the
Egyptians. Some of these stories are obviously legendary
in part, e.g. some give him Euripides as a companion, although the poet died in 406. This fact makes us rather
sceptical concerning the reports of the journeys in general;
but all the same, we cannot say with certainty that Plato
did *not* visit Egypt, and he may have done so. If he did
actually go to Egypt, he may have gone about 395 and
have returned to Athens at the outbreak of the Corinthian
wars. Professor Ritter thinks it very probable that Plato
was a member of the Athenian force in the first years of
the wars (395 and 394).

What is certain, however, is that Plato visited Italy and
Sicily, when he was forty years old.[9] Possibly he wished to
meet and converse with members of the Pythagorean School:
in any case he became acquainted with Archytas, the
learned Pythagorean. (According to Diogenes Laërtius,
Plato's aim in undertaking the journey was to see Sicily and
the volcanoes.) Plato was invited to the court of Dionysius
I, Tyrant of Syracuse, where he became a friend of Dion,
the Tyrant's brother-in-law. The story goes that Plato's out-
spokenness excited the anger of Dionysius, who gave him
into the charge of Pollis, a Lacedaemonian envoy, to sell
as a slave. Pollis sold Plato at Aegina (at that time at war
with Athens), and Plato was even in danger of losing
his life; but eventually a man of Cyrene, a certain Anniceris,
ransomed him and sent him to Athens.[10] It is difficult to
know what to make of this story, as it is not mentioned in
Plato's *Epistles:* if it really happened (Ritter accepts the
story) it must be dated 388 B.C.

On his return to Athens, Plato seems to have founded the Academy (388/7), near the sanctuary of the hero Academus. The Academy may rightly be called the first European university, for the studies were not confined to philosophy proper, but extended over a wide range of auxiliary sciences, like mathematics, astronomy and the physical sciences, the members of the School joining in the common worship of the Muses. Youths came to the Academy, not only from Athens itself, but also from abroad; and it is a tribute to the scientific spirit of the Academy and a proof that it was not simply a "philosophical-mystery" society, that the celebrated mathematician Eudoxus transferred himself and his School from Cyzicus to the Academy. It is as well to lay stress on this scientific spirit of the Academy, for though it is perfectly true that Plato aimed at forming statesmen and rulers, his method did not consist in simply teaching those things which would be of immediate practical application, e.g. rhetoric (as did Isocrates in his School), but in fostering the disinterested pursuit of science. The programme of studies culminated in philosophy, but it included as preliminary subjects a study of mathematics and astronomy, and no doubt harmonics, in a disinterested and not purely utilitarian spirit. Plato was convinced that the best training for public life is not a merely practical "sophistic" training, but rather the pursuit of science for its own sake. Mathematics, apart of course from its importance for Plato's philosophy of the Ideas, offered an obvious field for disinterested study, and it had already reached a high pitch of development among the Greeks. (The studies seem also to have included biological, e.g. botanical, researches, pursued in connection with problems of logical classification.) The politician so formed will not be an opportunist time-server, but will act courageously and fearlessly in accordance with convictions founded on eternal and changeless truths. In other words, Plato aimed at producing statesmen and not demagogues.

Besides directing the studies in the Academy, Plato himself gave lectures and his hearers took notes. It is important to notice that these lectures were not published, and that they stand in contrast to the dialogues, which were published works meant for "popular" reading. If we realise this fact, then some of the sharp differences that we naturally tend to discern between Plato and Aristotle (who entered the Academy in 367) disappear, at least in part. We possess Plato's popular works, his dialogues, but not his lectures. The situation is the exact opposite in regard to Aristotle, for while the works of Aristotle that are in our hands represent his lectures, his popular works or dialogues have not come down to us—only fragments remain. We cannot, therefore, by a comparison of Plato's dialogues with Aristotle's lectures, draw conclusions, without further evidence, as to a strong opposition between the two philosophers in point of literary ability, for instance, or emotional, aesthetic and "mystical" outlook. We are told that Aristotle used to relate how those who came to hear Plato's lecture on the Good, were often astonished to hear of nothing but arithmetic and astronomy, and of the limit and the One. In *Ep.* 7, Plato repudiates the accounts that some had published of the lecture in question. In the same letter he says: "So there is not, and may there never be, any treatise by me at least on these things, for the subject is not communicable in words, as other sciences are. Rather is it that after long association in the business itself and a shared life that a light is lit in the soul, kindled, as it were, by a leaping flame, and thenceforward feeds itself." Again in *Ep.* 2: "Therefore I have never myself written a word on these matters, and there neither is nor ever shall be any written treatise of Plato; what now bears the name belongs to Socrates, beautified and rejuvenated." [11] From such passages some draw the conclusion that Plato had not much opinion of the value of books for really educative purposes. This may well be so, but we should not put undue emphasis on this point, for Plato, after all, *did* publish books—and we must also remember that the passages in question may not be by Plato at all. Yet we must concede that the Ideal Theory, in the precise form in which it was taught in the Academy, was not given to the public in writing.

Plato's reputation as teacher and counsellor of statesmen must have contributed to bringing about his second journey to Syracuse in 367. In that year Dionysius I died, and Dion invited Plato to come to Syracuse in order to take in hand the education of Dionysius II, then about thirty years old. Plato did so, and set the Tyrant to a course of geometry. Soon, however, Dionysius' jealousy of Dion got the upper hand, and when Dion left Syracuse, the philosopher after some difficulty managed to return to Athens, whence he continued to instruct Dionysius by letter. He did not succeed in bringing about a reconciliation between the Tyrant and his uncle, who took up residence at Athens, where he consorted with Plato. In 361, however, Plato undertook a third journey to Syracuse at the earnest request of Dionysius, who wished to continue his philosophical studies. Plato apparently hoped to draft a constitution for a proposed confederation of Greek cities against the Carthaginian menace, but opposition proved too strong; moreover, he found himself unable to secure the recall of Dion, whose fortune was confiscated by his nephew. In 360, therefore, Plato returned to Athens, where he continued his activities in the Academy until his death in the year 348/7.[12] (In 357 Dion succeeded in making himself master of Syracuse, but he was murdered in 353, to the great grief of Plato, who felt that he had been disappointed in his dream of a philosopher-king.)

Chapter Eighteen

PLATO'S WORKS

A. Genuineness

In general it may be said that we possess the entire corpus
of Plato's works. As Professor Taylor remarks: "Nowhere in
later antiquity do we come on any reference to a Platonic
work which we do not still possess." [1] We may suppose,
then, that we possess all Plato's published dialogues. We
do not, however, as already remarked, possess a record of
the lectures that he delivered in the Academy (though we
have more or less cryptic references in Aristotle), and this
would be all the more to be regretted if those are right
who would see in the dialogues popular work designed for
the educated laymen, to be distinguished from the lectures
delivered to professional students of philosophy. (It has
been conjectured that Plato lectured without a manuscript.
Whether this be the fact or not, we have not got the
manuscript of any lectures delivered by Plato. All the same,
we have no right to draw an oversharp distinction between
the doctrines of the dialogues and the doctrine delivered
within the precincts of the Academy. After all, not all the
dialogues can easily be termed "popular" work, and certain
of them in particular show evident signs that Plato is therein
groping after the clarification of his opinions.) But to say
that we most probably possess all the dialogues of Plato,
is not the same as to say that all the dialogues that have
come down to us under the name of Plato are actually
by Plato himself: it still remains to sift the genuine from
the spurious. The oldest Platonic MSS. belong to an

arrangement attributed to a certain Thrasyllus, to be dated round about the beginning of the Christian era. In any case this arrangement, which was by "tetralogies," seems to have been based on an arrangement in "trilogies" by Aristophanes of Byzantium in the third century B.C. It would appear, then, that the thirty-six dialogues (reckoning the Epistles as one dialogue) were generally admitted by scholars of that period to be the work of Plato. The problem can thus be reduced to the question: "Are the thirty-six dialogues all genuine or are some of them spurious; and, if so, which?"

Doubts were cast upon some of the dialogues even in antiquity. Thus from Athenaeus (flor. c. 228 B.C.) we learn that some ascribed the Alcibiades II to Xenophon. Again, it would seem that Proclus not only rejected the Epinomis and Epistles, but even went so far as to reject the Laws and Republic. The assigning of spurious works was carried much further, as might be expected, in the nineteenth century, especially in Germany, the culmination of the process being reached under Ueberweg and Schaarschmidt. "If one includes the attacks of ancient and modern criticism, then of the thirty-six items of the tetralogies of Thrasyllus, only five have remained free from all attack." [2] Nowadays, however, criticism runs in a more conservative direction, and there is general agreement as to the genuineness of all the important dialogues, as also a general agreement as to the spurious character of certain of the less important dialogues, while the genuineness of a few of the dialogues remains a matter of dispute. The results of critical investigation may be summed up as follows:

(i) Dialogues which are generally rejected are: Alcibiades II, Hipparchus, Amatores or Rivales, Theages, Clitophon, Minus. Of this group, all except the Alcibiades II are probably contemporary fourth-century work, not deliberate forgeries but slighter works of the same character as the Platonic dialogues; and they may be taken, with some degree of justification, as contributing something to our knowledge of the conception of Socrates current in the fourth century. The Alcibiades II is probably later work.

(ii) The genuineness of the following six dialogues is disputed: Alcibiades I, Ion, Menexenus, Hippias Maior, Epinomis, Epistles. Professor Taylor thinks that the Alcibiades I is the work of an immediate disciple of Plato[3] and

Dr. Praechter, too, thinks that it is probably not the authentic work of the Master.[4] Praechter considers the *Ion* to be genuine, and Taylor remarks that it "may reasonably be allowed to pass as genuine until some good reason for rejecting it is produced." [5] The *Menexenus* is clearly taken by Aristotle to be of Platonic origin, and modern critics are inclined to accept this view.[6] The *Hippias Maior* is most probably to be taken as the genuine work of Plato, as it seems to be alluded to, though not by name, in the *Topics* of Aristotle.[7] As to the *Epinomis*, though Professor Jaeger ascribes it to Philippus of Opus,[8] Praechter and Taylor deem it authentic. Of the *Epistles*, 6, 7 and 8 are generally accepted and Professor Taylor thinks that the acceptance of these *Epistles* leads logically to the acceptance of all the rest, except 1 and possibly 2. It is true that one would not like to relinquish the *Epistles*, as they give us much valuable information concerning Plato's biography; but we must be careful not to let this very natural desire influence unduly our acceptance of *Epistles* as genuine.[9]

(iii) The genuineness of the remaining dialogues may be accepted; so that the result of criticism would seem to be that of the thirty-six dialogues of the tetralogies, six are generally rejected, six others may be accepted until proved unauthentic (except probably *Alcibiades I* and certainly *Epistle I*), while twenty-four are certainly the genuine work of Plato. We have, therefore, a very considerable body of literature on which to found our conception of the thought of Plato.

B. Chronology of Works

1. *Importance* of determining the chronology of the works.

It is obviously important in the case of any thinker to see how his thought developed, how it changed—if it did change—what modifications were introduced in the course of time, what fresh ideas were introduced. The customary illustration in this connection is that of the literary production of Kant. Our knowledge of Kant would scarcely be adequate, if we thought that his Critiques came in his early years and that he later reverted to a "dogmatic" position. We might also instance the case of Schelling. Schelling produced several philosophies in the course of his life, and for an understanding of his thought it is highly desirable that one should know that he began with the standpoint of Fichte, and that his theosophical flights belong to his later years.

2. Method of determining the chronology of the works.[10]

(i) The criterion that has proved of most help in determining the chronology of the works of Plato is that of *language*. The argument from language is all the surer in that, while differences of content may be ascribed to the conscious selection and purpose of the author, development of linguistic style is largely unconscious. Thus Dittenberger traces the frequent use of τί μήν; and the growing use of γε μήν and ἄλλα μήν, as formula of agreement, to the first Sicilian journey of Plato. The *Laws* certainly belong to Plato's old age,[11] while the *Republic* belongs to an earlier period. Now, not only is there a decreased vigour of dramatic power visible in the *Laws*, but we can also discern points of linguistic style which Isocrates had introduced into Attic prose and which do not appear in the *Republic*. This being so, we are helped in assessing the order of the intervening dialogues, according to the degree in which they approach the later style of writing.

But while the use of linguistic style as a criterion for determining the chronology of the dialogues has proved to be the most helpful method, one cannot, of course, neglect to make use of other criteria, which may often decide the matter at issue when the linguistic indications are doubtful or even contradictory.

(ii) One obvious criterion for assessing the order of the dialogues is that afforded by the direct testimony of the ancient writers, though there is not as much help to be had from this source as might perhaps be expected. Thus while Aristotle's assertion that the *Laws* were written later than the *Republic* is a valuable piece of information, the report of Diogenes Laërtius to the effect that the *Phaedrus* is the earliest of the Platonic dialogues cannot be accepted. Diogenes himself approves of the report, but it is evident that he is arguing from the subject-matter (love—in the first part of the dialogue) and from the poetic style.[12] We cannot argue from the fact that Plato treats of love to the conclusion that the dialogue must have been written in youth, while the use of poetic style and myth is not in itself conclusive. As Taylor points out, we should go far wrong were we to argue from the poetical and "mythical" flights of the second part of *Faust* to the conclusion that Goethe wrote the second part before the first.[13] A similar illustration might be taken from the case of Schelling, whose theosophical flights, as already mentioned, took place in his advanced age.

(iii) As for references within the dialogues to historical persons and acts, these are not so very many, and in any case they only furnish us with a *terminus post quem*. For example, if there were a reference to the death of Socrates, as in the *Phaedo,* the dialogue must clearly have been composed after the death of Socrates, but that does not tell us *how long after.* However, critics have obtained some help from this criterion. For instance, they have argued that the *Meno* was probably written when the incident of the corruption of Ismenias of Thebes was still fresh in people's memory.[14] Again, if the *Gorgias* contains a reply to a speech of Polycrates against Socrates (393/2), the *Gorgias* would probably have been written between 393 and 389, i.e. before the first Sicilian journey. It might, naïvely, be supposed that the age ascribed to Socrates in the dialogues is an indication of the date of composition of the dialogue itself, but to apply this criterion as a universal rule is clearly going too far. For instance, a novelist might well introduce his detective-hero as a grown man and as an already experienced police officer in his first novel, and then in a later novel treat of the hero's first case. Moreover, though one may be justified in supposing that dialogues dealing with the personal fate of Socrates were composed not long after his death, it would be clearly unscientific to take it for granted that dialogues dealing with the last years of Socrates, e.g. the *Phaedo* and the *Apology,* were all published at the same time.

(iv) References of one dialogue to another would obviously prove a help in determining the order of the dialogues, since a dialogue that refers to another dialogue must have been written after the dialogue to which it refers; but it is not always easy to decide if an apparent reference to another dialogue really *is* a reference. However, there are some cases in which there is a clear reference, e.g. the reference to the *Republic* that is contained in the *Timaeus.*[15] Similarly, the *Politicus* is clearly the sequel to the *Sophistes* and so must be a later composition.[16]

(v) In regard to the actual content of the dialogue, we have to exercise the greatest prudence in our use of this criterion. Suppose for instance, that some philosophical doctrine is found in a short summary sentence in dialogue X, while in dialogue Y it is found treated at length. A critic might say: "Very good, in dialogue X a preliminary sketch is given, and in dialogue Y the matter is explained at length." Might it not be that a short summary is given in dialogue X precisely because the doctrine has already been treated at length in dialogue Y? One critic[17] has maintained that the negative and critical examination of problems precedes the positive and constructive exposition. If this be taken as a criterion, then the *Theaetetus*, the *Sophistes*, the *Politicus*, the *Parmenides*, should precede in date of composition the *Phaedo* and the *Republic*, but investigation has shown that this cannot be so.

However, to say that the content-criterion has to be used with prudence, is not to say that it has no use. For example, the attitude of Plato towards the doctrine of Ideas suggests, that the *Theaetetus*, *Parmenides*, *Sophistes*, *Politicus*, *Philebus*, *Timaeus*, should be grouped together, while the connection of the *Parmenides*, *Sophistes* and *Politicus* with the Eleatic dialectic suggests that these dialogues stand in a peculiarly close relation with one another.

(vi) Differences in the artistic construction of the dialogues may also be of help in determining their relation to one another in regard to order of composition. Thus in certain dialogues the setting of the dialogue, the characterisation of the personages who take part in it, are worked out with great care: there are humorous and playful allusions, vivid interludes and so on. To this group of dialogues belongs the *Symposium*. In other dialogues, however, the artistic side retreats into the background, and the author's attention is obviously wholly occupied with the philosophic content. In dialogues of this second group—to which the *Timaeus* and the *Laws* would belong—form is more or less neglected: content is everything. A probably legitimate conclusion is that the dialogues written with more attention to artistic form are earlier than the others, as artistic vigour flagged in Plato's old age and his attention was engrossed by the theoretic philosophy. (This does not mean that the use of poetic *language* necessarily becomes less frequent, but that the power of conscious artistry tends to decrease with years.)

3. Scholars vary in their estimate of the results obtained

by the use of criteria such as the foregoing; but the following chronological schemes may be taken as, in the main, satisfactory (though it would hardly be acceptable to those who think that Plato did not write when he was directing the Academy in its early years).

1. Socratic Period

In this period Plato is still influenced by the Socratic intellectual determinism. Most of the dialogues end without any definite result having been attained. This is characteristic of Socrates' "not knowing."

i. *Apology.* Socrates' defence at his trial.
ii. *Crito.* Socrates is exhibited as the good citizen who, in spite of his unjust condemnation, is willing to give up his life in obedience to the laws of the State. Escape is suggested by Crito and others, and money is provided; but Socrates declares that he will abide by his principles.
iii. *Euthyphron.* Socrates awaits his trial for impiety. On the nature of piety. No result to the inquiry.
iv. *Laches.* On courage. No result.
v. *Ion.* Against the poets and rhapsodists.
vi. *Protagoras.* Virtue is knowledge and can be taught.
vii. *Charmides.* On temperance. No result.
viii. *Lysis.* On friendship. No result.
ix. *Republic.* Bk. I. On justice.

    (The *Apology* and *Crito* must obviously have been written at an early date. Probably the other dialogues of this group were also composed before the first Sicilian journey from which Plato returned by 388/7.)

2. Transition Period

Plato is finding his way to his own opinions.

x. *Gorgias.* The practical politician, or the rights of the stronger versus the philosopher, or justice at all costs.
xi. *Meno.* Teachability of virtue corrected in view of ideal theory.
xii. *Euthydemus.* Against logical fallacies of later Sophists.

xiii. *Hippias I.* On the beautiful.

xiv. *Hippias II.* Is it better to do wrong voluntarily or involuntarily?

xv. *Cratylus.* On the theory of language.

xvi. *Menexenus.* A parody on rhetoric.

> (The dialogues of this period were probably composed before the first Sicilian journey, though Praechter thinks that the *Menexenus* dates from after the journey.)

3. *Period of Maturity*

Plato is in possession of his own ideas.

xvii. *Symposium.* All earthly beauty is but a shadow of true Beauty, to which the soul aspires by Eros.

xviii. *Phaedo.* Ideas and Immortality.

xix. *Republic.* The State. Dualism strongly emphasised, i.e. metaphysical dualism.

xx. *Phaedrus.* Nature of love: possibility of philosophic rhetoric.

Tripartition of soul, as in *Rep.*

> (These dialogues were probably composed between the first and second Sicilian journeys.)

4. *Works of Old Age*

xxi. *Theaetetus.* (It may that the latter part was composed *after* the *Parmenides.*) Knowledge is not sense-perception or true judgment.

xxii. *Parmenides.* Defence of ideal theory against criticism.

xxiii. *Sophistes.* Theory of Ideas again considered.

xxiv. *Politicus.* The true ruler is the *knower*. The legal State is a makeshift.

xxv. *Philebus.* Relation of pleasure to good.

xxvi. *Timaeus.* Natural science. Demiurge appears.

xxvii. *Critias.* Ideal agrarian State contrasted with imperialistic sea-power, "Atlantis."

xxviii. *Laws* and *Epinomis.* Plato makes concessions to real life, modifying the Utopianism of the *Republic.*
> (Of these dialogues, some may have been written between the second and third Sicilian journeys, but the *Timaeus, Critias, Laws* and *Epinomis* were probably written after the third journey.)

xxix. Letters 7 and 8 must have been written after the death
of Dion in 353.

Note

Plato never published a complete, nicely rounded-off and
finished philosophical system: his thought continued to develop as fresh problems, other difficulties to be considered,
new aspects of his doctrine to be emphasised or elaborated,
certain modifications to be introduced, occurred to his
mind.[18] It would, therefore, be desirable to treat Plato's
thought genetically, dealing with the different dialogues in
their chronological order, so far as this can be ascertained.
This is the method adopted by Professor A. E. Taylor in his
outstanding work, *Plato, the Man and His Work*. In a book
such as this, however, such a course is scarcely practicable,
and so I have thought it necessary to divide up the thought
of Plato into various compartments. None the less, in order
to avoid, as much as can be, the danger of cramming together views that spring from different periods of Plato's
life, I will attempt not to lose sight of the gradual genesis
of the Platonic doctrines. In any case, if my treatment of
Plato's philosophy leads the reader to turn his attention to
the actual dialogues of Plato, the author will consider himself amply rewarded for any pains he has taken.

Chapter Nineteen

THEORY OF KNOWLEDGE

Plato's theory of knowledge cannot be found systematically expressed and completely elaborated in any one dialogue. The *Theaetetus* is indeed devoted to the consideration of problems of knowledge, but its conclusion is negative, since Plato is therein concerned to refute false theories of knowledge, especially the theory that knowledge is sense-perception. Moreover, Plato had already, by the time he came to write the *Theaetetus*, elaborated his theory of degrees of "knowledge," corresponding to the hierarchy of being in the *Republic*. We may say, then, that the positive treatment preceded the negative and critical, or that Plato, having made up his mind what knowledge is, turned later to the consideration of difficulties and to the systematic refutation of theories which he believed to be false.[1] In a book like the present one, however, it seems best to treat first of the negative and critical side of the Platonic epistemology, before proceeding to consider his positive doctrine. Accordingly, we propose first of all to summarise the argument of the *Theaetetus*, before going on to examine the doctrine of the *Republic* in regard to knowledge. This procedure would seem to be justified by the exigencies of logical treatment, as also by the fact that the *Republic* is not primarily an epistemological work at all. Positive epistemological doctrine is certainly contained in the *Republic*, but some of the *logically prior* presuppositions of that doctrine are contained in the later dialogue, the *Theaetetus*.

The task of summarising the Platonic epistemology and

giving it in systematic form is complicated by the fact that it is difficult to separate Plato's epistemology from his ontology. Plato was not a critical thinker in the sense of Immanuel Kant, and though it is possible to read into his thoughts an anticipation of the Critical Philosophy (at least, this is what some writers have endeavoured to do), he is inclined to assume that we can have knowledge and to be primarily interested in the question what is the true object of knowledge. This means that ontological and epistemological themes are frequently intermingled or treated *pari passu*, as in the *Republic*. We will make an attempt to separate the epistemology from the ontology, but the attempt cannot be wholly successful, owing to the very character of the Platonic epistemology.

1. *Knowledge is not Sense-perception*

Socrates, interested like the Sophists in practical conduct, refused to acquiesce in the idea that truth is relative, that there is no stable norm, no abiding object of knowledge. He was convinced that ethical conduct must be founded on knowledge, and that that knowledge must be knowledge of eternal values which are not subject to the shifting and changing impressions of sense or of subjective opinion, but are the same for all men and for all peoples and all ages. Plato inherited from his Master this conviction that there can be knowledge in the sense of objective and universally valid knowledge; but he wished to demonstrate this fact theoretically, and so he came to probe deeply into the problems of knowledge, asking what knowledge is and of what.

In the *Theaetetus* Plato's first object is the refutation of false theories. Accordingly he sets himself the task of challenging the theory of Protagoras that knowledge is perception, that what appears to an individual to be true is true for that individual. His method is to elicit dialectically a clear statement of the theory of knowledge implied by the Heraclitean ontology and the epistemology of Protagoras, to exhibit its consequences and to show that the conception of "knowledge" thus attained does not fulfil the requirements of true knowledge at all, since knowledge must be, Plato assumes, (i) infallible, and (ii) of what *is*. Sense-perception is neither the one nor the other.

The young mathematical student Theaetetus enters into

conversation with Socrates, and the latter asks him what he thinks knowledge to be. Theaetetus replies by mentioning geometry, the sciences and the crafts, but Socrates points out that this is no answer to his question, for he had asked, not *of* what knowledge is, but *what* knowledge is. The discussion is thus meant to be epistemological in character, though, as has already been pointed out, ontological considerations cannot be excluded, owing to the very character of the Platonic epistemology. Moreover, it is hard to see how in any case ontological questions can be avoided in an epistemological discussion, since there is no knowledge *in vacuo:* knowledge, if it is knowledge at all, must necessarily be knowledge of something, and it may well be that knowledge is necessarily related to some particular type of object.

Theaetetus, encouraged by Socrates, makes another attempt to answer the question proposed, and suggests that "knowledge is nothing but perception," [2] thinking no doubt primarily of vision, though in itself perception has, of course, a wider connotation. Socrates proposes to examine this idea of knowledge, and in the course of conversation elicits from Theaetetus an admission of Protagoras' view that perception means appearance, and that appearances vary with different subjects. At the same time he gets Theaetetus to agree that knowledge is always of something that *is*, and that, as being knowledge, it must be infallible. [3] This having been established, Socrates next tries to show that the objects of perception are, as Heraclitus taught, always in a state of flux: they never *are*, they are always *becoming*. (Plato does not, of course, accept Heraclitus' doctrine that *all* is becoming, though he accepts the doctrine in regard to the objects of sense-perception, drawing the conclusion that sense-perception cannot be the same as knowledge.) Since an object may appear white to one at one moment, grey at another, sometimes hot and sometimes cold, etc., "appearing to" must mean "becoming for," so that perception is always of that which is in process of becoming. My perception is true for me, and if I know what appears to me, as I obviously do, then my knowledge is infallible. So Theaetetus has said well that perception is knowledge.

This point having been reached, Socrates proposes to examine the idea more closely. He raises the objection that if knowledge is perception, then no man can be wiser than any other man, for I am the best judge of my own sense-perception as such. What, then, is Protagoras' justification for setting himself up to teach others and to take a handsome fee for doing so? And where is our ignorance that makes us sit at his feet? For is not each one of us the measure of his own wisdom? Moreover, if knowledge and perception are the same, if there is no difference between seeing and knowing, it follows that a man who has come to know (i.e. see) a thing in the past and still remembers it, does not know it—although he remembers it—since he does not see it. Conversely, granted that a man can remember something he has formerly perceived and can *know* it, even while no longer perceiving it, it follows that knowledge and perception cannot be equated (even if perception were a kind of knowledge).

Socrates then attacks Protagoras' doctrine on a broader basis, understanding "Man is the measure of all things," not merely in reference to sense-perception, but also to all truth. He points out that the majority of mankind believe in knowledge and ignorance, and believe that they themselves or others can hold something to be true which in point of fact is not true. Accordingly, anyone who holds Protagoras' doctrine to be false is, according to Protagoras himself, holding the truth (i.e. if the man who is the measure of all things is the individual man).

After these criticisms Socrates finishes the claims of perception to be knowledge by showing (i) that perception is not the whole of knowledge, and (ii) that even within its own sphere perception is not knowledge.

(i) Perception is not the whole of knowledge, for a great part of what is generally recognised to be knowledge consists of truths involving terms which are not objects of perception at all. There is much we know about sensible objects, which is known by intellectual reflection and not immediately by perception. Plato gives existence or non-existence as examples.[4] Suppose that a man sees a mirage. It is not immediate sense-perception that can inform him as to the objective existence or non-existence of the mirage perceived: it is only rational reflection that can tell him this. Again, the conclusions and arguments of mathematics are not apprehended by sense. One might add that our knowledge of a person's character is something more than can be explained by the definition, "Knowledge is perception," for our knowledge of a person's character is certainly not given in bare sensation.

(ii) Sense-perception, even within its own sphere, is not knowledge. We cannot really be said to know anything if we have not attained truth about it, e.g. concerning its existence or non-existence, its likeness to another thing or its unlikeness. But truth is given in reflection, in the judgment, not in bare sensation. The bare sensation may give, e.g. one white surface and a second white surface, but in order to judge the similarity between the two, the mind's activity is necessary. Similarly, the railway lines *appear* to converge: it is in intellectual reflection that we know that they are really parallel.

Sense-perception is not, therefore, worthy of the name of knowledge. It should be noted how much Plato is influenced by the conviction that sense-objects are not proper objects of knowledge and cannot be so, since knowledge is of what is, of the stable and abiding, whereas objects of sense cannot really be said to *be—qua* perceived, at least—but only to *become*. Sense-objects are objects of apprehension in some sort, of course, but they elude the mind too much to be objects of real knowledge, which must be, as we have said, (i) infallible, (ii) of what *is*.

(It is noteworthy that Plato, in disposing of the claim of perception to be the whole of knowledge, contrasts the private or peculiar objects of the special senses—e.g. colour, which is the object of vision alone—with the "common terms that apply to everything," and which are the objects of the mind, not of the senses. These "common terms" correspond to the Forms or Ideas which are, ontologically, the stable and abiding objects, as contrasted with the particulars or *sensibilia*.)

2. Knowledge is not simply "True Judgment"

Theaetetus sees that he cannot say that judgment *tout simple* is knowledge, for the reason that false judgments are possible. He therefore suggests that knowledge is true judgment, at least as a provisional definition, until examination of it shows whether it is correct or false. (At this point a digression occurs, in which Socrates tries to find out how false judgments are possible and come to be made at all. Into this discussion I cannot enter at any length, but I will mention one or two suggestions that are made in its course. For example, it is suggested that one class of false judgments arises through the confusion of two objects of different sorts, one a present object of sense-perception, the other a memory-image. A man may judge—mistakenly—that he sees his friend some way off. There is someone there, but it is not his friend. The man has a memory-image of his friend, and something in the figure he sees recalls to him this memory-image: he then judges falsely that it is his friend who is over there. But, obviously, not all cases of false judgment are instances of the confusion of a memory-image with a present object of sense-perception: a mistake in mathematical calculation can hardly be reduced to this. The famous simile of the "aviary" is introduced, in an attempt to show how other kinds of false judgment may arise, but it is found to be unsatisfactory; and Plato concludes that the problem of false judgment cannot be advantageously treated until the nature of knowledge has been determined. The discussion of false judgment was resumed in the *Sophistes*.)

In the discussion of Theaetetus' suggestion that knowledge is true judgment, it is pointed out that a judgment may be true without the fact of its truth involving knowledge on the part of the man who makes the judgment. The relevance of this observation may be easily grasped. If I were to make at this moment the judgment, "Mr. Churchill is talking to President Truman over the telephone," it *might* be true; but it would not involve knowledge on my part. It would be a guess or random shot, as far as I am concerned, even though the judgment were objectively true. Similarly, a man might be tried on a charge of which he was actually not guilty, although the circumstantial evidence was very strong against him and he could not prove his innocence. If, now, a skilful lawyer defending the innocent man were able, for the sake of argument, so to manipulate the evidence or to play on the feelings of the jury, that they gave the verdict "Not guilty," their judgment would actually be a true judgment; but they could hardly be said to *know* the innocence of the prisoner, since *ex hypothesi* the evidence is against him. Their verdict would be a true judgment, but it would be based on persuasion rather than on knowledge. It follows, then, that knowledge is not simply true judgment, and Theaetetus is called on to make another suggestion as to the right definition of knowledge.

3. *Knowledge is not True Judgment plus an "Account"*

True judgment, as has been seen, may mean no more than true belief, and true belief is not the same thing as knowledge. Theaetetus, therefore, suggests that the addition of an "account" or explanation (λόγος) would convert true belief into knowledge. Socrates begins by pointing out that if giving an account or explanation means the enumeration of elementary parts, then these parts must be known or knowable: otherwise the absurd conclusion would follow that knowledge means adding to true belief the reduction of the complex to unknown or unknowable elements. But what does giving an account mean?

1. It cannot mean merely that a correct judgment, in the sense of true belief, is expressed in words, since, if that were the meaning, there would be no difference between true belief and knowledge. And we have seen that there is a difference between making a judgment that happens to be correct and making a judgment that one *knows* to be correct.

2. If "giving an account" means analysis into elementary parts (i.e. knowable parts), will addition of an account in this sense suffice to convert true belief into knowledge? No, the mere process of analysing into elements does not convert true belief into knowledge, for then a man who could enumerate the parts which go to make up a wagon (wheels, axle, etc.) would have a scientific knowledge of a wagon, and a man who could tell you what letters of the alphabet go to compose a certain word would have a grammarian's scientific knowledge of the word. (N.B. We must realise that Plato is speaking of the mere enumeration of parts. For instance, the man who could recount the various steps that lead to a conclusion in geometry, simply because he had seen them in a book and had learnt them by heart, without having really grasped the necessity of the premisses and the necessary and logical sequence of the deduction, would be able to enumerate the "parts" of the theorem; but he would not have the scientific knowledge of the mathematician.)

3. Socrates suggests a third interpretation of "plus account." It may mean "being able to name some mark by which the thing one is asked about differs from everything else." [5] If this is correct, then to know something means the ability to give the distinguishing characteristic of that thing.

But this interpretation too is disposed of, as being inadequate to define knowledge.

(a) Socrates points out that if knowledge of a thing means the addition of its distinguishing characteristic to a correct notion of that thing, we are involved in an absurd position. Suppose that I have a correct notion of Theaetetus. To convert this correct notion into knowledge I have to add some distinguishing characteristic. But unless this distinguishing characteristic were *already* contained within my correct notion, how could the latter be called a *correct* notion? I cannot be said to have a correct notion of Theaetetus, unless this correct notion includes Theaetetus' distinguishing characteristics: if these distinguishing characteristics are not included, then my "correct notion" of Theaetetus would equally well apply to all other men; in which case it would *not* be a correct notion of Theaetetus.

(b) If, on the other hand, my "correct notion" of Theaetetus includes his distinguishing characteristics, then it would also be absurd to say that I convert this correct notion into knowledge by adding the *differentia*, since this would be equivalent to saying that I convert my correct notion of Theaetetus into knowledge by adding to Theaetetus, as already apprehended in distinction from others, that which distinguishes him from others.

N.B. It is to be noted that Plato is not speaking here of *specific* differences, he is speaking of individual, sensible objects, as is clearly shown by the examples that he takes—the sun and a particular man, Theaetetus.[6] The conclusion to be drawn is not that no knowledge is attained through definition by means of a difference, but rather that the individual, sensible object is indefinable and is not really the proper object of knowledge at all. This is the real conclusion of the dialogue, namely, that true knowledge of sensible objects is unattainable, and—by implication—that true knowledge must be knowledge of the universal and abiding.

4. True Knowledge

1. Plato has assumed from the outset that knowledge is attainable, and that knowledge must be (i) infallible and (ii) of the *real*. True knowledge must possess both these characteristics, and any state of mind that cannot vindicate its claim to both these characteristics cannot be true knowledge.

In the *Theaetetus* he shows that neither sense-perception nor true belief are possessed of both these marks; neither, then, can be equated with true knowledge. Plato accepts from Protagoras the belief in the relativity of sense and sense-perception, but he will not accept a universal relativism: on the contrary, knowledge, absolute and infallible knowledge, is attainable, but it cannot be the same as sense-perception, which is relative, elusive and subject to the influence of all sorts of temporary influences on the part of both subject and object. Plato accepts, too, from Heraclitus the view that the objects of sense-perception, individual and sensible particular objects, are always in a state of becoming, of flux, and so are unfit to be the objects of true knowledge. They come into being and pass away, they are indefinite in number, cannot be clearly grasped in definition and cannot become the objects of scientific knowledge. But Plato does not draw the conclusion that there are no objects that are fitted to be the objects of true knowledge, but only that sensible particulars cannot be the objects sought. The object of true knowledge must be stable and abiding, fixed, capable of being grasped in clear and scientific definition, which is of the *universal*, as Socrates saw. The consideration of different states of mind is thus indissolubly bound up with the consideration of the different objects of those states of mind.

If we examine those judgments in which we think we attain knowledge of the essentially stable and abiding, we find that they are judgments concerning *universals*. If, for example, we examine the judgment "The Athenian Constitution is good," we shall find that the essentially stable element in this judgment is the concept of goodness. After all, the Athenian Constitution might be so changed that we would no longer qualify it as good, but as bad. This implies that the concept of goodness remains the same, for if we term the changed Constitution "bad," that can only be because we judge it in reference to a fixed concept of goodness. Moreover, if it is objected that, even though the Athenian Constitution may change as an empirical and historical fact, we can still say "The Athenian Constitution is good," if we mean the particular form of the Constitution that we once called good (even though it may in point of fact have since been changed), we can point out in answer that in this case our judgment has reference, not so much to the Athenian Constitution as a given empirical fact, as to a certain *type* of constitution. That this type of constitution happens at any given historical moment to be embodied in the Athenian Constitution is more or less irrelevant: what we really mean is that this universal type of constitution (whether found at Athens or elsewhere) carries with it the universal quality of goodness. Our judgment, as far as it attains the abiding and stable, really concerns a universal.

Again, scientific knowledge, as Socrates saw (predominantly in connection with ethical valuations), aims at the definition, at crystallising and fixing knowledge in the clear and unambiguous definition. A scientific knowledge of goodness, for instance, must be enshrined in the definition "Goodness is . . . ," whereby the mind expresses the essence of goodness. But definition concerns the universal. Hence true knowledge is knowledge of the universal. Particular constitutions change, but the concept of goodness remains the same, and it is in reference to this stable concept that we judge of particular constitutions in respect of goodness. It follows, then, that it is the universal that fulfils the requirements for being an object of knowledge. Knowledge of the highest universal will be the highest kind of knowledge, while "knowledge" of the particular will be the lowest kind of "knowledge."

But does not this view imply an impassable gulf between true knowledge on the one hand and the "real" world on the other—a world that consists of particulars? And if true knowledge is knowledge of universals, does it not follow that true knowledge is knowledge of the abstract and "unreal"? In regard to the second question, I would point out that the essence of Plato's doctrine of Forms or Ideas is simply this: that the universal concept is not an abstract form devoid of objective content or references, but that to each true universal concept there corresponds an objective reality. How far Aristotle's criticism of Plato (that the latter hypostatised the objective reality of the concepts, imagining a transcendent world of "separate" universals) is justified, is a matter for discussion by itself: whether justified or unjustified, it remains true that the essence of the Platonic theory of Ideas is not to be sought in the notion of the "separate" existence of universal realities, but in the belief that universal concepts have objective reference, and that the corresponding reality is of a higher order than sense-perception as such. In regard to the first question (that of the gulf between true

knowledge and the "real" world), we must admit that it was
one of Plato's standing difficulties to determine the precise
relation between the particular and the universal; but to this
question we must return when treating of the theory of
Ideas from the ontological viewpoint: at the moment one can
afford to pass it over.

2. Plato's positive doctrine of knowledge, in which degrees
or levels of knowledge are distinguished according to objects, is set out in the famous passage of the *Republic* that
gives us the simile of the Line.[7] I give here the usual sche-
matic diagram, which I will endeavour to explain. It must
be admitted that there are several important points that remain very obscure, but doubtless Plato was feeling his way
towards what he regarded as the truth; and, as far as we
know, he never cleared up his precise meaning in unambiguous terms. We cannot, therefore, altogether avoid conjecture.

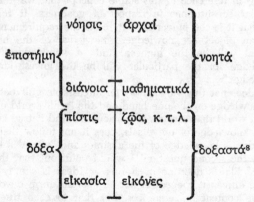

The development of the human mind on its way from ignorance to knowledge, lies over two main fields, that of δόξα
(opinion) and that of ἐπιστήμη (knowledge). It is only
the latter that can properly be termed knowledge. How are
these two functions of the mind differentiated? It seems
clear that the differentiation is based on a differentiation of
object. δόξα (opinion), is said to be concerned with
"images," while ἐπιστήμη, at least in the form of νόησις,
is concerned with originals or archetypes, ἀρχαί. If a man
is asked what justice is, and he points to imperfect embodiments of justice, particular instances which fall short of

the universal ideal, e.g. the action of a particular man, a particular constitution or set of laws, having no inkling that there exists a principle of absolute justice, a norm and standard, then that man's state of mind is a state of δόξα: he sees the images or copies and mistakes them for the originals. But if a man has an apprehension of justice in itself, if he can rise above the images to the Form, to the Idea, to the universal, whereby all the particular instances must be judged, then his state of mind is a state of knowledge, of ἐπιστήμη or γνῶσις. Moreover, it is possible to progress from one state of mind to the other, to be "converted," as it were; and when a man comes to realise that what he formerly took to be originals are in reality only images or copies, i.e. imperfect embodiments of the ideal, imperfect realisations of the norm or standard, when he comes to apprehend in some way the original itself, then his state of mind is no longer that of δόξα, he has been converted to ἐπιστήμη.

The line, however, is not simply divided into two sections; each section is subdivided. Thus there are two degrees of ἐπιστήμη and two degrees of δόξα. How are they to be interpreted? Plato tells us that the lowest degree, that of εἰκασία, has as its object, in the first place, "images" or "shadows," and in the second place "reflections in water and in solid, smooth, bright substances, and everything of the kind." [9] This certainly sounds rather peculiar, at least if one takes Pluto to imply that any man mistakes shadow and reflections in water for the original. But one can legitimately extend the thought of Plato to cover in general images of images, imitations at second hand. Thus we said that a man whose only idea of justice is the embodied and imperfect justice of the Athenian Constitution or of some particular man, is in a state of δόξα in general. If, however, a rhetorician comes along, and with specious words and reasonings persuades him that things are just and right, which in reality are not even in accord with the empirical justice of the Athenian Constitution and its laws, then his state of mind is that of εἰκασία. What he takes for justice is but a shadow or caricature of what is itself only an image, if compared to the universal Form. The state of mind, on the other hand, of the man who takes as justice the justice of the law of Athens or the justice of a particular just man is that of πίστις.

Plato tells us that the objects of the πίστις section are the real objects corresponding to the images of the εἰκασία section of the line, and he mentions "the animals about us, and the whole world of nature and of art." [10] This implies, for instance, that the man whose only idea of a horse is that of particular real horses, and who does not see that particular horses are imperfect "imitations" of the ideal horse, i.e. of the specific type, the universal, is in a state of πίστις. He has not got knowledge of the horse, but only opinion. (Spinoza might say that he is in a state of *imagination*, of inadequate knowledge.) Similarly, the man who judges that external nature is true reality, and who does not see that it is a more or less "unreal" copy of the invisible world (i.e. who does not see that sensible objects are imperfect realisations of the specific type) has only πίστις. He is not so badly off as the dreamer who thinks that the images that he sees are the real world (εἰκασία), but he has not got ἐπιστήμη : he is devoid of real scientific knowledge.

The mention of art in the above quotation helps us to understand the matter a little more clearly. In the tenth book of the *Republic,* Plato says that artists are at the third remove from truth. For example, there is the specific form of man, the ideal type that all individuals of the species strive to realise, and there are particular men who are copies or imitations or imperfect realisations of the specific types. The artist now comes and paints a man, the painted man being an imitation of an imitation. Anyone who took the painted man to be a real man (one might say anyone who took the wax policeman at the entrance of Madame Tussaud's to be a real policeman) would be in a state of εἰκασία, while anyone whose idea of a man is limited to the particular men he has seen, heard of or read about, and who has no real grasp of the specific type, is in a state of πίστις. But the man who apprehends the ideal man, i.e. the ideal type, the specific form of which particular men are imperfect realisations, has νόησις. [11] Again, a just man may imitate or embody in his actions, although imperfectly, the idea of justice. The tragedian then proceeds to imitate this just man on the stage, but without knowing anything of justice in itself. He merely imitates an imitation.

Now, what of the higher division of the line, which corresponds in respect of object to νοητά, and in respect of state of mind to ἐπιστήμη? In general it is connected, not

with ὁρατά or sensible objects (lower part of the line), but
with ἀόρατά, the invisible world, νοητά. But what of the
subdivision? How does νόησις in the restricted sense differ
from διάνοια? Plato says that the object of διάνοια is
what the soul is compelled to investigate by the aid of the
imitations of the former segments, which it employs as
images, starting from hypothesis and proceeding, not to a
first principle, but to a conclusion.[12] Plato is here speaking of
mathematics. In geometry, for instance, the mind proceeds
from hypotheses, by the use of a visible diagram, to a conclusion. The geometer, says Plato, assumes the triangle, etc.,
as known, adopts these "materials" as hypotheses, and then,
employing a visible diagram, argues to a conclusion, being
interested, however, not in the diagram itself (i.e. in this
or that particular triangle or particular square or particular
diameter). Geometers thus employ figures and diagrams, but
"they are really endeavouring to behold those objects which
a person can only see with the eye of thought." [13]

One might have thought that the mathematical objects
of this kind would be numbered among the Forms or ἀρχαί,
and that Plato would have equated the scientific knowledge
of the geometer with νόησις proper; but he expressly de-
clined to do so, and it is impossible to suppose (as some
have done) that Plato was fitting his epistemological doctrines to the exigencies of his simile of the line with its
divisions. Rather must we suppose that Plato really meant
to assert the existence of a class of "intermediaries," i.e. of
objects which are the object of ἐπιστήμη, but which are all
the same inferior to ἀρχαί, and so are the objects of διάνοια
and not of νόησις.[14] It becomes quite clear from the close
of the sixth book of the Republic[15] that the geometers have
not got νοῦς or νόησις in regard to their objects; and that
because they do not mount up above their hypothetical
premisses, "although taken in connection with a first principle these objects come within the domain of the pure reason." [16] These last words show that the distinction between
the two segments of the upper part of the line is to be referred to a distinction of state of mind and not only to a distinction of object. And it is expressly stated that understanding or διάνοια is intermediate between opinion (δόξα)
and pure reason (διάνοῦς).

This is supported by the mention of hypotheses. Nettleship thought that Plato's meaning is that the mathematician

accepts his postulates and axioms as if they were self-contained truth: he does not question them himself, and if anyone else questions them, he can only say that he cannot argue the matter. Plato does not use the word "hypothesis" in the sense of a judgment which is taken as true while it *might* be untrue, but in the sense of a judgment which is treated as if it were self-conditioned, not being seen in its ground and in its necessary connection with being.[17] Against this it might be pointed out that the examples of "hypotheses" given in 510 c are all examples of entities and not of judgments, and that Plato speaks of destroying hypotheses rather than of reducing them to self-conditioned or self-evident propositions. A further suggestion on this matter is given at the close of this section.

In the *Metaphysics*,[18] Aristotle tells us that Plato held that mathematical entities are "between forms and sensible things." "Further, besides sensible things and forms, he says there are the objects of mathematics, which occupy an intermediate position, differing from sensible things in being eternal and unchangeable, from Forms in that there are many alike, while the Form itself is in each case unique." In view of this statement by Aristotle, we can hardly refer the distinction between the two segments of the upper part of the line to the state of mind alone. There must be a difference of object as well. (The distinction would be drawn between the states of mind exclusively, if, while τὰ μαθηματικά belonged *in their own right* to the same segment as αἱ ἀρχαί, the mathematician, acting precisely as such, accepted his "materials" hypothetically and then argued to conclusions. He would be in the state of mind that Plato calls διάνοια, for he treats his postulates as self-conditioned, without asking further questions, and argues to a conclusion by means of visible diagrams; but his reasoning would concern, not the diagrams as such but ideal mathematical objects, so that, if he were to take his hypotheses "in connection with a first principle," he would be in a state of νόησις instead of διάνοια, although the true object of his reasoning, the ideal mathematical objects, would remain the same. This interpretation, i.e. the interpretation that would confine the distinction between the two segments of the upper part of the line to states of mind, might well seem to be favoured by the statement of Plato that mathematical questions, when "taken in connection with a first principle, come within the domain of the pure reason"; but Aristotle's remarks on the subject, if they are a correct statement of the thought of Plato, evidently forbid this interpretation, since he clearly thought that Plato's mathematical entities were supposed to occupy a position between αἱ ἀρχαί and τὰ ὁρατά.)

If Aristotle is correct and Plato really meant τὰ μαθηματικά to constitute a class of objects on their own, distinct from other classes, in what does this distinction consist? There is no need to dwell on the distinction between τὰ μαθηματικά and the objects of the lower part of the line, τὰ ὁρατά, since it is clear enough that the geometrician is concerned with ideal and perfect objects of thought, and not with empirical circles or lines, e.g. cart-wheels or hoops or fishing-rods, or even with geometrical diagrams as such, i.e. as sensible particulars. The question, therefore, resolves itself into this: in what does the distinction between τὰ μαθηματικά, as objects of διάνοια, and αἱ ἀρχαί, as objects of νόησις, really consist?

A natural interpretation of Aristotle's remarks in the *Metaphysics* is that, according to Plato, the mathematician is speaking of intelligible particulars, and not of sensible particulars, nor of universals. For example, if the geometer speaks of two circles intersecting, he is not speaking of the sensible circles drawn nor yet of circularity as such—for how could circularity intersect circularity? He is speaking of intelligible circles, of which there are many alike, as Aristotle would say. Again, to say that "two and two make four" is not the same as to say what will happen if twoness be added to itself—a meaningless phrase. This view is supported by Aristotle's remark that for Plato "there must be a first 2 and 3, and the numbers must not be addable to one another." [19] For Plato, the integers, including 1, form a series in such a way that 2 is *not* made up of two 1's, but is a unique numerical form. This comes more or less to saying that the integer 2 is twoness, which is not composed of two "onenesses." These integer numbers Plato seems to have identified with the Forms. But though it cannot be said of the integer 2 that there are many alike (any more than we can speak of many circularities), it is clear that the mathematician who does not ascend to the ultimate formal principles, does in fact deal with a plurality of 2's and a plurality of circles. Now, when the geometer speaks

of intersecting circles, he is not treating of sensible particulars, but of intelligible objects. Yet of these intelligible
objects there are many alike, hence they are not real
universals but constitute a class of intelligible particulars,
"above" sensible particulars, but "below" true universals. It is
reasonable, therefore, to conclude that Plato's τὰ μαθηματικά
are a class of intelligible particulars.

Now, Professor A. E. Taylor,[20] if I understand him cor-
rectly, would like to confine the sphere of τὰ μαθηματικά
to ideal spatial magnitudes. As he points out, the properties
of e.g. curves can be studied by means of numerical equa-
tions, but they are not themselves numbers; so that they
would not belong to the highest section of the line, that of
αἱ ἀρχαί or Forms, which Plato identified with Numbers.
On the other hand, the ideal spatial magnitudes, the
objects which the geometrician studies, are not sensible
objects, so that they cannot belong to the sphere of τὰ ὁρατά.
They therefore occupy an intermediate position between
Number-Forms and Sensible Things. That this is true of the
objects with which the geometer deals (intersecting circles,
etc.) I willingly admit; but is one justified in excluding from
τὰ μαθηματικά the objects with which the arithmetician
deals? After all, Plato, when treating of those whose state
of mind is that of διάνοια, speaks not only of students of
geometry, but also of students of arithmetic and the kindred
sciences.[21] It would certainly not appear from this that we
are justified in asserting that Plato confined τὰ μαθηματικά
to ideal spatial magnitudes. Whether or not we think that
Plato ought to have so confined the sphere of mathematical
entities, we have to consider, not only what Plato *ought*
to have said, but also what he *did* say. Most probably,
therefore, he understood, as comprised in the class of
τὰ μαθηματικά, the objects of the arithmetician as well as
those of the geometer (and not only of these two, as can be
inferred from the remark about "kindred sciences"). What,
then, becomes of Aristotle's statement that for Plato numbers
are not addable (ἀσύμβλητοι)? I think that it is certainly
to be accepted, and that Plato saw clearly that numbers as
such are unique. On the other hand, it is equally clear
that we add groups or classes of objects together, and speak
of the characteristic of a class as a number. These we add,
but they stand for the classes of individual objects, though
they are themselves the objects, not of sense but of intelli-

gence. They may, therefore, be spoken of as intelligible particulars, and they belong to the sphere of τὰ μαθηματικά, as well as the ideal spatial magnitudes of the geometer. Aristotle's own theory of number may have been erroneous, and he may thus have misrepresented Plato's theory in some respects; but if he definitely stated, as he did, that Plato posited an intermediate class of mathematical entities, it is hard to suppose that he was mistaken, especially as Plato's own writings would seem to leave no reasonable doubt, not only that he actually posited such a class, but also that he did not mean to confine this class to ideal spatial magnitudes.

(Plato's statement that the hypotheses of the mathematicians—he mentions "the odd and the even and the figures and three kinds of angles and the cognates of these in their several branches of science" [22]—when taken in connection with a first principle, are cognisable by the higher reason, and his statement that the higher reason is concerned with first principles, which are self-evident, suggest that he would welcome the modern attempts to reduce pure mathematics to their logical foundations.)

It remains to consider briefly the highest segment of the line. The state of mind in question, that of νόησις, is the state of mind of the man who uses the hypotheses of the διάνοια segment as starting-points, but passes beyond them and ascends to first principles. Moreover, in this process (which is the process of Dialectic) he makes no use of "images," such as are employed in the διάνοια segment, but proceeds in and by the ideas themselves,[23] i.e. by strictly abstract reasoning. Having clearly grasped the first principles, the mind then descends to the conclusions that follow from them, again making use only of abstract reasoning and not of sensible images.[24] The objects corresponding to νόησις are αἱ ἀρχάι, the first principles or Forms. They are not merely epistemological principles, but also ontological principles, and I will consider them more in detail later; but it is as well to point out the following fact. If it were merely a question of seeing the ultimate principles of the hypotheses of the διάνοια section (as e.g. in the modern reduction of pure mathematics to their logical foundations), there might be no very great difficulty in seeing what Plato was driving at; but he speaks expressly of dialectic as "destroying the hypotheses," ἀναιροῦσα τὰς ὑποθέσεις,[25]

which is a hard saying, since, though dialectic may well
show that the postulates of the mathematician need revi-
sion, it is not so easy, at first sight at least, to see how it
can be said to destroy the hypotheses. As a matter of
fact, Plato's meaning becomes clearer if we consider one
particular hypothesis he mentions—the odd and the even.
It would appear that Plato recognised that there are numbers which are neither even nor odd, i.e. irrational numbers, and that in the *Epinomis*[26] he demands the recognition
of quadratic and cubic "surds" as *numbers*.[27] If this is so,
then it would be the task of dialectic to show that the
traditional hypotheses of the mathematician, that there are
no irrational numbers, but that all numbers are integers and
are either even or odd, is not strictly true. Again, Plato
refused to accept the Pythagorean idea of the point-unit
and spoke of the point as "the beginning of a line," [28] so that
the point-unit, i.e. the point as having magnitude of its own,
would be a fiction of the geometer, "a geometrical fiction," [29]
an hypothesis that needs to be "destroyed."

3. Plato further illustrated his epistemological doctrine by
the famous allegory of the Cave in the seventh book of the
Republic.[30] I will briefly sketch the allegory, since it is
valuable as showing clearly, if any further proof be needed,
that the ascent of the mind from the lower sections of the
line to the higher is an epistemological progress, and that
Plato regarded this process, not so much as a continuous
process of evolution as a series of "conversions" from a less
adequate to a more adequate cognitive state.

Plato asks us to imagine an underground cave which has
an opening towards the light. In this cave are living human
beings, with their legs and necks chained from childhood
in such a way that they face the inside wall of the cave and
have never seen the light of the sun. Above and behind
them, i.e. between the prisoners and the mouth of the cave,
is a fire, and between them and the fire is a raised way and
a low wall, like a screen. Along this raised way there pass
men carrying statues and figures of animals and other objects, in such a manner that the objects they carry appear
over the top of the low wall or screen. The prisoners, facing
the inside wall of the cave, cannot see one another nor the
objects carried behind them, but they see the shadows of
themselves and of these objects thrown on to the wall they
are facing. They see only shadows.

These prisoners represent the majority of mankind, that multitude of people who remain all their lives in a state of εἰκασία, beholding only shadows of reality and hearing only echoes of the truth. Their view of the world is most inadequate, distorted by "their own passions and prejudices, and by the passions and prejudices of other people as conveyed to them by language and rhetoric." [31] And though

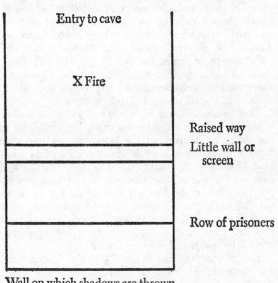

Entry to cave

X Fire

Raised way

Little wall or screen

Row of prisoners

Wall on which shadows are thrown

they are in no better case than children, they cling to their distorted views with all the tenacity of adults, and have no wish to escape from their prison-house. Moreover, if they were suddenly freed and told to look at the realities of which they had formerly seen the shadows, they would be blinded by the glare of the light, and would imagine that the shadows were far more real than the realities.

However, if one of the prisoners who has escaped grows accustomed to the light, he will after a time be able to look at the concrete sensible objects, of which he had formerly seen but the shadows. This man beholds his fellows in the light of the fire (which represents the visible sun) and is in a state of πίστις, having been "converted" from the shadow-world of εἰκόνες, prejudices and passions and sophistries, to the real world of ζῷα, though he has not yet ascended to the world of intelligible, nonsensible realities. He sees the prisoners for what they are, namely prisoners, prisoners in the bonds of passion and sophistry. Moreover, if he perseveres and comes out of the cave into the sunlight, he will see the world of sun-illumined and clear objects (which represent intelligible realities), and lastly, though only by an effort, he will be able to see the sun itself, which represents the Idea of the Good, the highest Form, "the universal cause of all things right and beautiful —the source of truth and reason." [32] He will then be in a state of νόησις. (To this Idea of the Good, as also to the political considerations that concerned Plato in the *Republic*, I shall return in later chapters.)

Plato remarks that if someone, after ascending to the sunshine, went back into the cave, he would be unable to see properly because of the darkness, and so would make himself "ridiciulous"; while if he tried to free another and lead him up to the light, the prisoners, who love the darkness and consider the shadows to be true reality, would put the offender to death, if they could but catch him. Here we may understand a reference to Socrates, who endeavoured to enlighten all those who would listen and make them apprehend truth and reason, instead of letting themselves be misled by prejudice and sophistry.

This allegory makes it clear that the "ascent" of the line was regarded by Plato as a progress, though this progress is not a continuous and automatic process: it needs effort and mental discipline. Hence his insistence on the great importance of *education*, whereby the young may be brought gradually to behold eternal and absolute truths and values, and so saved from passing their lives in the shadow-world of error, falsehood, prejudice, sophistical persuasion, blindness to true values, etc. This education is of primary importance in the case of those who are to be statesmen. Statesmen and rulers will be blind leaders of the blind, if they dwell in the spheres of εἰκασία or πίστις, and the wrecking of the ship of State is a more terrible thing than the wreck of anyone's individual barque. Plato's interest in the epistemological ascent is thus no mere academic or narrowly critical interest: he is concerned with the conduct of life, tendence of the soul and with the good of the

State. The man who does not realise the true good of man will not, and cannot, lead the truly good human life, and the statesman who does not realise the true good of the State, who does not view political life in the light of eternal principles, will bring ruin on his people.

The question might be raised, whether or not there are religious implications in the epistemology of Plato, as illustrated by the simile of the Line and the allegory of the Cave. That the conceptions of Plato were given a religious colouring and application by the Neo-Platonists is beyond dispute: moreover, when a Christian writer, such as the Pseudo-Dionysius, traces the mystic's ascent to God by the *via negativa*, beyond visible creatures to their invisible Source, the light of which blinds by excess of light, so that the soul is in a state of, so to speak, luminous obscurity, he certainly utilises themes which came from Plato *via* the Neo-Platonists. But it does not necessarily follow that Plato himself understood the ascent from a religious viewpoint. In any case this difficult question cannot be profitably touched on until one has considered the ontological nature and status of Plato's Idea of the Good; and even then one can scarcely reach definitive certainty.

Chapter Twenty

THE DOCTRINE OF FORMS

In this chapter I propose to discuss the theory of Forms or Ideas in its ontological aspect. We have already seen that in Plato's eyes the object of true knowledge must be stable and abiding, the object of intelligence and not of sense, and that these requirements are fulfilled by the universal, as far as the highest cognitive state, that of νόησις, is concerned. The Platonic epistemology clearly implies that the universals which we conceive in thought are not devoid of objective reference, but we have not yet examined the important question, in what this objective reference consists. There is indeed plenty of evidence that Plato continued to occupy himself throughout his years of academic and literary activity with problems arising from the theory of Forms, but there is no real evidence that he ever radically changed his doctrine, still less that he abandoned it altogether, however much he tried to clarify or modify it, in view of difficulties that occurred to him or that were suggested by others. It has sometimes been asserted that the mathematisation of the Forms, which is ascribed to Plato by Aristotle, was a doctrine of Plato's old age, a relapse into Pythagorean "mysticism," [1] but Aristotle does not say that Plato *changed* his doctrine, and the only reasonable conclusion to be drawn from Aristotle's words would appear to be that Plato held more or less the same doctrine, at least during the time that Aristotle worked under him in the Academy. (Whether Aristotle misinterpreted Plato or not is naturally another question.) But though Plato continued to maintain the doctrine of Ideas, and though he sought to clarify his meaning and the ontological and logical implications of his thought, it does not follow that we can always clearly grasp what he actually meant. It is greatly to be regretted that we have no adequate record of his lectures in the Academy, since this would doubtless throw great light on the interpretation of his theories as put forward in the dialogues, besides conferring on us the inestimable benefit of knowing what Plato's "real" opinions were, the opinions that he transmitted only through oral teaching and never published.

In the *Republic* it is assumed that whenever a plurality of individuals have a common name, they have also a corresponding idea or form.[2] This is the universal, the common nature or quality which is grasped in the concept, e.g. beauty. There are many beautiful things, but we form one universal concept of beauty itself: and Plato assumed that these universal concepts are not merely subjective concepts, but that in them we apprehend objective essences. At first hearing this sounds a peculiarly naïve view, perhaps, but we must recall that for Plato it is thought that grasps reality, so that the object of thought, as opposed to sense-perception, i.e. universals, must have reality. How could they be grasped and made the object of thought unless they were real? We *discover* them: they are not simply invented by us. Another point to remember is that Plato seems first to have concerned himself with moral and aesthetic universals (as also with the objects of mathematical science), as was only natural, considering the main interest of Socrates, and to think of Absolute Goodness or Absolute Beauty existing in their own right, so to speak, is not unreasonable, particularly if Plato identified them, as we believe that he did. But when Plato came to turn his attention more to natural objects than he had formerly done, and to consider class-concepts, such as those of man or horse, it was obviously rather difficult to suppose that universals corresponding to these class-concepts existed in their own right as objective essences. One may identify Absolute Goodness and Absolute Beauty, but it is not so easy to identify the objective essence of man with the objective essence of horse: in fact, to attempt to do so would be ludicrous. But some principle of unity had to be found, if the essences were not to be left in isolation one from another, and Plato came to devote attention to this

principle of unity, so that all the specific essences might be
unified under or subordinated to one supreme generic essence. Plato tackles this problem from the logical viewpoint,
it is true, inquiring into the problem of logical classification;
but there is no real evidence that he ever abandoned the
view that universals have an ontological status, and he
doubtless thought that in settling the problem of logical classification, he was also settling the problem of ontological
unification.

To these objective essences Plato gave the name of Ideas
or Forms (ἰδέαι or εἴδη), words which are used inter-
changeably. The word εἶδος in this connection appears
suddenly in the *Phaedo*.[3] But we must not be misled by this
use of the term "Idea." "Idea" in ordinary parlance means
a subjective concept in the mind, as when we say: "That is
only an idea and nothing real"; but Plato, when he speaks of
Ideas or Forms, is referring to the objective content or reference of our universal concepts. In our universal concepts
we apprehend objective essences, and it is to these objective
essences that Plato applied the term "Ideas." In some dialogues, e.g. in the *Symposium*, the word "Idea" is not used,
but the *meaning* is there, for in that dialogue Plato speaks of
essential or absolute Beauty (αὐτὸ ὃ ἔστι καλόν), and this
is what Plato would mean by the Idea of Beauty. Thus it
would be a matter of indifference, whether he spoke of the
Absolute Good or of the Idea of the Good: both would
refer to an objective essence, which is the source of goodness in all the particular things that are truly good.

Since by Ideas or Forms Plato meant objective essences,
it becomes of paramount importance for an understanding
of the Platonic ontology to determine, as far as possible,
precisely how he regarded these objective essences. Have
they a transcendental existence of their own, apart from
particular things, and, if so, what is their relation to one
another and to the concrete particular objects of this world?
Does Plato duplicate the world of sense-experience by postulating a transcendental world of invisible, immaterial essences? If so, what is the relation of this world of essences
to God? That Plato's language often implies the existence
of a separate world of transcendental essences cannot be
denied, but it must be remembered that language is primarily
designed to refer to the objects of our sense-experience, and
is very often found inadequate for the precise expression

of metaphysical truths. Thus we speak, and cannot well help speaking, of "God forseeing," a phrase that, as it stands, implies that God is in time, whereas we know that God is not in time but is eternal. We cannot, however, speak adequately of the eternity of God, since we have no experience of eternity ourselves, and our language is not designed to express such matters. We are human beings and have to use human language—we can use no other: and this fact should make us cautious in attaching too much weight to the mere language or phrases used by Plato in dealing with abstruse, metaphysical points. We have to endeavour to get at the meaning behind those phrases. By this I do not mean to imply that Plato did not believe in the subsistence of universal essences, but simply to point out that, if we find that he did in fact hold this doctrine, we must beware of the temptation to put that doctrine in a ludicrous light by stressing the phrases used by Plato, without due consideration of the meaning to be attached to those phrases.

Now, what we might call the "vulgar" presentation of the Platonic theory of Ideas has generally been more or less as follows. In Plato's view the objects which we apprehend in universal concepts, the objects with which science deals, the objects corresponding to universal terms of predication, are objective Ideas or subsistent Universals, existing in a transcendental world of their own—somewhere "out there"—apart from sensible things, understanding by "apart from" practically spatial separation. Sensible things are copies or participations in these universal realities, but the latter abide in an unchanging heaven of their own, while sensible things are subject to change, in fact are always becoming and can never truly be said to *be*. The Ideas exist in their heaven in a state of isolation one from another, and apart from the mind of any Thinker. Plato's theory having been thus presented, it is pointed out that the subsistent universals either *exist* (in which case the real world of our experience is unjustifiably duplicated) or they do not exist, but have independent and *essential reality* in some mysterious way (in which case a wedge is unjustifiably driven between existence and essence). (The Thomist School of Scholastic philosophers, be it remarked in passing, admit a "real distinction" between essence and the act of existence in created being; but, for them, the distinction is *within* the creature. Uncreated Being is Absolute Existence and Absolute Essence

in identity.) Of the reasons which have led to this traditional presentation of the doctrine of Plato one may enumerate three.

(i) Plato's way of speaking about the Ideas clearly supposes that they exist in a sphere apart. Thus in the *Phaedo*
he teaches that the soul existed before its union with the
body in a transcendental realm, where it beheld the subsistent intelligible entities or Ideas, which would seem to
constitute a plurality of "detached" essences. The process of
knowledge, or getting to know, consists essentially in recollection, in remembering the Ideas which the soul once beheld
clearly in its state of pre-existence.

(ii) Aristotle asserts in the *Metaphysics*[4] that Plato "separated" the Ideas, whereas Socrates had not done so. In
his criticism of the theory of Ideas he constantly supposes
that, according to the Platonists, Ideas exist apart from
sensible things. Ideas constitute the reality or "substance"
of things; "how, therefore," asks Aristotle, "can the Ideas,
being the substance of things, exist apart?"[5]

(iii) In the *Timaeus* Plato clearly teaches that God or the
"Demiurge" forms things of this world according to the model
of the Forms. This implies that the Forms or Ideas exist
apart, not only from the sensible things that are modelled
on them, but also from God, Who takes them as His model.
They are therefore hanging in the air, as it were.

In this way, say the critics, Plato—

(a) Duplicates the "real" world;
(b) Posits a multitude of subsistent essences with no sufficient metaphysical ground or basis (since they are
independent even of God);
(c) Fails to explain the relation between sensible things
and the Ideas (except by metaphorical phrases like
"imitation" or "participation"); and
(d) Fails to explain the relation of the Ideas to one another, e.g. of species to genus, or to find any real
principle of unity. Accordingly, if Plato was trying to
solve the problem of the One and the Many, he failed
lamentably and merely enriched the world with one
more fantastic theory, which was exploded by the
genius of Aristotle.

It must be left to an examination of Plato's thought in more
detail to show what truth there is in this presentation of the

theory of Ideas; but we would point out at once that these critics tend to neglect the fact that Plato saw clearly that the plurality of Ideas needs some principle of unity, and that he tried to solve this problem. They also tend to neglect the fact that we have indications not only in the dialogues themselves, but also in the allusions of Aristotle to Plato's theory and Plato's lectures, *how* Plato tried to solve the problem, namely, by a new interpretation, and application of the Eleatic doctrine of the One. Whether Plato actually solved the problems that arise out of his theories is a matter for dispute, but it will not do to speak as though he never saw any of the difficulties that Aristotle afterwards brought against him. On the contrary, Plato anticipated some of the very objections raised by Aristotle and thought that he had solved them more or less satisfactorily. Aristotle evidently thought otherwise, and he may have been right, but it is unhistorical to speak as though Aristotle raised objections which Plato had been too foolish to see. Moreover, if it is an historical fact, as it is, that Plato brought difficulties against himself, one should be careful in attributing to him an opinion that is fantastic—unless, of course, we are compelled by the evidence to believe that he held it.

Before going on to consider the theory of Ideas as presented in the dialogues, we will make some preliminary observations in connection with the three reasons that we enumerated in support of the traditional presentation of Plato's Ideal Theory.

(i) It is an undeniable fact that Plato's way of speaking about the Ideas very often implies that they exist "apart from" sensible things. I believe that Plato really did hold this doctrine; but there are two cautionary observations to be made.

(a) If they exist "apart from" sensible things, this "apart from" can only mean that the Ideas are possessed of a reality independent of sensible things. There can be no question of the Ideas being in a place, and, strictly speaking, they would be as much "in" as "out of" sensible things, for *ex hypothesi* they are incorporeal essences and incorporeal essences cannot be in a place. As Plato had to use human language, he would naturally express the essential reality and independence of the Ideas in spatial terminology (he could not do anything else); but he would not *mean* that the Ideas were spatially separate from things. Transcendence in this connection would mean that the Ideas do not change and perish with sensible particulars: it would no more mean that they are in a heavenly place of their own than God's transcendence implies for us that God is in a place, different from the places or spaces of the sensible objects He has created. It is absurd to speak as though the Platonic Theory involved the assumption of an Ideal Man with length, breadth, depth, etc., existing in the heavenly place. To do so is to make the Platonic theory gratuitously ridiculous: whatever the transcendence of the Ideas might mean, it could not mean *that*.

(b) We should be careful not to place too much weight on doctrines such as that of the pre-existence of the soul and the process of "recollection." Plato sometimes, as is well known, makes use of "Myth," giving a "likely account," which he does not mean to be taken with the same exactitude and seriousness as more scientifically argued themes. Thus in the *Phaedo* "Socrates" gives an account of the soul's future life, and then expressly declares that it does not become a man of sense to affirm that these things are exactly as he has described them.[6] But while it is clear enough that the account of the soul's future life is conjectural and admittedly "mythical" in character, it appears altogether unjustifiable to extend the concept of "myth" to include the whole doctrine of immortality, as some would do, for in the passage alluded to in the *Phaedo* Socrates declares that, though the picture of the future life is not to be understood literally or positively affirmed, the soul is "certainly immortal." And, as Plato couples together immortality after death with pre-existence, it hardly seems that one is warranted in dismissing the whole conception of pre-existence as "mythical." It may possibly be that it was no more than an hypothesis in Plato's eyes (so that, as I said, we should not attach too much weight to it); but, all things considered, we are not justified in simply asserting that it actually is myth, and, unless its mythical character can be demonstrated satisfactorily, we ought to accept it as a seriously-meant doctrine. Yet even if the soul pre-existed and contemplated the Forms in that state of pre-existence, it would *not* follow that the Forms or Ideas in any *place*, save metaphorically. Nor does it even necessarily follow that they are "detached" essences, for they might all be included in some ontological principle of unity.

(ii) In regard to the statements of Aristotle in the *Metaphysics* it is as well to point out at once that Aristotle must have known perfectly well what Plato taught in the Academy and that Aristotle was no imbecile. It is absurd to speak as though Aristotle's insufficient knowledge of contemporary mathematical developments would necessarily lead to his essentially perverting Plato's doctrine of the Forms, at least in its non-mathematical aspects. He may or may not have fully understood Plato's mathematical theories: it does not follow from this alone that he made an egregious blunder in his interpretation of the Platonic ontology. If Aristotle declares that Plato "separated" the Forms, we cannot pass over this statement as mere ignorant criticism. All the same, we have to be careful not to assume *a priori* what Aristotle meant by "separation," and in the second place we have to inquire whether Aristotle's criticism of the Platonic theory necessarily implies that Plato himself drew the conclusions that Aristotle attacks. It *might* be that some of the conclusions attacked by Aristotle were conclusions that he (Aristotle) considered to be logical consequences of the Platonic theory, although Plato may not have drawn those conclusions himself. If this were the case, then we should have to inquire whether the conclusions really did flow from Plato's premisses. But as it would be impracticable to discuss Aristotle's criticism until we have seen what Plato himself said about the Ideas in his published works, it is best to reserve till later a discussion of Aristotle's criticism, although it is true that, since one has to rely largely on Aristotle for knowledge of what Plato taught in his lectures, one cannot help drawing upon him in an exposition of the Platonic doctrine. It is, however, important (and this is the burden of these preliminary remarks) that we should put out of our heads the notion that Aristotle was an incompetent fool, incapable of understanding the true thought of the Master.[7] Unjust he may have been, but he was no fool.

(iii) It can scarcely be denied that Plato in the *Timaeus* speaks as though the Demiurge, the Efficient Cause of order in the world, fashions the objects of this world after the pattern of the Forms as Exemplary Cause, thus implying that the Forms or Ideas are quite distinct from the Demiurge, so that, if we call the Demiurge "God," we should have to conclude that the Forms are not only "outside" the things of this world, but also "outside" God. But though Plato's language in the *Timaeus* certainly implies this interpretation, there is some reason, as will be seen later, to think that the Demiurge of the *Timaeus* is an *hypothesis* and that Plato's "theism" is not to be over-stressed. Moreover, and this is an important fact to remember, Plato's doctrine, as given in his lectures, was not precisely the same as that given in the dialogues: or it might be better to say that Plato developed aspects of his doctrine in his lectures that scarcely appear in the dialogues. The remarks of Aristotle concerning Plato's lecture on the Good, as recorded by Aristoxenus, would seem to indicate that in dialogues such as the *Timaeus*, Plato revealed some of his thoughts only in a pictorial and figurative way. To this question I return later: we must now endeavour to ascertain, as far as possible, what Plato's doctrine of Ideas actually was.

1. In the *Phaedo*, where the discussion centres round the problem of immortality, it is suggested that truth is not to be attained by the bodily senses, but by reason alone, which lays hold of the things that "really are." [8] What are the things that "really are," i.e. that have true being? They are the essences of things, and Socrates gives as examples justice itself, beauty itself, and goodness itself, abstract equality, etc. These essences remain always the same, while particular objects of sense do not. That there really exist such essences is assumed by Socrates: he lays it down "as an hypothesis that there is a certain abstract beauty, and goodness, and magnitude," and that a particular beautiful object, for instance, is beautiful because it partakes of that abstract beauty.[9] (In 102 b the word Idea is applied to these essences; they are termed εἴδη.) In the *Phaedo* the existence of these essences is used as an aid in the proof of immortality. It is pointed out that the fact that a man is able to judge of things as more or less equal, more or less beautiful, implies knowledge of a standard, of the essence of beauty or equality. Now, men do not come into the world and grow up with a clear knowledge of universal essences: how is it, then, that they can judge of particular things in reference to a universal standard? Is it not because the soul pre-existed before its union with the body, and had knowledge of the essences in its state of pre-existence? The process of learning would thus be a process of reminiscence, in which particular embodiments of the essence acted as

reminders of the essences previously beheld. Moreover, since rational knowledge of essences in this life involves transcending the bodily senses and rising to the intellectual plane, should we not suppose that the soul of the philosopher beholds these essences after death, when he is no longer hampered and shackled by the body?

Now, the natural interpretation of the doctrine of the Ideas as given in the *Phaedo* is that the Ideas are subsistent universals; but it is to be remembered that, as already mentioned, the doctrine is put forward tentatively as an "hypothesis," i.e. as a premiss which is assumed until connection with an evident first principle either justifies it or "destroys" it, or shows that it stands in need of modification or correction. Of course, one cannot exclude the possibility that Plato put forward the doctrine tentatively because he (Plato) was not yet certain of it, but it would appear legitimate to suppose that Plato makes Socrates put forward the doctrine in a tentative fashion precisely because he knew very well that the historical Socrates had not reached the metaphysical theory of the Ideas, and that in any case he had not arrived at Plato's final Principle of the Good. It is significant that Plato allows Socrates to divine the Ideal Theory in his "swan-song," when he becomes "prophetic." [10] This might well imply that Plato allows Socrates to divine a certain amount of his (i.e. Plato's) theory, but not all. It is also to be noted that the theory of pre-existence and reminiscence is referred, in the *Meno*, to "priests and priestesses," [11] just as the sublimest part of the *Symposium* is referred to "Diotima." Some have concluded that these passages were avowedly "Myths" in Plato's eyes, but it might equally well be the case that these hypothetical passages (hypothetical for *Socrates*) reveal something of Plato's own doctrine, as distinct from that of Socrates. (In any case we should not use the doctrine of reminiscence as an excuse for attributing to Plato an explicit anticipation of Neo-Kantian theory. The Neo-Kantians may think that the *a priori* in the Kantian sense is the truth that Plato was getting at or that underlies his words, but they cannot be justified in fathering the explicit doctrine on to Plato, without much better evidence than they can offer.) I conclude, then, that the theory of Ideas, as put forward in the *Phaedo*, represents but a part of Plato's doctrine. It should not be inferred that for Plato himself the Ideas were *"detached"* subsistent universals. Aristotle clearly stated that Plato identified the One with the Good; but this unifying principle, whether already held by Plato when he composed the *Phaedo* (as is most probable) or only later elaborated, certainly does not appear in the *Phaedo*.

2. In the *Symposium*, Socrates is represented as reporting a discourse made to him by one Diotima, a "Prophetess," concerning the soul's ascent to true Beauty under the impulse of Eros. From beautiful forms (i.e. bodies), a man ascends to the contemplation of the beauty that is in souls, and thence to science, that he may look upon the loveliness of wisdom, and turn towards the "wide ocean of beauty" and the "lovely and majestic forms which it contains," until he reaches the contemplation of a Beauty that is "eternal, unproduced, indestructible; neither subject to increase nor decay; not partly beautiful and partly ugly; not at one time beautiful and at another time not; not beautiful in relation to one thing and deformed in relation to another; not here beautiful and there ugly; not beautiful in the estimation of some people and deformed in that of others. Nor can this supreme beauty be figured to the imagination like a beautiful face, or beautiful hands, or any other part of the body, nor like any discourse, nor any science. Nor does it subsist in any other thing that lives or is, either in earth, or in heaven, or in any other place; but it is eternally self-subsistent and monoeidic with itself. All other things are beautiful through a participation of it, with this condition, that although they are subject to production and decay, it never becomes more or less, or endures any change." This is the divine and pure, the monoeidic beautiful itself.[12] It is evidently the Beauty of the *Hippias Maior*, "from which all beautiful things derive their beauty." [13]

The priestess Diotima, into whose mouth Socrates puts his discourse on Absolute Beauty and the ascent thereto under the impulse of Eros, is represented as suggesting that Socrates may not be able to follow her to such sublime heights, and she urges him to strain all his attention to reach the obscure depth of the subject.[14] Professor A. E. Taylor interprets this to mean that Socrates is too modest to claim the mystical vision for himself (although he has really experienced it), and so represents himself as but reporting the words of Diotima. Taylor will have nothing to do with the suggestion that the speech of Diotima represents *Plato's* personal conviction, never attained by the historical Socrates. "Much unfortunate nonsense has been written about the meaning of Diotima's apparent doubt whether Socrates will be able to follow her as she goes on to speak of the 'full and perfect vision...' It has even been seriously argued that Plato is here guilty of the arrogance of professing that he has reached philosophical heights to which the 'historical' Socrates could not ascend." [15] That such a procedure would be indicative of arrogance on Plato's part might be true, if there were question of a mystical vision, as Taylor apparently thinks there is; but it is by no means certain that there is any question of religious mysticism in the speech of Socrates, and there seems no real reason why Plato should not be able to claim a greater philosophic penetration in regard to the ultimate Principle than Socrates, without thereby laying himself open to any justifiable charge of arrogance. Moreover, if as Taylor supposes, the opinions put into the mouth of Socrates in the *Phaedo* and the *Symposium* are those of the historic Socrates, how does it come about that in the *Symposium* Socrates speaks as though he had actually grasped the ultimate Principle, the Absolute Beauty, while in the *Phaedo* the theory of Ideas (in which abstract beauty finds a place) is put forward as a tentative hypothesis, i.e. in the very dialogue that purports to give Socrates' conversation before his death? Might we not be justified in expecting that if the historic Socrates had really apprehended the final Principle for certain, some sure indication of this would have been given in his final discourse? I prefer, then, the view that in the *Symposium* the speech of Diotima does not represent the certain conviction of the historic Socrates. In any case, however, this is an academic point: whether the report of Diotima's words represents the conviction of the historic Socrates or of Plato himself, the evident fact remains that some hint (at the very least) of the existence of an Absolute is therein given.

Is this Beauty in itself, the very essence of Beauty, a subsistent essence, "separate" from beautiful things, or is it not? It is true that Plato's words concerning science might be taken to imply a scientific appreciation of the mere universal concept of Beauty which is embodied in varying degrees in various beautiful objects; but the whole tenor of Socrates' discourse in the *Symposium* leads one to suppose that this essential Beauty is no mere concept, but has ob-

jective reality. Does this imply that it is "separate"? Beauty
in itself or Absolute Beauty is "separate" in the sense that
it is real, subsistent, but not in the sense that it is in a
world of its own, spatially separate from things. For *ex
hypothesi* Absolute Beauty is spiritual; and the categories
of time and space, of local separation, simply do not apply
in the case of that which is essentially spiritual. In the
case of that which transcends space and time, we cannot
even legitimately raise the question, *where* it is. It is nowhere,
as far as local presence is concerned (though it is not nowhere in the sense of being unreal). The Χωρισμός or separation would thus seem to imply, in the case of the Platonic
essence, a reality beyond the subjective reality of the abstract
concept—a subsistent reality, but not a local separation. It is,
therefore, just as true to say that the essence is immanent,
as that it is transcendent: the great point is that it is *real*
and independent of particulars, unchanged and abiding. It
is foolish to remark that if the Platonic essence is real, it
must be somewhere. Absolute Beauty, for instance, does not
exist outside us in the sense in which a flower exists outside us—for it might just as well be said to exist inside us,
inasmuch as spatial categories simply do not apply to it.
On the other hand, it cannot be said to be inside us in the
sense that it is purely subjective, is confined to us, comes
into being with us, and perishes through our agency or
with us. It is both transcendent and immanent, inaccessible
to the senses, apprehensible only by the intellect.

   To the means of ascent to Absolute Beauty, the signification
of Eros, and the question whether a mystical approach is
implied, we must return later: at the present I wish simply
to point out that in the *Symposium* indications are not wanting that Absolute Beauty is the ultimate Principle of unity.
The passage[16] concerning the ascent from different sciences
to one science—the science of universal Beauty—suggests that
"the wide ocean of intellectual beauty," containing "lovely
and majestic forms," is subordinate to or even comprised in
the ultimate Principle of Absolute Beauty. And if Absolute
Beauty is a final and unifying Principle, it becomes necessary
to identify it with the Absolute Good of the *Republic*.

   3. In the *Republic* it is clearly shown that the true philosopher seeks to know the essential nature of each thing. He
is not concerned to know, for example, a multiplicity of
beautiful things or a multiplicity of good things, but rather

to discern the essence of beauty and the essence of goodness, which are embodied in varying degrees in particular beautiful things and particular good things. Non-philosophers, who are so taken up with the multiplicity of appearances that they do not attend to the essential nature and cannot distinguish, e.g. the essence of beauty from the many beautiful phenomena, are represented as having only opinion (δόξα) and as lacking in scientific knowledge. They are not concerned with not-being, it is true, since not-being cannot be an object of "knowledge" at all, but is completely unknowable; yet they are no more concerned with true being or reality, which is stable and abiding: they are concerned with fleeting phenomena or appearances, objects which are in a state of *becoming*, constantly coming to be and passing away. Their state of mind is thus one of δόξα and the object of their δόξα is the phenomenon that stands half-way between being and not-being. The state of mind of the philosopher, on the other hand, is one of knowledge, and the object of his knowledge is Being, the fully real, the essential, the Idea or Form.

So far, indeed, there is no direct indication that the essence or Idea is regarded as subsistent or "separate" (so far as the latter term is applicable at all to non-sensual reality); but that it *is* so regarded may be seen from Plato's doctrine concerning the Idea of the Good, the Idea that occupies a peculiar position of pre-eminence in the *Republic*. The Good is there compared to the sun, the light of which makes the objects of nature visible to all and so is, in a sense, the source of their worth and value and beauty. This comparison is, of course, but a comparison, and as such should not be pressed: we are not to suppose that the Good exists as an object among objects, as the sun exists as an object among other objects. On the other hand, as Plato clearly asserts that the Good gives being to the objects of knowledge and so is, as it were, the unifying and all-comprehensive Principle of the essential order, while itself excelling even essential being in dignity and power,[17] it is impossible to conclude that the Good is a mere concept or even that it is a non-existent end, a teleological principle, as yet unreal, towards which all things are working: it is not only an epistemological principle, but also—in some, as yet, ill-defined sense—an *ontological* principle, a principle of being. It is, therefore, real in itself and subsistent.

It would seem that the Idea of the Good of the *Republic* must be regarded as identical with the essential Beauty of the *Symposium*. Both are represented as the high-peak of an intellectual ascent, while the comparison of the Idea of the Good with the sun would appear to indicate that it is the source not only of the goodness of things, but also of their beauty. The Idea of the Good gives being to the Forms or essences of the intellectual order, while science and the wide ocean of intellectual beauty is a stage on the ascent to the essentially beautiful. Plato is clearly working towards the conception of the Absolute, the absolutely Perfect and exemplary Pattern of all things, the ultimate ontological Principle. This Absolute is immanent, for phenomena embody it, "copy" it, partake in it, manifest it, in their varying degrees; but it is also transcendent, for it is said to transcend even being itself, while the metaphors of participation (μέθεξις) and imitation (μίμησις)[18] imply a distinction between the participation and the Partaken of, between the imitation and the Imitated or Exemplar. Any attempt to reduce the Platonic Good to a mere logical principle and to disregard the indications that it is an ontological principle, necessarily leads to a denial of the sublimity of the Platonic metaphysic—as also, of course, to the conclusion that the Middle Platonist and Neo-Platonist philosophers entirely misunderstood the essential meaning of the Master.

At this point in the discussion there are two important observations to be made:

(i) Aristotle in the *Eudemian Ethics*[19] says that Plato identifies the Good with the One, while Aristoxenus, recalling Aristotle's account of Plato's lecture on the Good, tells us that the audience, who went to the lecture expecting to hear something about human goods, such as wealth, happiness, etc., were surprised when they found themselves listening to a discourse on mathematics, astronomy, numbers and *the identity of the good and one*. In the *Metaphysics*, Aristotle says that "Of those who maintain the existence of the unchangeable substances, some say that the one itself is the good itself, but they thought its substance lay mainly in its unity." [20] Plato is not mentioned by name in this passage, but elsewhere[21] Aristotle distinctly says that, for Plato, "the Forms are the cause of the essence of all other things, and the One is the cause of the essence of the Forms." Now, in the *Republic*,[22] Plato speaks of the ascent of the mind to the first principle of the whole, and asserts that the Idea of the Good is inferred to be "the universal author of all things beautiful and right, parent of light and of the lord of light in this world, and the *source of truth and reason* in the other." Hence it would seem only reasonable to conclude that the One, the Good and the essential Beauty are the same for Plato, and that the intelligible world of Forms owes its being in some way to the One. The word "emanation" (so dear to the Neo-Platonists) is nowhere used, and it is difficult to form any precise notion how Plato derived the Forms from the One; but it is clear enough that the One is the unifying Principle. Moreover, the One itself, though immanent in the Forms, is also transcendent, in that it cannot be simply equated with the single Forms. Plato tells us that "the good is not essence, but far exceeds essence in dignity and power," while on the other hand it is "not only the source of intelligibility in all objects of knowledge, but also of their being and essence," [23] so that he who turns his eye towards the Good, turns it towards "that place where is the full perfection of being." [24] The implication is that the Idea of the Good may rightly be said to transcend being, since it is above all visible and intelligible objects, while on the other hand, as the Supremely Real, the true Absolute, it is the Principle of being and essence in all things.

In the *Timaeus*, Plato says that "It is hard to find the maker and father of the universe, and having found him, it is impossible to speak of him to all." [25] That the position occupied by the Demiurge in the *Timaeus* suggests that these words apply to him, is true; but we must remember (a) that the Demiurge is probably a symbol for the operation of Reason in the universe, and (b) that Plato explicitly said that there were subjects on which he refused to write,[26] one of these subjects being without doubt his full doctrine of the One. The Demiurge belongs to the "likely account." [27] In his second letter, Plato says that it is a mistake to suppose that any of the predicates we are acquainted with apply to the "king of the universe," [28] and in his sixth letter he asks his friends to swear an oath of loyalty "in the name of the God who is captain of all things present and to come, and of the Father of that captain and cause." [29] Now, if the "Captain" is the Demiurge, the "Father" cannot be the Demiurge too, but must be the One; and I think that

Plotinus was right in identifying the Father with the One or Good of the *Republic*.

The One is thus Plato's ultimate Principle and the source of the world of Forms, and Plato, as we have seen, thinks that the One transcends human predicates. This implies that the *via negativa* of Neo-Platonist and Christian philosophers is a legitimate approach to the One, but it should not be immediately concluded that the approach to the One is an "ecstatic" approach, as in Plotinus. In the *Republic* it is definitely asserted that the approach is *dialectical*, and that a man attains the vision of the Good by "pure intelligence." [30] By dialectic the highest principle of the soul is raised "to the contemplation of that which is best in existence." [31] To this subject we must return later.

(ii) If the Forms proceed from the One—in some undefined manner—what of particular sensible objects? Does not Plato make such a rift between intelligible and visible worlds that they can be no longer interconnected? It would appear that Plato, who in the *Republic*[32] appears to condemn empirical astronomy, was forced by the progress of empirical science to modify his views, and in the *Timaeus* he himself considers nature and natural questions. (Moreover, Plato came to see that the dichotomy between an unchanging, intelligible world of reality and a changing world of unreality is hardly satisfactory. "Shall we be easily persuaded that change and life and soul and wisdom are not really present to what completely is, that it is neither living nor intelligent but is something awful and sacred in its thoughtless and static stability?") [33] In the *Sophist* and *Philebus* it is implied that διάνοια and αἴσθησις (which belong to different segments of the Line) unite together in the scientific judgment of perception. Ontologically speaking, the sensible particular can become the object of judgment and knowledge only in so far as it is really subsumed under one of the Ideas, "partaking" in the specific Form: in so far as it is a class-instance, it is real and can be known. The sensible particular *as such*, however, considered precisely in its particularity, is indefinable and unknowable, and is not truly "real." To this conviction Plato clung, and it is obviously an Eleatic legacy. The sense-world is, therefore, not wholly illusion, but it contains an element of unreality. Yet it can hardly be denied that even this position, with its sharp distinction between the formal and material elements of the particular, would leave the problem of the "separation" of the intelligible world from the sensible world really unresolved. It is this "separation" that Aristotle attacked. Aristotle thought that determinate form and the matter in which it is embodied are inseparable, both belonging to the real world, and, in his opinion, Plato simply ignored this fact and introduced an unjustifiable separation between the two elements. The real universal, according to Aristotle, is the *determined* universal, and the determined universal is an inseparable aspect of the real: it is a λόγος ἔνυλος or definition embodied in matter. Plato did not see this.

(Professor Julius Stenzel made the brilliant suggestion[34] that when Aristotle criticised Plato's "separation," he was criticising Plato for his failure to see that there is no genus alongside the species. He appeals to *Metaph.*, 1037 b 8 ff., where Aristotle attacks Plato's method of logical division for supposing that in the resulting definition the intermediate *differentiae* must be recapitulated, e.g. Plato's method of division would result in our defining man as a "two-footed animal." Aristotle objects to this on the ground that "footedness" is not something alongside "two-footedness." Now, that Aristotle objected to this method of division is true; but his criticism of the Platonic theory of Forms on the ground of the Χωρισμός it introduces, cannot be reduced to the criticism of a logical point, for Aristotle is not criticising Plato merely for putting a generic form alongside the specific form, but for putting Forms in general alongside particulars.[35] It may well be, however, that Aristotle considered that Plato's failure to see that there is no genus alongside the species, i.e. no merely determinable universal, helped to conceal from him the Χωρισμός he was introducing between Forms and particulars—and here Stenzel's suggestion is valuable; but the Χωρισμός attacked by Aristotle cannot be confined to a logical point. That is clear from the whole tenor of Aristotle's criticism.)

4. In the *Phaedrus* Plato speaks of the soul who beholds "real existence, colourless, formless and intangible, visible only to the intelligence" (ἡ ἀχρώματός τε καὶ ἀσχημάτιστος καὶ ἀναφὴς οὐσία ὄντως οὖσα, ψυχῆς, κυβερνήτῃ μόνῳ θεατὴ νῷ),[36] and which sees distinctly "absolute justice, and absolute temperance, and absolute science; not such as they appear in creation, nor under the variety of forms to which we nowadays give the name of realities, but the

justice, the temperance, the science, which exist in that which
is real and essential being" (τὴν ἐν τῷ ὅ ἐστιν ὂν ὄντως
ἐπιστήμην οὖσαν). This would seem to me to imply that
these Forms or *Ideals* are comprised in the Principle of
Being, in the One, or at least that they owe their essence
to the One. Of course, if we use the imagination and try to
picture to ourselves absolute justice or temperance existing
on its own account in a heavenly world, we shall no doubt
think Plato's words childishly naïve and ludicrous; but we
should ask ourselves what Plato *meant* and should beware
of attributing hastily to him such an extraordinary conception. Most probably Plato means to imply, by his figurative
account, that the Ideal of Justice, the Ideal of Temperance,
etc., are objectively grounded in the Absolute Principle of
Value, in the Good, which "contains" within itself the ideal
of human nature and so the ideal of the virtues of human
nature. The Good or Absolute Principle of Value has thus the
nature of a τέλος; but it is not an unrealised τέλος, a
non-existent end-to-be-achieved; it is an existent τέλος,
an ontological Principle, the Supremely Real, the perfect
Exemplary Cause, the Absolute or One.

5. It is to be noted that at the beginning of the *Parmenides*
the question is raised what Ideas Socrates is prepared to
admit.[37] In reply to Parmenides, Socrates admits that there
are Ideas of "likeness" and "of the one and many," and
also of "the just and the beautiful and the good," etc. In
answer to a further question, he says that he is often un-
decided, whether he should or should not include Ideas of
man, fire, water, etc.; while, in answer to the question
whether he admits Ideas of hair, mud, dirt, etc., Socrates
answers, "Certainly not." He admits, however, that he
sometimes gets disturbed and begins to think that there is
nothing without an Idea, though no sooner has he taken up
this position than he "runs away," afraid that he "may fall
into a bottomless pit of nonsense and perish." He returns,
therefore, "to the Ideas of which I was just now speaking."

Julius Stenzel uses this discussion in an attempt to prove
that εἶδος had at first for Plato a definitely valuational connotation, as was but natural in the inheritor of Socrates. It
was only later that the term came to be extended to cover
all class-concepts. I believe that this is, in the main, correct,
and that it was largely this very extension of the term Idea
(i.e. *explicit* extension, since it already contained an implicit

extension) which forced on Plato's attention difficulties of the type considered in the *Parmenides*. For, as long as the term εἶδος is "laden with moral and aesthetic qualities," [38] as long as it has the nature of a valuational τέλος, drawing men under the impulse of Eros, the problem of its internal unity or multiplicity does not so obviously arise: it is the Good and the Beautiful in One. But once Ideas of man and other particular objects of our experience are explicitly admitted, the Ideal World threatens to become a Many, a reduplication of this world. What is the relation of the Ideas to one another, and what is their relation to particular things? Is there any real unity at all? The Idea of the Good is sufficiently remote from sensible particulars not to appear as an unwelcome reduplication of the latter; but if there is an Idea of man, for instance, "separate" from individual men, it might well appear as a mere reduplication of the latter. Moreover, is the Idea wholly present in every individual man, or is it only partially present in every individual man? Again, if it is legitimate to speak of a likeness between individual men and the Idea of Man, must you not postulate a τρίτος ἄνθρωπος, in order to account for this resemblance and so proceed on an infinite regress? This type of objection was brought against the Ideal Theory by Aristotle, but it was already anticipated by Plato himself. The difference is, that while Plato (as we shall see later) thought that he had answered the objections, Aristotle did not think that Plato had answered them.

In the *Parmenides*, therefore, the question of the relation of individual objects to the Idea is discussed, objections being raised to the Socratic explanation. According to Socrates the relation may be described in two ways: (i) As a participation (μέθεξις, μετέχειν) of the particular object in the Idea; (ii) as an imitation (μίμησις) of the Idea by the particular object, the particular objects being ὁμοιώματα and μιμήματα of the Idea, the latter being the exemplar or παράδειγμα. (It does not seem possible to refer the two explanations to different periods of Plato's philosophical development—at least, not in any rigid way—since both explanations are found together in the *Parmenides*,[39] and both thoughts occur in the *Symposium*.)[40] The objections raised by Parmenides against these Socratic theories are, no doubt, intended to be serious criticism—as, indeed, they are—and not a mere *jeu d'esprit*, as has been suggested. The objections are real objections, and it would appear that Plato tried to develop his theory of Ideas in an attempt to meet some such criticisms as that which he puts into the mouths of the Eleatics in the *Parmenides*.

Do particular objects participate in the whole Idea or only in part of it? This is the dilemma proposed by Parmenides as a logical consequence of the participation-explanation of the relation between Ideas and particular objects. If the first of the alternatives be chosen, then the Idea, which is one, would be entirely in each of many individuals. If the second of the alternatives be chosen, then the Form or Idea is unitary and divisible (or many) at the same time. In either case a contradiction is involved. Moreover, if equal things are equal by the presence of a certain amount of equality, then they are equal by what is less than equality. Again, if something is big by participation in bigness it is big by possessing that which is less than bigness—which seems to be a contradiction. (It is to be noted that objections of this kind suppose that the Ideas are what amount to individual objects on their own account, and so they serve to show the impossibility of regarding the Idea in this way.)

Socrates suggests the imitation-theory, that particular objects are copies of the Ideas, which are themselves patterns or exemplars; the resemblance of the particular objects to the Idea constitutes its participation in it. Against this Parmenides argues that, if white things are like whiteness, whiteness is also like white things. Hence, if the likeness between white things is to be explained by postulating a Form of whiteness, the likeness between whiteness and white things should also be explained by postulating an archetype, and so on indefinitely. Aristotle argued in much the same way, but all that really follows from the criticism is that the Idea is not simply another particular object, and that the relation between the particular objects and the Idea cannot be the same as that between different particular objects.[41] The objection, then, is to the point as showing the necessity for further consideration of the true relations, but this does not show that the Ideal Theory is totally untenable.

The objection is also raised that on Socrates' theory the Ideas would be unknowable. Man's knowledge is concerned with the objects of this world, and with the relations between individual objects. We can, for example, know the relation between the individual master and the individual slave, but this knowledge is insufficient to inform us as to the relationship between absolute mastership (the Idea of Mastership) and absolute slavery (the Idea of Slavery). For that purpose we should require absolute knowledge and this we do not possess. This objection, too, shows the hopelessness of regarding the Ideal World as merely parallel to this world: if we are to know the former, then there must be some objective basis in the latter which enables us to know it. If the two worlds are merely parallel, then, just as we would know the sensible world without being able to know the Ideal World, so a divine intelligence would know the Ideal World without being able to know the sensible world.

The objections raised are left unanswered in the *Parmenides,* but it is to be noticed that Parmenides was not concerned to deny the existence of an intelligible world: he freely admits that if one refuses to admit the existence of absolute Ideas at all, then philosophic thinking goes by the board. The result of the objections that Plato raises against himself in the *Parmenides* is, therefore, to impel him to further exact consideration of the nature of the Ideal World and of its relation to the sensible world. It is made clear by the difficulties raised that some principle of unity is required which will, at the same time, not annihilate the many. This is admitted in the dialogue, though the unity considered is a unity in the world of Forms, as Socrates "did not care to solve the perplexity in reference to visible objects, but only in reference to thought and to what may be called ideas." [42] The difficulties are, therefore, not solved in the *Parmenides;* but the discussion must not be regarded as a destruction of the Ideal Theory, for the difficulties simply indicate that the theory must be expounded in a more satisfactory way than Socrates has expounded it hitherto.

In the second part of the dialogue Parmenides himself leads the discussion and undertakes to exemplify his "art," the method of considering the consequences which flow from a given hypothesis and the consequences which flow from denying that hypothesis. Parmenides proposes to start from the hypothesis of the One and to examine the consequences which are seen to flow from its assertion and its denial. Subordinate distinctions are introduced, the argument is long and complicated and no satisfactory conclusion is arrived at. Into this argument one cannot enter in a book like the present one, but it is necessary to point out that this second part of the *Parmenides* is no more a refutation of the doctrine of the One than the first part was of the Ideal Theory. A real refutation of the doctrine of the One would certainly not be put into the mouth of Parmenides himself, whom Plato greatly respected. In the *Sophist* the Eleatic Stranger apologises for doing violence to "father Parmenides," [43] but, as Mr. Hardie aptly remarks, this apology "would hardly be called for if in another dialogue father Parmenides had done violence to himself." [44] Moreover, at the end of the *Parmenides* agreement is voted as to the assertion that, "If One is not, then nothing is." The participants may not be sure of the status of the many or of their relation to the One or even of the precise nature of the One; but they are at least agreed that there *is* a One.

6. In the *Sophist* the object before the interlocutors is to define the Sophist. They have a notion, of course, what the Sophist is, but they wish to *define* the Sophist's nature, to pin him down, as it were, in a clear formula (λόγος). It will be remembered that in the *Theaetetus* Socrates rejected the suggestion that knowledge is true belief plus an account (λόγος); but in that dialogue the discussion concerned particular sensible objects, while in the *Sophist* the discussion turns on class-concepts. The answer which is given to the problem of the *Theaetetus* is, therefore, that knowledge consists in apprehending the class-concept by means of genus and difference, i.e. by *definition*. The method of arriving at definition is that of analysis or division (διαίρεσις, διαιρεῖν κατ᾽ εἴδη), whereby the notion or name to be defined is subsumed under a wider genus or class, which latter is then divided into its natural components. One of these natural components will be the notion to be defined. Previous to the division a process of synthesis or collecting (συνάγειν εἰς ἕν, συναγωγή) should take place, through which terms that are at least *prima facie* interrelated are grouped together and compared, with a view to determining the genus from which the process of division is to start. The wider class chosen is divided into two mutually-exclusive sub-classes, distinguished from one another by the presence or absence of some peculiar characteristic; and the process is continued until the *definiendum* is finally tracked down and defined by means of its genus and differences. (There is an amusing fragment of Epicrates, the comic poet, de-

scribing the classification of a pumpkin in the Academy.)

There is no need to enter either upon the actual process of tracking down the Sophist, or upon Plato's preliminary example of the method of division (the definition of the angler); but it must be pointed out that the discussion makes it clear that the Ideas may be one and many at the same time. The class-concept "Animal," for example, is one; but at the same time it is many, in that it contains within itself the sub-classes of "Horse," "Fox," "Man," etc. Plato speaks as though the generic Form pervades the subordinate specific Form or is dispersed throughout them, "blending" with each of them, yet retaining its own unity. There is a communion (κοινωνία) between Forms, and one Form partakes of (μετέχειν) another (as in "Motion exists" it is implied that Motion blends with Existence); but we should not suppose that one Form partakes of another in the same sense in which the individual partakes of the specific Form, for Plato would not speak of the individual blending with the specific Form. The Forms thus constitute a hierarchy, subordinate to the One as the highest and all-pervading Form; but it is to be remembered that for Plato the "higher" the Form is, the richer it is, so that his point of view is the opposite to that of the Aristotelian, for whom the more "abstract" the concept, the poorer it is.

There is one important point to be noticed. The process of division (Plato, of course, believed that the logical division detects the grades of real being) cannot be prolonged indefinitely, since ultimately you will arrive at the Form that admits of no further division. These are the *infimae species* or ἄτομα εἴδη. The Form of Man, for instance, is indeed "many" in this sense, that it contains the genus and all relative differences, but it is not many in the sense of containing further subordinate specific classes into which it could be divided. On the contrary, below the ἄτομον εἴδος Man there stand *individual men*. The ἄτομα εἴδη, therefore, constitute the lowest rung of the ladder or hierarchy of Forms, and Plato very probably considered that by bringing down the Forms, by the process of division, to the border of the sensible sphere, he was providing a connecting link between τὰ ἀόρατα and τὰ ὁρατά. It may be that the relation between the individuals and the *infimae species* was to be elucidated in the *Philosopher*, the dialogue which, it is conjectured, was once intended by Plato to follow the

Statesman and which was never written; but it cannot be said that the chasm was ever satisfactorily bridged, and the problem of the Χωρισμός remained. (Julius Stenzel put forward the suggestion that Plato adopted from Democritus the principle of dividing until the atom is reached, which, in Plato's hands, becomes the intelligible "atomic Form." It is certainly significant that geometrical shape was a feature of the atom of Democritus, while geometrical shapes play an important part in Plato's picture of the formation of the world in the *Timaeus;* but it would seem that the relation of Plato to Democritus must always remain conjectural and something of a puzzle.)[45]

I have mentioned the "blending" of the Forms, but it is also to be noticed that there are Forms which are incompatible, at least in their "particularity," and will not "blend," e.g. Motion and Rest. If I say: "Motion does not rest," my statement is true, since it expresses the fact that Motion and Rest are incompatible and do not blend: if, however, I say: "Motion is Rest," my statement is false, since it expresses a combination that is not objectively verified. Light is thus thrown on the nature of false judgment which perplexed Socrates in the *Theaetetus;* though more relevant to the actual problem of the *Theaetetus* is the discussion of false statement in 262 e ff. of the *Sophist.* Plato takes as an example of a true statement, "Theaetetus sits," and as an example of a false statement, "Theaetetus flies." It is pointed out that Theaetetus is an existent subject and that Flying is a real Form, so that false statement is not a statement about *nothing.* (Every significant statement is about *something,* and it would be absurd to admit non-existent facts or objective falsehoods.) The statement has a meaning, but the relation of participating between the actual "sitting" of Theaetetus and the different Form "Flying" is missing. The statement, therefore, has a meaning, but the statement as a whole does not correspond with the fact as a whole. Plato meets the objection that there can be no false statement because there is nothing for it to mean, by an appeal to the Theory of Forms (which does not appear in the *Theaetetus,* with the consequence that in that dialogue the problem could not be solved). "We can have discourse only through the weaving together of Forms."[46] It is not meant that all significant statements must concern Forms exclusively (since we can make significant statements about

singular things like Theaetetus), but that every significant
statement involves the use of at least one Form, e.g. "Sitting" in the true statement, "Theaetetus sits." [47]

The *Sophist* thus presents us with the picture of a
hierarchy of Forms, combining among themselves in an
articulated complex; but it does not solve the problem of
the relation of the particulars to the "atomic Forms." Plato
insists that there are εἴδωλα or things which are not non-
existent, but which at the same time are not fully real; but
in the *Sophist* he realises that it is no longer possible to
insist on the completely unchanging character of all Reality.
He still holds that the Forms are changeless, but somehow
or other spiritual motion must be included in the Real. "Life,
soul, understanding" must have a place in what is perfectly
real, since, if Reality as a whole excludes all change, intelligence (which involves life) will have no real existence
anywhere at all. The conclusion is that "we must admit
that what changes and change itself are real things," [48]
and that "Reality or the sum of things is both at once—all
that is unchangeable and all that is in change." [49] Real
being must accordingly include life, soul and intelligence,
and the change implied by them; but what of the εἴδωλα,
the purely sensible and perpetually changing, mere becoming?
What is the relation of this half-real sphere to Real Being?
This question is not answered in the *Sophist*.

7. In the *Sophist* [50] Plato clearly indicates that the whole
complex of Forms, the hierarchy of genera and species, is
comprised in an all-pervading Form, that of Being, and he
certainly believed that in tracing out the structure of the
hierarchy of Forms by means of διαίρεσις he was detecting,
not merely the structure of logical Forms, but also the
structure of ontological Forms of the Real. But whether
successful or not in his division of the genera and species,
was it of any help to him in overcoming the Χωρισμός,
the separation between the particulars and the *infimae
species*? In the *Sophist* he showed how division is to be continued until the ἄτομον εἶδος is reached, in the apprehension of which δόξα and αἴσθησις are involved, though
it is λόγος alone that determines the "undetermined" plurality. The *Philebus* assumes the same, that we must be able
to bring the division to an end by setting a limit to the
unlimited and comprehending sense-particulars in the lowest
class, so far as they can be comprehended. (In the *Philebus*

Ideas are termed ἑνάδες or μονάδες.) The important point to notice is that for Plato the sense-particulars *as such* are the unlimited and the undetermined: they are limited and determined only in so far as they are, as it were, brought within the ἄτομον εἶδος. This means that the sense-particulars in so far as they are not brought within the ἄτομον εἶδος and cannot be brought within it, are not true objects at all: they are not fully real. In pursuing the διαίρεσις as far as the ἄτομον εἶδος Plato was, in his own eyes, comprehending all Reality. This enables him to use the words: "But the form of the infinite must not be brought near to the many until one has observed its full number, the number between the one and the infinite; when this has been learnt, each several individual thing may be forgotten and dismissed into the infinite." [51] In other words, the division must be continued until particulars in their intelligible reality are comprehended in the ἄτομον εἶδος: when this has been done, the remainder, i.e. the sense-particulars, in their non-intelligible aspect, as impenetrable to λόγος, may be dismissed into the sphere of what is fleeting and only semi-real, that which cannot truly be said to *be*. From Plato's own point of view, therefore, the problem of the Χωρισμός may have been solved; but from the point of view of anyone who will not accept his doctrine of sense-particulars, it is very far from being solved.

8. But though Plato may have considered that he had solved the problem of the Χωρισμός, it still remained to show how the sense-particulars come into existence at all. Even if the whole hierarchy of Forms, the complex structure comprised in the all-embracing One, the Idea of Being, or the Good is an ultimate and self-explanatory principle, the Real and the Absolute, it is none the less necessary to show how the world of appearance, which is not simply not-being, even if it is not fully being, came into existence? Does it proceed from the One? If not, what is its cause? Plato made an attempt to answer this question in the *Timaeus*, though I can here only summarise very briefly his answer, as I shall return later to the *Timaeus* when dealing with the physical theories of Plato.

In the *Timaeus* the Demiurge is pictured as conferring geometrical shapes upon the primary qualities within the Receptacle or Space, and so introducing order into disorder, taking as his model in building up the world the intelligible realm of Forms. Plato's account of "creation" is most probably not meant to be an account of creation in time or *ex nihilo:* rather is it an analysis, by which the articulate structure of the material world, the work of a rational cause, is distinguished from the "primeval" chaos, without its being necessarily implied that the chaos was ever actual. The chaos is probably primeval only in the logical, and not in the temporal or historic sense. But if this is so, then the non-intelligible part of the material world is simply assumed: it exists "alongside of" the intelligible world. The Greeks, it would seem, never really envisaged the possibility of creation out of nothing (*ex nihilo sui et subiecti*). Just as the logical process of διαίρεσις stops at the ἄτομον εἶδος and Plato in the *Philebus* dismisses the merely particular εἰς τὸ ἄπειρον, so in the physical analysis of the *Timaeus* the merely particular, the non-intelligible element (that which, logically considered, cannot be comprehended under the ἄτομον εἶδος) is dismissed into the sphere of that which is "in discordant and unordered motion,"[52] the factor that the Demiurge "took over." Therefore, just as, from the viewpoint of the Platonic logic, the sense-particulars as such cannot be deduced, cannot be rendered fully intelligible (did not Hegel declare that Herr Krug's pen could not be deduced?), so, in the Platonic physics, the chaotic element, that into which order is "introduced" by Reason, is not explained: doubtless Plato thought that it was inexplicable. It can neither be *deduced* nor has it been *created out of nothing.* It is simply there (a fact of experience), and that is all that we can say about it. The Χωρισμός accordingly remains, for, however "unreal" the chaotic may be, it is not not-being *tout simple:* it is a factor in the world, a factor that Plato leaves unexplained.

9. I have exhibited the Ideas or Forms as an ordered, intelligible structure, constituting in their totality a One in Many, in such a way that each subordinate Idea is itself one in many, as far as the ἄτομον εἶδος, below which is τὸ ἄπειρον. This complex of Forms is the Logical-Ontological Absolute. I must now raise the question, whether Plato regarded the Ideas as the Ideas of God or as independent of God. For the Neo-Platonists, the Ideas were the Thoughts of God: how far can such a theory be ascribed to Plato himself? If it could be so ascribed, it would clearly go a

long way towards showing how the "Ideal World" is at
once a unity and a plurality—a unity as contained in the
Divine Mind, or Nous, and as subordinated to the Divine
Plan, a plurality as reflecting the richness of the Divine
Thought-content, and as only realisable in Nature in a mul-
titude of existent objects.

In the tenth book of the *Republic*[53] Plato says that God
is the Author (Φυτουργός) of the ideal bed. More than
that, God is the Author of all other things—"things" in the
context meaning other essences. From this it might appear
that God created the ideal bed by *thinking* it, i.e. by comprising within His intellect the Idea of the world, and so
of man and of all his requirements. (Plato did not, of
course, imagine that there was a material ideal bed.)
Moreover, since Plato speaks of God as "king" and "truth"
(the tragic poet is at the third remove ἀπὸ βασιλέως καὶ
τῆς ἀληθείας), while he has already spoken of the Idea of
the Good as κυρία ἀλήθειαν καὶ νοῦν παραχομένη[54] and
as Author of being and essence in intelligible objects
(Ideas),[55] it might well appear that Plato means to Identify
God with the Idea of the Good.[56] Those who wish to
believe that this was really Plato's thought, and who
proceed to interpret "God" in a theistic sense, would naturally appeal to the *Philebus*,[57] where it is implied that the
Mind that orders the universe is possessed of soul (Socrates
certainly says that wisdom and mind cannot exist without
soul), so that God would be a living and intelligent being.
We should thus have a personal God, Whose Mind is the
"place" of Ideas, and Who orders and rules the universe,
"king of heaven and earth." [58]

That there is much to be said for this interpretation of
Plato's thought, I would not deny: moreover, it is naturally
attractive to all those who desire to discover a tidy
system in Plato and a theistic system. But common honesty
forces one to admit the very serious difficulties against this
tidy interpretation. For example, in the *Timaeus* Plato pictures the Demiurge as introducing order into the world and
forming natural objects according to the model of the Ideas
or Forms. The Demiurge is probably a symbolic figure representing the Reason that Plato certainly believed to be operative in the world. In the *Laws* he proposes the institution
of a Nocturnal Council or Inquisition for the correction and
punishment of atheists. Now, "atheist" means, for Plato, first

and foremost the man who denies the operation of Reason in the world. Plato certainly admits that soul and intelligence belong to the Real, but it does not seem possible to assert with certainty that, in Plato's view, the Divine Reason is the "place" of the Ideas. It might, indeed, be argued that the Demiurge is spoken of as desiring that "all things should come as near as possible to being like himself," and that "all things should be good" [59]—phrases which suggest that the separation of the Demiurge from the Ideas is a Myth and that, in Plato's real thought, he is the Good and the ultimate Source of the Ideas. That the *Timaeus* never says that the Demiurge created the Ideas or is their Source, but pictures them as distinct from him (the Demiurge being depicted as Efficient Cause and the Ideas as Exemplary Cause), does not seem to be conclusive evidence that Plato did *not* bring them together; but it should at least make us beware of asserting positively that he *did* bring them together. Moreover, if the "Captain" and God of the sixth letter is the Demiurge or Divine Reason, what of the "Father"? If the "Father" is the One, then it would not look as though the One and the whole hierarchy of the Ideas can be explained as thoughts of the Demiurge. [60]

But if the Divine Reason is not the ultimate, is it possible that the One is the ultimate, not only as ultimate Exemplary Cause, but also as ultimate Productive Cause, being itself "beyond" mind and soul as it is "beyond" essence? If so, can we say that the Divine Reason proceeds in some way (timelessly, of course) from the One, and that this Reason either contains the Ideas as thoughts or exists "alongside" the Ideas (as depicted in the *Timaeus*)? In other words, can we interpret Plato on Neo-Platonic lines? [61] The remark about the "Captain" and the "Father" in the sixth letter might be understood in support of this interpretation, while the fact that the Idea of the Good is never spoken of as a *soul* might mean that the Good is beyond soul, i.e. more than soul, not less than soul. The fact that in the *Sophist* Plato says, through the mouth of the Eleatic Stranger, that "Reality or the sum of things" must include soul, intelligence and life, [62] implies that the One or total Reality (the Father of *Ep.* 6) comprises not only the Ideas but also mind. If so, what is the relation of Mind to the World-soul of the *Timaeus*? The World-soul and the Demiurge are distinct in that dialogue (for the Demiurge is depicted as "making" the World-soul); but in the *Sophist* it is said that intelligence must have life, and that both these must have soul "in which they reside." [63] It is, however, possible that the making of the World-soul by the Demiurge is not to be taken literally at all, especially as it is stated in the *Phaedrus* that soul is a beginning and uncreated,[64] and that the World-soul and the Demiurge represent together the Divine Reason immanent in the world. If this were so, then we should have the One, the Supreme Reality, embracing and in some sense the Source (though not the Creator in time) of the Divine Reason (= Demiurge = World-soul) and the Forms. We might then speak of the Divine Reason as the "Mind of God" (if *we* equated God with the One) and the Forms as Ideas of God; but we should have to bear in mind that such a conception would bear a closer resemblance to later Neo-Platonism than to specifically Christian philosophy.

That Plato had some idea of what he meant hardly needs to be stressed, but in view of the evidence at our disposal we must avoid dogmatic pronouncements as to what he *did* mean. Therefore, although the present writer is inclined to think that the second interpretation bears some resemblance to what Plato actually thought, he is very far from putting it forward as certainly the authentic philosophy of Plato.

10. We must now touch briefly on the vexed question of the mathematical aspect of the Ideal Theory.[65] According to Aristotle,[66] Plato declared that:

(i) The Forms are Numbers;

(ii) Things exist by participation in Numbers;

(iii) Numbers are composed of the One and the great-and-small or "indeterminate duality" (ἀόριστος

(iv) δυάς) instead of, as the Pythagoreans thought, the unlimited (ἄπειρον) and limit (πέρας);
τὰ μαθηματικά occupy an intermediate position between Forms and things.

With the subject of τὰ μαθηματικά or the "intermediates" I have already dealt when treating of the Line: it remains, therefore, to consider the following questions:

(i) Why did Plato identify Forms with Numbers and what did he mean?

(ii) Why did Plato say that things exist by participation in numbers?

   (iii) What is meant by composition from the One and
      the great-and-small?

With these questions I can only deal very briefly. Not
only would an adequate treatment require a much greater
knowledge of mathematics, both ancient and modern, than
the present writer possesses; but it is also doubtful if, with the
material at our disposal, even the mathematically-gifted specialist could give a really adequate and definitive treatment.

   (i) Plato's motive in identifying Forms with Numbers
seems to be that of rationalising or rendering intelligible the
mysterious and transcendental world of Forms. To render intelligible in this case means to find the *principle of order*.

   (ii) Natural objects embody the principle of order to some
extent: they are, for example, instances of the logical universal and tend towards the realisation of their form: they
are the handiwork of intelligence and exhibit design.

   (*a*) This truth is expressed in the *Timaeus* by saying that
the sensible characters of bodies are dependent on the geometrical structure of their corpuscles. This geometrical structure is determined by that of their faces, and that of their
faces by the structure of the two types of triangles (isosceles
right-angled and right-angled scalene) from which they are
built up. The ratios of the sides of the triangles to one
another may be expressed numerically.

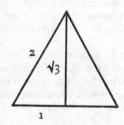

Half-equilateral or right-
angled scalene

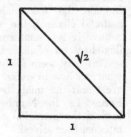

Half-square or right-
angled isosceles

   (*b*) Another expression of the same truth is the doctrine
of the *Epinomis* that the apparently mazy movements of
the heavenly bodies (the primary objects of official cult)
really conform to mathematical law and so express the
wisdom of God.[67]

(*c*) Natural bodies, therefore, embody the principle of order and may, to a greater or less extent, be "mathematicised." On the other hand, they cannot be entirely "mathematicised"—they are not Numbers—for they embody also contingency, an irrational element, "matter." They are thus not said to *be* Numbers, but to *participate* in Numbers.

(iii) This partly irrational character of natural objects gives us the key to the understanding of the "great and the small."

(*a*) The triplet of numbers which gives the ratio of the sides to one another is, in the case of the isosceles right-angled triangle, 1, 1, $\sqrt{2}$, and in the case of the right-angled scalene, 1, $\sqrt{3}$, 2. In either case, then, there is an irrational element which expresses the *contingency* in natural objects.

(*b*) Taylor points out that in a certain sequence of fractions—nowadays derived from a "continual fraction," but actually alluded to by Plato himself[68] and by Theo of Smyrna[69]—alternate terms converge upwards to $\sqrt{2}$ as limit and upper bound, while alternate other terms converge downwards to $\sqrt{2}$ as limit and lower bound. The terms of the whole sequence, therefore, in their original order, are in consequence alternately "greater and less" than $\sqrt{2}$, while jointly converging to $\sqrt{2}$ as their unique limit. We have, then, the characteristics of the great and the small or the indeterminate duality. The "endlessness" of the continued fraction, the "irrationality," seems to be identified with the material element, the element of non-being, *in all that becomes*. It is a mathematical expression of the Heraclitean flux-character of natural entities.

This may seem fairly clear as regards natural bodies. But what are we to make of Aristotle's dictum that "from the great and the small, by participation in the One, come the Forms, i.e. the Numbers"?[70] In other words, how can we explain the extension of the form-matter composition to the integers themselves?

If we take the series $1 + \frac{1}{2} + \frac{1}{4} + \frac{1}{8} + \ldots + \frac{1}{2}n + \ldots$ we have a series that converges to the number 2. It is clear, then, that an infinite series of rational fractions may converge towards a rational limit, and examples could be given in which the μέγα καὶ μικρόν are involved. Plato would seem to have extended this composition from the μέγα καὶ μικρόν to the integers themselves, passing over, however, the fact that 2 as the limit of convergence cannot be identified with the integer 2, since the integers are *presupposed* as a series from which the convergents are formed. In the Platonic Academy the integers were derived or "educed" from One by the help of the ἀόριστος δυάς, which seems to have been identified with the *integer* 2, and to have been given the function of "doubling." The result is that the integers are derived in a non-rational series. On the whole we may say that, pending new light from philologically exact mathematical history, the theory of the composition of the integers from the One and the great-and-small will continue to look like a puzzling excrescence on the Platonic theory of Ideas.

11. In regard to the whole tendency to pan-mathematisation I cannot but regard it as unfortunate. That the real is rational is a presupposition of all dogmatic philosophy, but it does not follow that the whole of reality can be rationalised by us. The attempt to reduce all reality to mathematics is not only an attempt to rationalise all reality—which is the task of philosophy, it may be said—but presupposes that all reality can be rationalised *by us,* which is an assumption. It is perfectly true that Plato admits an element in Nature that cannot be submitted to mathematisation, and so to rationalisation, but his attempt to rationalise reality and the extension of this attempt to the spiritual sphere has a flavour about it which may well remind us of Spinoza's deterministic and mechanistic view of reality (expressed in his *Ethica more geometrico demonstrata*) and of Hegel's attempt to comprehend the inner essence of ultimate Reality or God within the formulae of logic.

It may at first sight appear strange that the Plato who composed the *Symposium,* with its ascent to Absolute Beauty under the inspiration of Eros, should have been inclined to pan-mathematicism; and this apparent contrast might seem to support the view that the Socrates of the Platonic dialogues does not give Plato's opinions, but his own, that while Socrates invented the Ideal Theory as it appears in the dialogues, Plato "arithmetised" it. Yet, apart from the fact that the "mystical" and predominantly religious interpretation of the *Symposium* is very far from having been demonstrated as the certain interpretation, the apparent contrast between the *Symposium*—assuming for the moment that the "ascent" is a religious and mystical one—and Plato's mathematical interpretation of the Forms, as related to us by Aristotle, would hardly seem to be a compelling argument for the view that the Platonic Socrates is the historic Socrates, and that Plato reserved most of his personal views for the Academy, and, in the dialogues, for expression by other *dramatis personae* than the figure of Socrates. If we turn to Spinoza, we find a man who, on the one hand, was possessed by the vision of the unity of all things in God, and who proposed the ideal intuition of the *amor intellectualis Dei*, and who, on the other hand, sought to extend the mechanical aspect of Physics to all reality. Again, the example of Pascal should be sufficient to show us that mathematical genius and a deeply religious, even mystical, temperament are not at all incompatible.

Moreover, pan-mathematicism and idealism might even be held to lend support to one another. The more Reality is mathematicised, the more, in a sense, it is transferred on to an ideal plane, while, conversely, the thinker who desires to find the true reality and being of Nature in an ideal world might easily grasp the proffered hand of mathematics as an aid in the task. This would apply especially in the case of Plato, since he had before him the example of the Pythagoreans, who combined not only an interest in mathematics, but also a trend towards pan-mathematicism with religious and psychological interests. We are, therefore, in no way entitled to declare that Plato *could not* have combined in himself religious and transcendentalist tendencies with a tendency to pan-mathematicism, since, whether incompatible or not from the abstract viewpoint, history has shown that they are not incompatible from the psychological standpoint. If the Pythagoreans were possible, if Spinoza and Pascal were possible, then there is no reason why we should say, i.e. *a priori*, that Plato could not have written a mystical book and delivered the lecture on the Good in which, we learn, he spoke of arithmetic and astronomy and identified the One and the Good. But, though we cannot assert this *a priori*, it still remains to inquire whether in actual fact Plato meant such a passage as the speech of Socrates in the *Symposium* to be understood in a religious sense.

12. By what process does the mind arrive at the apprehension of the Ideas, according to Plato? I have already spoken briefly of the Platonic dialectic and method of διαίρεσις, and nobody will deny the importance of dialectic in the Platonic theory; but the question arises whether

Plato did or did not envisage a religious, even a mystical, approach to the One or Good. *Prima facie* at least the *Symposium* contains mystical elements, and, if we come to the dialogue with our minds full of the interpretation given it by Neo-Platonist and Christian writers, we shall probably find in it what we are seeking. Nor can this interpretation be set aside *ab initio*, for certain modern scholars of great and deserved repute have lent their powerful support thereto.

Thus, referring to Socrates' speech in the *Symposium*, Professor Taylor comments: "In substance, what Socrates is describing is the same spiritual voyage which St. John of the Cross describes, for example, in the well-known song, *En una noche oscura*, which opens his treatise on the *Dark Night*, and Crashaw hints at more obscurely all through his lines on *The Flaming Heart*, and Bonaventura charts for us with precision in the *Itinerarium Mentis in Deum*." [71] Others, however, will have none of this; for them Plato is no mystic at all, or if he does display any mystical leanings, it is only in the weakness of old age that he does so. Thus Professor Stace declares, that "the Ideas are rational, that is to say, they are apprehended through reason. The finding of the common element in the manifold is the work of inductive reason, and through this alone is the knowledge of the Ideas possible. This should be noted by those persons who imagine that Plato was some sort of benevolent mystic. The imperishable One, the absolute reality, is apprehended, not by intuition or in any kind of mystic ecstasy, but only by rational cognition and laborious thought." [72] Again, Professor C. Ritter says that he would like "to direct a critical remark against the recent attempts, oft repeated, to stamp Plato as a mystic. These are wholly based on forged passages of the *Epistles*, which I can only consider as inferior achievements of a spiritual poverty which seeks to take refuge in occultism. I am astonished that anyone can hail them as enlightened wisdom, as the final result of Platonic philosophising." [73] Professor Ritter is, needless to say, perfectly well aware that certain passages in the certainly authentic works of Plato lend themselves to interpretation in the mystical sense; but, in his view, such passages are not only poetical and mythical in character, but were understood as such by Plato himself. In his earlier works Plato throws out suggestions, is feeling his way, as it were, and sometimes clothes his half-formed thoughts in poetical and mythical language; but when, in later dialogues, he applies himself to a more scientific treatment of his epistemological and ontological doctrines, he no longer brings in priestesses or uses poetic symbolism.

It would seem that, if we regard the Good predominantly in its aspect as Ideal or τέλος, Eros might well be understood as simply the impulse of man's higher nature towards the good and virtue (or, in the language of the doctrine of pre-existence and reminiscence, as the natural attraction of man's higher nature towards the Ideal which he beheld in the state of pre-existence). Plato, as we have seen, would not accept a merely relativistic ethic: there are absolute standards and norms, absolute ideals. There is thus an ideal of justice, an ideal of temperance, an ideal of courage, and these ideals are real and absolute, since they do not vary but are the unchanging standards of conduct. They are not "things," for they are ideal; yet they are not merely subjective, because they "rule," as it were, man's acts. But human life is not lived out atomistically, apart from Society and the State, nor is man a being entirely apart from nature; and so we can arrive at the apprehension of an all-embracing Ideal and τέλος, to which all particular Ideals are subordinate. This universal Ideal is the Good. It is apprehended by means of dialectic, i.e. *discursively;* but in man's higher nature there is an attraction towards the truly good and beautiful. If man mistakenly takes sensible beauty and good, e.g. the beauty of physical objects, as his true good, then the impulse of attraction of Eros is directed towards these inferior goods, and we have the earthly and sensual man. A man may, however, be brought to see that the soul is higher and better than the body, and that beauty of soul is of more value than beauty of body. Similarly, he may be brought to see the beauty in the formal sciences[74] and the beauty of the Ideals: the power of Eros then attracts him "towards the wide ocean of intellectual beauty" and "the sight of the lovely and majestic forms which it contains." [75] Finally, he may come to apprehend how all the particular ideals are subordinate to one universal Ideal or τέλος, the Good-in-itself, and so to enjoy "the science" of this universal beauty and good. The rational soul is akin to the Ideal,[76] and so is able to contemplate the Ideal and to delight in its contemplation once the sensual appetite has been restrained.[77] "There is none so worthless whom Love cannot impel, as it were by a divine inspiration, towards virtue." [78] The true life for man is thus the philosophic life or the life of wisdom, since it is only the philosopher who attains true universal science and apprehends the rational character of Reality. In the *Timaeus* the Demiurge is depicted as forming the world according to the Ideal or Exemplary Pattern, and as endeavouring to make it as much like the Ideal as the refractory matter at his disposal will permit. It is for the philosopher to apprehend the Ideal and to endeavour to model his own life and that of others according to the Pattern. Hence the place accorded to the Philosopher-King in the *Republic*.

Eros or Love is pictured in the *Symposium*[79] as "a great god," holding an intermediate place between the divine and the mortal. Eros, in other words, "the child of Poverty and plenty," is *desire*, and desire is for what is not yet possessed, but Eros, though poor, i.e. not yet possessing, is the "earnest desire for the possession of happiness and that which is good." The term "Eros" is often confined to one species of Eros—and that by no means the highest—but it is a term of wider connotation than physical desire, and is, in general, "the desire of generation in the beautiful, both with relation to the body and the soul." Moreover, since Eros is the desire that good be for ever present with us, it must of necessity be also the desire for immortality.[80] By the lower Eros men are compelled to seek immortality through the production of children: through a higher Eros poets like Homer and statesmen like Solon leave a more enduring progeny "as the pledges of that love which subsisted between them and the beautiful." Through contact with Beauty itself the human being becomes immortal and produces true virtue.

Now all this might, it seems, be understood of a purely intellectualist, in the sense of discursive, process. None the less, it is true that the Idea of the Good or the Idea of Beauty is an ontological Principle, so there can be no *a priori* reason why it should not itself be the object of Eros and be apprehended intuitively. In the *Symposium* the soul at the summit of the ascent is said to behold Beauty "on a sudden," while in the *Republic* the Good is asserted to be seen last of all and only with an effort—phrases which might imply an intuitional apprehension. What we might call the "logical" dialogues may give little indication of any mystical approach to the One; but that does not necessarily mean that Plato never envisaged any such approach, or that, if he ever envisaged it, he had rejected it by the time he came to write

the *Parmenides,* the *Theaetetus* and the *Sophist.* These dialogues deal with definite problems, and we have no right to
expect Plato to present all aspects of his thought in any one
dialogue. Nor does the fact that Plato never proposes the
One or the Good as the object of official religious cult necessarily militate against the possibility of his admitting an
intuitional and mystical approach to the One. In any case we
would scarcely expect Plato to propose the radical transfor-
mation of the popular Greek religion (though in the *Laws* he
does propose its purification, and hints that true religion consists in a virtuous life and recognition of Reason's operation
in the universe, e.g. in the movements of the heavenly
bodies); while, if the One is "beyond" being and soul, it
might never occur to him that it could be the object of a
popular cult. After all, Neo-Platonists, who certainly admitted an "ecstatic" approach to the One, did not hesitate
to lend their support to the traditional and popular religion.

In view of these considerations, it would appear that we are
forced to conclude that (*a*) we are certain as to the *dialectical* approach, and (*b*) we are uncertain as to any mystical
approach, while not denying that some passages of Plato's
writings could be understood as implying such an approach,
and may *possibly* have been meant by Plato to be so
understood.

13. It is evident that the Platonic Theory of Forms constitutes an enormous advance on pre-Socratic Philosophy. He
broke away from the *de facto* materialism of the pre-Socratics, asserting the existence of immaterial and invisible
Being, which is not but a shadow of this world but is real
in a far deeper sense than the material world is real. While
agreeing with Heraclitus, that sensible things are in a state of
flux, of becoming, so that they can never really be said to *be,*
he saw that this is but one side of the picture: there is
also true Being, a stable and abiding Reality, which can
be known, which is indeed the supreme object of knowledge.
On the other hand, Plato did not fall into the position of
Parmenides, who by equating the universe with a static One,
was forced to deny all change and becoming. For Plato the
One is transcendent, so that becoming is not denied but is
fully admitted in the "created" world. Moreover, Reality itself is not without Mind and life and soul, so that there is
spiritual movement in the Real. Again, even the transcendent
One is not without the Many, just as the objects of this

world are not entirely without unity, for they participate in or imitate the Forms and so partake in order to some extent. They are not fully real, but they are not mere Not-being; they have a share in being, though true Being is not material. Mind and its effect, order, are present in the world: Mind or Reason permeates, as it were, this world and is not a mere *Deus ex machina*, like the Nous of Anaxagoras.

But if Plato represents an advance on the pre-Socratics, he represents an advance also on the Sophists and on Socrates himself. On the Sophists, since Plato, while admitting the relativism of bare αἴσθησις, refused, as Socrates had before him, to acquiesce in the relativity of science and moral values. On Socrates himself, since Plato extended his investigations beyond the sphere of ethical standards and definitions into those of logic and ontology. Moreover, while there is no certain indication that Socrates attempted any systematic unification of Reality, Plato presents us with a Real Absolute. Thus while Socrates and the Sophists represent a reaction to the foregoing systems of cosmology and to the speculations concerning the One and the Many (though in a true sense Socrates' pre-occupation with definiteness concerns the One and the Many), Plato took up again the problems of the Cosmologists, though on a much higher plane and without abandoning the position won by Socrates. He may thus be said to have attempted the synthesis of what was valuable, or appeared to him valuable, in the pre-Socratic and Socratic philosophies.

It must, of course, be admitted that the Platonic Theory of Forms is unsatisfactory. Even if the One or Good represents for him the ultimate Principle, which comprises all the other Forms, there remains the Χωρισμός between the intelligible and the purely sensible world. Plato may have thought that he had solved the problem of the Χωρισμός from the epistemological standpoint, by his doctrine of the union of λόγος, δόξα and αἴσθησις in the apprehension of the ἄτομα εἴδη; but, ontologically speaking, the sphere of pure Becoming remains unexplained. (It is, however, doubtful if the Greeks *ever* "explained" it.) Thus Plato does not appear to have cleared up satisfactorily the meaning of μέθεξις and μίμησις. In the *Timaeus*[81] he says explicitly that the Form never enters "into anything else anywhere," a statement which shows clearly that Plato did *not* regard the Form or Idea as an intrinsic constituent of the physical object. Therefore, in view of Plato's own statements, there is no point in trying to delete the difference between him and Aristotle. Plato may well have apprehended important truths to which Aristotle failed to do justice, but he certainly did not hold the same view of the universal as that held by Aristotle. Consequently, "participation" for Plato should not be taken to mean that there is an "ingredience" of "eternal objects" into "events." "Events" or physical objects are thus, for Plato, no more than imitations or mirror-images of the Ideas, and the conclusion is inescapable that the sensible world exists "alongside" the intelligible world, as the latter's shadow and fleeting image. The Platonic Idealism is a grand and sublime philosophy which contains much truth (for the purely sensible world is indeed neither the only world nor yet the highest and most "real" world); but, since Plato did not claim that the sensible world is mere illusion and not-being, his philosophy inevitably involves a Χωρισμός, and it is useless to attempt to slur over the fact. After all, Plato is not the only great philosopher whose system has landed him in difficulties in regard to "particularity," and to say that Aristotle was right in detecting the Χωρισμός in the Platonic philosophy is not to say that the Aristotelian view of the universal, when taken by itself, obviates all difficulties. It is far more probable that these two great thinkers emphasised (and perhaps over-emphasised) different aspects of reality which need to be reconciled in a more complete synthesis.

But, whatever conclusions Plato may have arrived at, and whatever imperfections or errors there may be in his Theory of Ideas, we must never forget that Plato meant to establish ascertained truth. He firmly held that we can, and do, apprehend essences in thought, and he firmly held that these essences are not purely subjective creations of the human mind (as though the ideal of justice, for instance, were purely man's creation and relative in character): we do not create them, we discover them. We judge of things according to standards, whether moral and aesthetic standards or generic and specific types: all judgment necessarily implies such standards, and if the scientific judgment is objective, then these standards must have objective reference. But they are not found, and cannot be found, in the sense-world as such: therefore they must be transcendent of the fleeting world of sense-particulars. Plato really did not raise the "critical problem," though he undoubtedly believed that experience is inexplicable, unless the objective existence of the standards is maintained. We should not attribute to Plato the position of a Neo-Kantian, for even if (which we do not mean to admit) the truth underlying the doctrines of pre-existence and reminiscence is the Kantian *a priori*, there is no evidence that Plato himself used these "myths" as figurative expressions for the doctrine of a purely subjective *a priori*. On the contrary, all the evidence goes to show that Plato believed in the truly objective reference of concepts. Reality can be known and Reality is rational; what cannot be known is not rational, and what is not fully real is not fully rational. This Plato held to the last, and he believed that if our experience (in a wide sense) is to be explained or rendered coherent, it can only be explained on the basis of his theory. If he was no Kantian, he was, on the other hand, no mere romancer or mythologist: he was a *philosopher*, and the theory of Forms was put forward as a philosophic and rational theory (a philosophic "hypothesis" for the explanation of experience), not as an essay in mythology or popular folklore, nor as the mere expression of the longing for a better world than this one.

It is, then, a great mistake to change Plato into a poet, as though he were simply an "escapist" who desired to create a supercorporeal world, an ideal world, wherein he could dwell away from the conditions of daily experience. If Plato could have said with Mallarmé, "La chair est triste, hélas! et j'ai lu tous les livres, Fuir! là-bas fuir . . . ," [82] it would have been because he believed in the *reality* of a supersensual and intelligible world, which it is given to the philosopher to *discover*, not to create. Plato did not seek to transmute "reality" into dream, creating his own poetical world, but to rise from this inferior world to the superior world of the pure Archetypal Ideas. Of the subsistent reality of these Ideas he was profoundly convinced. When Mallarmé says: "Je dis: une fleur, et hors de l'oubli où ma voix relègue aucun contour, en tant que quelque chose d'autre, que les calices sus, musicalement se lève, idée même et suave, l'absente de tous bouquets," he is thinking of the creation of the ideal flower, not of the discovery of the Archetypal Flower in the Platonic sense. Just as in a symphony the instruments may transmute a landscape into music, so the poet transmutes the concrete flowers of experience into idea, into the music of dream-thought. Moreover, in actual practice Mallarmé's emptying-out of particular circumstances served rather the purpose of widening the associative, evocative and allusive scope of the idea or image. (And because these were so personal, it is so difficult to understand his poetry.) In any case, however, all this is foreign to Plato, who, whatever his artistic gifts may have been, is primarily a philosopher, not a poet.

Nor are we entitled to regard Plato's aim as that of transmuting reality in the fashion of Rainer Maria Rilke. There may be truth in the contention that we build up a world of our own by clothing it, as it were, from within ourselves—the sunlight on the wall may mean more to us than it means "in itself," in terms of atoms and electrons and light-waves, because of our subjective impressions, and the allusions, associations, overtones and undertones that we supply—but Plato's effort was not to enrich, beautify and transmute this world by subjective evocations, but to pass beyond the sensible world to the world of thought, the Transcendental Reality. Of course, it still remains open to us, if we are so inclined, to discuss the psychological origins of Plato's thought (it *might* be that he was psychologically an escapist); but, if we do so, we must at the same time remember that this is not equivalent to an interpretation of what Plato meant. Whatever "subconscious" motives he may or may not have had, he certainly meant to pursue a serious, philosophic and scientific inquiry.

Nietzsche accused Plato of being an enemy to this world, of setting up a transcendental world out of enmity to this world, of contrasting a "There" with a "Here" out of dislike of the world of experience and of human life and out of moral presuppositions and interests. That Plato was influenced by disappointments in actual life, e.g. by the political conduct of the Athenian State or by his disappointment in Sicily, is probably true; but he was not actively hostile to this world; on the contrary, he desired to train statesmen of the true type, who would, as it were, carry on the work of the Demiurge in bringing order into disorder. He was hostile to life and this world, only in so far as they are disordered and fragmentary, out of harmony with or not expressing what he believed to be stable realities and stable norms of surpassing value and universal significance. The point is not so much what influences contributed to the formation of

Plato's metaphysic, whether as causes, conditions or occasions, as the question: "Did Plato prove his position or did he not?"—and with this question a man like Nietzsche does not concern himself. But we cannot afford to dismiss *a priori* the notion that what there is of order and intelligibility in this world has an objective foundation in an invisible and transcendent Reality, and I believe that Plato not only attained a considerable measure of truth in his metaphysic, but also went a long way towards showing that it *was* the truth. If a man is going to talk at all, he is certain to make valuational judgments, judgments which presuppose objective norms and standards, values which can be apprehended with varying degrees of insight, values which do not "actualise" themselves but depend for their actualisation on the human will, co-operating with God in the realisation of value and the ideal in human life. We have, of course, no direct intuition of the Absolute, as far as natural knowledge is concerned (and in so far as the Platonic theory implies such a knowledge it is inadmissible, while in so far as it identifies true knowledge with direct apprehension of the Absolute it might seem to lead, unwittingly, to scepticism), but by rational reflection we can certainly come to the knowledge of objective (and indeed transcendentally-grounded) values, ideals and ends, and this after all is Plato's main point.

Chapter Twenty-One

THE PSYCHOLOGY OF PLATO

1. Plato in no way fell a victim to the crude psychology of the former Cosmological Schools, in which the soul was reduced to air or fire or atoms: he was neither materialist nor epiphenomenalist, but an uncompromising spiritualist. The soul is clearly distinct from the body; it is man's most valuable possession, and the true tendance of the soul must be its chief concern. Thus at the close of the *Phaedrus*, Socrates prays: "Beloved Pan, and all ye other Gods who here are present, grant me to be beautiful in the inner man, and all I have of outer things to be consonant with those within. May I count the wise man only rich. And may my store of gold be such none but the temperate man can bear." [1] The reality of the soul and its pre-eminence over the body finds emphatic expression in Plato's psychological dualism, which corresponds to his metaphysical dualism. In the *Laws*[2] Plato defines the soul as "self-initiating motion" (τὴν δυναμένην αὐτὴν κινεῖν κίνησιν) or the "source of motion." This being so, the soul is prior to the body in the sense that it is superior to the body (the latter being moved without being the source of motion) and must rule the body. In the *Timaeus* Plato says that "the only existing thing which properly possesses intelligence is soul, and this is an invisible thing, whereas fire, water, earth and air are all visible bodies";[3] and in the *Phaedo* he shows that the soul cannot be a mere epiphenomenon of the body. Simmias suggests that the soul is only the harmony of the body and perishes when the body, of which it is the harmony, perishes;

232

but Socrates points out that the soul can rule the body and
its desires, whereas it is absurd to suppose that a mere
harmony can rule that of which it is the harmony.[4] Again,
if the soul were a mere harmony of the body, it would follow
that one soul could be more of a soul than another (since
a harmony will admit of increase or diminution), which
is an absurd supposition.

But although Plato asserts an essential distinction between
soul and body, he does not deny the influence that may be
exercised on the soul by or through the body. In the
Republic he includes physical training among the constitu-
ents of true education, and he rejects certain types of music
because of the deleterious effect they have on the soul. In
the *Timaeus,* again, he admits the evil influence that can be
wrought by bad physical education and by bodily habits
of vice, which may even bring about an irremediable state
in which the soul is enslaved,[5] and in the *Laws* he stresses
the influence of heredity.[6] In fact, a defective constitution
inherited from the parents and a faulty education or environment are responsible for most of the soul's ills. "No one is
willingly bad; the bad man becomes bad because of some
faulty habit of body and a stupid upbringing, and these are
unwelcome evils that come to any man without his choice." [7]
Even if, therefore, Plato speaks on occasion as though the
soul merely dwelt in the body and used it, we must not
represent him as denying any interaction of soul and body on
one another. He may not have *explained* interaction, but
this is a most difficult task in any case. Interaction is an
obvious fact, and has to be accepted: the situation is certainly not bettered by denying interaction, because one cannot fully explain it, or by reducing soul to body in order
to do away with the necessity of giving any explanation at
all or of confessing that one has not got one to give.

2. In the *Republic* we find the doctrine of the tripartite
nature of the soul,[8] a doctrine which is said to have been
borrowed from the Pythagoreans.[9] The doctrine recurs in the
Timaeus, so we can hardly be justified in supposing that
Plato ever abandoned it.[10] The soul consists of three "parts"
—the rational "part" (τὸ λογιστικόν), the courageous or
spirited "part" (τὸ θυμοειδές) and the appetitive "part"
(τὸ ἐπιθυμητικόν). The word "part" may justifiably be used
in this connection, since Plato himself employs the term
μέρος; but I put it just now in inverted commas in order

to indicate that it is a metaphorical term and should not be taken to mean that the soul is extended and material. The word μέρος appears in 444 b 3 of the fourth book of the *Republic,* and before this Plato uses the word εἶδος, a word that shows that he regarded the three parts as forms or functions or principles of action, not as parts in the material sense.

Τὸ λογιστικόν is what distinguishes man from the brute, and is the highest element or formality of the soul, being immortal and akin to the divine. The two other formalities, τὸ θυμοειδές and τὸ ἐπιθυμητικόν, are perishable. Of these the spirited part is the nobler (in man more akin to moral courage), and is, or should be, the natural ally of reason, though it is found in animals. Τὸ ἐπιθυμητικόν refers to bodily desires, for the rational part of the soul has its own desires, e.g. the passion for truth, Eros, which is the rational counterpart of the physical Eros. In the *Timaeus*[11] Plato locates the rational part of the soul in the head, the spirited part in the breast, and the appetitive part below the midriff. The location of the spirited element in heart and lungs was an ancient tradition, going back to Homer; but whether or not Plato understood these locations literally, it is hard to say. He may have meant that these locations are the points of interaction on the body of the several principles of the soul: did not Descartes (who certainly believed in the spirituality of the soul) locate the point of interaction in the pineal gland? But it is difficult to believe that Plato ever worked out his psychology systematically, as may be seen from the following considerations.

Plato declared that the soul is immortal, and the *Timaeus* certainly teaches that only the rational part of the soul enjoys this privilege.[12] But if the other parts of the soul are mortal and perishable, then they must be separable from the rational part in some mysterious way or they must form a different soul or souls. The apparent insistence on the simplicity of the soul in the *Phaedo* might be referred to the rational part; but in the Myths (e.g. of the *Republic* and the *Phaedrus*) it is implied that the soul survives in its totality, at least that it preserves memory in the state of separation from the body. I do not mean to suggest that all that is contained in the Myths is to be taken literally, but only to point out that their evident supposition that the soul after death retains memory and is affected by its previous life in the body, whether for good or evil, implies the possibility of the soul surviving in its totality and retaining at least the remote potentiality of exercising the spirited and appetitive functions, even though it could not exercise them actually in the state of separation from the body. However, this remains no more than a possible interpretation, and in view of Plato's own express statements and in view of his general dualistic position, it would seem probable that for him only τὸ λογιστικόν survives, and that the other parts of the soul perish entirely. If the conception of the three elements of the souls as three μέρη conflicts with the conception of three εἴδη, then that is simply a proof that Plato never fully elaborated his psychology or worked out the implications of the statements he made.

3. Why did Plato assert the tripartite nature of the soul? Mainly owing to the evident fact of the conflict within the soul. In the *Phaedrus* occurs the celebrated comparison in which the rational element is likened to a charioteer, and the spirited and appetitive elements to two horses.[13] The one horse is good (the spirited element, which is the natural ally of reason and "loves honour with temperance and modesty"), the other horse is bad (the appetitive element, which is "a friend to all riot and insolence"); and, while the good horse is easily driven according to the directions of the charioteer, the bad horse is unruly and tends to obey the voice of sensual passion, so that it must be restrained by the whip. Plato, therefore, takes as his *point de départ* the fact of experience that there are frequently rival springs of action within man; but he never really discusses how this fact can be reconciled with the unity of consciousness, and it is significant that he expressly admits that "to explain what the soul is, would be a long and most assuredly a godlike labour," whereas "to say what it resembles is a shorter and a human task."[14] We may conclude, then, that the tendency to regard the three principles of action as principles of one unitary soul and the tendency to regard them as separable μέρη remain unreconciled in Plato's psychology.

Plato's main interest is, however, evidently the ethical interest of insisting on the right of the rational element to rule, to act as charioteer. In the *Timaeus* the rational part of the soul, the immortal and "divine" element, is said to be made by the Demiurge out of the same ingredients as the World-Soul, while the mortal parts of the soul, together with the body, are made by the celestial gods.[15] This is doubtless a mythical expression of the fact that the rational element of the soul is the highest and is born to rule, has a natural right to rule, because it is more akin to the divine. It has a natural affinity with the invisible and intelligible world, which it is able to contemplate, whereas the other elements of the soul are bound up essentially with the body, i.e. with the phenomenal world, and have no direct part in reason and rational activity and cannot behold the world of Forms. This dualistic conception reappears in Neo-Platonism, in St. Augustine, in Descartes, etc.[16] Moreover, in spite of the adoption of the Peripatetic doctrine of the soul by St. Thomas Aquinas and his School, the Platonic *way of speaking* remains and must always remain the "popular" way of speaking among Christians, since the *fact* that influenced Plato's thought, the fact of the interior conflict in man, naturally looms large in the minds of all those who support the Christian Ethic. It should, however, be noted that the fact that we feel this conflict *within ourselves* demands a more unified view of the soul than is afforded by the Platonic psychology. For, if there were a plurality of souls within man—the rational and irrational—then our consciousness of the conflict as taking place within ourselves and the consciousness of moral responsibility would be inexplicable. I do not mean to imply that Plato was entirely blind to the truth, but rather to suggest that he laid such stress on one aspect of the truth that he tended to neglect the other aspect, and so failed to give any really satisfactory rational psychology.

4. That Plato asserted the immortality of the soul is clear enough. From his explicit assertions it would appear, as we have seen, that this is confined to one part of the soul, τὸ λογιστικόν, though it is just possible that the soul survives in its totality, although it cannot, obviously enough, exercise its lower functions in a state of separation from the body. It is true, however, that the latter position might appear to lead to the conclusion that the soul is more imperfect and worse off in a state of separation from the body than it is in this mortal life—a conclusion which Plato would certainly refuse to accept.

Complete rejection of the Platonic Myths would seem to be prompted, to a certain extent at least, by the desire to get rid of any notion of sanctions after death, as if a doctrine of rewards and punishments were irrelevant—and even hostile—to morality. But is it fair or in accordance with principles of historical criticism to father this attitude on Plato? It is one thing to admit that the details of the Myths are not meant to be taken seriously (all admit this), and quite another thing to say that the conception of a future life, the character of which is determined by conduct in this life, is itself "mythical." There is no real evidence that Plato himself regarded the Myths in their entirety as mere moonshine: if he did, why did he put them forward at all? It seems to the present writer that Plato was by no means indifferent to the theory of sanctions, and that this was one of the reasons why he postulated immortality. He would have agreed with Leibniz that "in order to satisfy the hope of the human race, it must be proved that the God Who governs all is just and wise, and that He will leave nothing without recompense and without punishment. These are the great foundations of ethics." [17]

How did Plato attempt to prove immortality?

(i) In the *Phaedo*[18] Socrates argues that contraries are produced from contraries, as "from stronger, weaker," or "from sleeping, awaking, and from awaking, sleeping." Now, life and death are contraries, and from life is produced death. We must, therefore, suppose that from death life is produced.

This argument rests on the unproved assumption of an eternal cyclic process: it also supposes that a contrary is produced from a contrary, as the matter out of which it proceeds or is made. The argument would hardly satisfy us: besides, it says nothing of the condition of the soul in its state of separation from the body, and would, by itself, lead to the doctrine of the wheel of rebirth. The soul in one "period" on earth might have no conscious remembrance of any former period on earth, so that all that is "proved" is that the soul survives, not that the individual survives *qua* individual.

(ii) The next argument adduced in the *Phaedo*[19] is that from the *a priori* factor in knowledge. Men have a knowledge of standards and absolute norms, as is implied in their comparative judgments of value. But these absolutes do not exist in the sense-world: therefore man must have beheld them in a state of pre-existence. Similarly, sense-perception cannot give us knowledge of the necessary and universal.

But a youth, even one who has had no mathematical education, can, by a process of questioning alone, without
teaching, be induced to "give out" mathematical truths. As
he has not learnt them from anybody and cannot get them
from sense-perception, the implication is that he apprehended them in a state of pre-existence, and that the process of "learning" is simply a process of reminiscence (cf.
Meno, 84 ff.).

As a matter of fact, the process of questioning employed
by Socrates in the *Meno* is really a way of teaching, and
in any case a certain amount of mathematical knowledge
is tacitly presupposed. However, even if the mathematical
science cannot be accounted for by "abstraction," mathematics could still be an *a priori* science, without our being
compelled to postulate pre-existence. Even supposing that
mathematics could, theoretically at least, be worked out
entirely *a priori* by the slave boy of *Meno,* that would not
necessitate his having pre-existed: there is always an alternative on Kantian lines.[20]

Simmias points out[21] that this argument proves no more
than that the soul existed before its union with the body:
it does not prove that the soul survives death. Socrates
accordingly observes that the argument from reminiscence
must be taken in conjunction with the preceding argument.

(iii) The third argument in the *Phaedo* (or second, if the
two previous arguments are taken together) is from the
uncompounded and deiform nature of the soul—from its
spirituality, as we would say.[22] Visible things are composite
and subject to dissolution and death—and the body is of
their number. Now, the soul can survey the invisible and
unchanging and imperishable Forms, and by coming thus
into contact with the Forms, the soul shows itself to be
more like them than it is to visible and corporeal things,
which latter are mortal. Moreover, from the fact that the
soul is naturally destined to rule the body, it appears
to be more like the divine than the mortal. The soul, as
we may think, is "divine"—which for the Greeks meant immortal and unchanging.

(This argument has developed into the argument from
the higher activities of the soul and the spirituality of the
concept to the spiritual and uncompounded nature of the
soul.)

(iv) Another argument of the *Phaedo* occurs in Socrates'

answer to the objections of Cebes. (To Socrates' refutation of the "epiphenomenalism" suggested by Simmias, I have referred earlier.) Cebes suggests[23] that the expenditure of energy which is undergone by the soul in its successive bodily lives may "wear it out," so that in the end it will "perish altogether in some one of the deaths." To this Socrates replies with another proof of immortality.[24] The existence of Forms is admitted. Now, the presence of one Form will not admit of the presence of a contrary Form, nor will a thing that is what it is by virtue of its participation in one Form admit of the simultaneous presence of a contrary Form, e.g. though we cannot say that fire is *warmth*, it is *warm*, and will not admit of the opposite predicate "cold" simultaneously. Soul is what it is by virtue of its participation in the Form of Life: therefore it will not admit of the presence of the contrary Form, "death." When, therefore, death approaches, the soul must either perish or withdraw. That it does not perish is assumed. Strictly speaking, then, this argument should not be termed an argument for the imperishability of the soul, once granted its spirituality. Cebes is understood by Socrates to accept the spirituality of the soul, but to be arguing that it might wear itself out. Socrates' answer practically comes to this, that a spiritual principle cannot wear itself out.

(v) In the *Republic*[25] Socrates assumes the principle that a thing cannot be destroyed or perish except through some evil that is inherent in it. Now, the evils of the soul are "unrighteousness, intemperance, cowardice, ignorance"; but these do not destroy it, for a thoroughly unjust man may live as long or longer than a just man. But if the soul is not destroyed by its own internal corruption, it is unreasonable to suppose that it can be destroyed by any external evil. (The argument evidently supposes dualism.)

(vi) In the *Phaedrus*[26] it is argued that a thing which moves another, and is moved by another, may cease to live as it may cease to be moved. The soul, however, is a self-moving principle,[27] a source and beginning of motion, and that which is a beginning must be uncreated, for if it were not uncreated, it would not be a beginning. But if uncreated, then indestructible, for if soul, the beginning of motion were destroyed, all the universe and creation would "collapse and come to a standstill."

Now, once granted that the soul is the principle of motion,

it must always have existed (if motion is from the beginning), but obviously this does little to prove personal
immortality. For all this argument shows, the individual soul
might be an emanation from the World-Soul, to which it
returns at bodily death. Yet on reading the *Phaedo* in
general and the Myths of the *Phaedo*, *Gorgias* and *Republic*,
one cannot avoid the impression that Plato believed in real
personal immortality. Moreover, passages such as that in
which Socrates speaks of this life as a preparation for
eternity,[28] and remarks like that made by Socrates in the
Gorgias,[29] that Euripides might be right in saying that life
here is really death and death really life (a remark which has
an Orphic ring about it), can hardly permit one to suppose
that Plato, in teaching immortality, meant to affirm a mere
persistence of τὸ λογιστικόν without any personal consciousness or continued self-identity. It is far more reasonable
to suppose that he would have agreed with Leibniz when
the latter asks: "Of what use would it be to you, sir, to
become king of China on condition of forgetting what you
have been? Would it not be the same as if God at the
same time that he destroyed you, created a king in China?" [30]

To consider the Myths in detail is not necessary, for they
are but pictorial representations of the truth that Plato
wished to convey, namely, that the soul persists after death,
and that the soul's life hereafter will be in accordance with
its conduct on this earth. How far Plato seriously intended
the doctrine of successive reincarnations, which is put forward in the Myths, is uncertain: in any case it would appear
that there is a hope for the philosophic soul of escaping from
the wheel of reincarnation, while it would also appear that
there may be incurable sinners who are flung for ever into
Tartarus. As already mentioned, the presentation of the future
life in the Myths is hardly consonant with Plato's assertion
that only τὸ λογιστικόν survives, and in this sense I
should agree with Ritter when he says: "It cannot be
maintained with certainty that Plato was convinced of the
immortality of the soul, as that is taught in the Myths of
the *Gorgias*, the *Phaedo* and the *Republic*." [31]

Plato's psychological doctrine is, therefore, not a systematically elaborated and consistent body of "dogmatic" statements: his interest was undoubtedly largely ethical in character. But this is not to say that Plato did not make many
acute psychological observations, which may be found scat-

tered throughout the dialogues. We have only to think of the illustrations he gives in the *Theaetetus* of the process of forgetting and remembering, or the distinction between memory and recollection in the *Philebus*.[32]

Chapter Twenty-Two

MORAL THEORY

1. *The Summum Bonum*

Plato's ethic is eudaemonistic, in the sense that it is directed towards the attainment of man's highest good, in the possession of which true happiness consists. This highest good of man may be said to be the true development of man's personality as a rational and moral being, the right cultivation of his soul, the general harmonious well-being of life. When a man's soul is in the state it ought to be in, then that man is happy. At the beginning of the *Philebus* two extreme positions are taken up by Protarchus and Socrates *causa argumenti*. Though they are both agreed that the good must be a state of soul, Protarchus is prepared to maintain that the good consists in *pleasure*, while Socrates will maintain that the good consists in *wisdom*. Socrates proceeds to show that pleasure as such cannot be the true and sole human good, since a life of unmixed pleasure (bodily pleasure is understood), in which neither mind nor memory nor knowledge nor true opinion had any share, "would be, not a human life, but that of a *pulmo marinus* or an oyster." [1] Not even Protarchus can think such a life desirable for a human being. On the other hand, a life of "unmixed mind," which was destitute of pleasure, could not be the sole good of man; even if intellect is the highest part of man and intellectual activity (especially the contemplation of the Forms) is man's highest function, man is not pure intellect. Thus the good life for man must be a "mixed" life, neither exclusively the life of the mind nor yet exclusively the life of sense-pleasure. Plato, therefore, is prepared to admit those pleasures which are not preceded by pain, e.g. the intellectual pleasures,[2] but also pleasures which consist in the satisfaction of desire, provided that they are innocent and are enjoyed in moderation. Just as honey and water must be mixed in due proportion in order to make a pleasing drink, so pleasant feeling and intellectual activity must be mixed in due proportion in order to make the good life of man.[3]

First of all, Plato says, the good life must include all knowledge of the truer type, the exact knowledge of timeless objects. But the man who was acquainted only with the exact and perfect curves and lines of geometry, and had no knowledge at all of the rough approximations to them which we meet with in daily life, would not even know how to find his way home. So second-class knowledge, and not only the first-class variety, must be admitted into the mixture: it will do a man no harm, provided that he recognises the second-class objects for what they are, and does not mistake the rough approximations for the exact truth. In other words, a man need not turn his back completely on this mortal life and the material world in order to lead the truly good life, but he must recognise that this world is not the only world, nor yet the highest world, but a poor copy of the ideal. (Music, says Protarchus, must be admitted, "if human life is to be a life at all," in spite of the fact that it is, according to Socrates, "full of guesswork and imitation" and "wanting in purity.")[4]

All the "water" having thus been admitted to the mixing-bowl, the question arises, how much "honey" to put in. The deciding vote in this question, how much pleasure to admit, rests with knowledge. Now, knowledge, says Plato, would claim kinship with the class of "true" and "unmixed" pleasures; but, as to the rest, knowledge will accept only those which accompany health and a sober mind and any form of goodness. The pleasures of "folly and badness" are quite unfit to find a place in the blend.

The secret of the blend which forms the good life is thus measure or proportion: where this is neglected, there exists, not a genuine mixture, but a mess. The good is thus a form of the beautiful, which is constituted by measure and proportion, and συμμετρία, καλόν and ἀλήθεια will be the three forms or notes found in the good. The first place goes to "seasonableness," τὸ καίριον, the second to proportion or beauty or completeness (τὸ σύμμετρον καὶ καλόν καὶ τὸ τέλεον καὶ ἱκανόν), the third to νοῦς καὶ φρόνησις, the fourth to ἐπιστῆμαι καὶ τέχναι καὶ δόξαι ὀρθαί, the fifth to the pleasures which have no pain mixed with them (whether involving actual sensation or not), and the sixth to the moderate satisfaction of appetite when, of course, this is harmless. Such, then, is man's true good, the good life, εὐδαιμονία, and the compelling motive in the search for it is Eros, the desire or longing for good or happiness.

Man's *summum bonum* or happiness includes, of course, knowledge of God—obviously so if the Forms are the Ideas of God; while, even if the *Timaeus* were taken literally and God were supposed to be apart from the Forms and to contemplate them, man's own contemplation of the Forms, which is an integral constituent of his happiness, would make him akin to God. Moreover, no man could be happy who did not recognise the Divine operation in the world. Plato can say, therefore, that the Divine happiness is the pattern of man's happiness.[5]

Now, happiness must be attained by the pursuit of virtue, which means becoming as like to God as it is possible for man to become. We must become "like the divine so far as we can, and that again is to become righteous with the help of wisdom." [6] "The gods have a care of anyone whose desire is to become just and to be like God, as far as man can attain to the divine likeness, by the pursuit of virtue." [7] In the *Laws* Plato declares that "God is the measure of all things, in a sense far higher than any man, as they say, can ever hope to be." (He thus answers Protagoras.) "And he who would be dear to God, must as far as possible be like Him and such as He is. Wherefore the temperate man is the friend of God, for he is like Him. . . ." He goes on to say that to offer sacrifice to the gods and pray to them is "the noblest and best of all things, and also the most conducive to a happy life," but points out that the sacrifices of the wicked and impious are unacceptable to the gods.[8] Worship and virtue belong, therefore, to happiness, so that although the pursuit of virtue and the leading of a virtuous life is the means of attaining happiness, virtue itself is not external to happiness, but is integral to it. Man's good is a condition of soul primarily, and it is only the truly virtuous man who is a truly good man and a truly happy man.

2. *Virtue*

1. In general we may say that Plato accepted the Socratic identification of virtue with knowledge. In the *Protagoras*[9] Socrates shows, as against the Sophist, that it is absurd to suggest that justice can be impious or piety unjust, so that the several virtues cannot be entirely disparate. Furthermore, the intemperate man is one who pursues what is really harmful to man while the temperate man pursues what is truly good and beneficial. Now, to pursue what is truly good and beneficial is wise, while to pursue what is harmful is foolish. Hence temperance and wisdom cannot be entirely disparate. Again, true valour or courage means, e.g. standing your ground in battle when you know the risks to which you are exposed; it does not mean mere foolhardiness. Thus courage can no more be separated from wisdom than can temperance. Plato does not, of course, deny that there are distinct virtues, distinguished according to their objects or the parts of the soul of which they are the habits; but all these distinct virtues form a unity, inasmuch as they are the expressions of the same knowledge of good and evil. The distinct virtues are, therefore, unified in prudence or the knowledge of what is truly good for man and of the means to attain that good. It is made clear in the *Meno* that *if* virtue is knowledge or prudence, it can be taught, and it is shown in the *Republic* that it is only the philosopher who has true knowledge of the good for man. It is not the Sophist, content with "popular" notions of virtue, who can teach virtue, but only he who has exact knowledge, i.e. the philosopher. The doctrine that virtue is knowledge is really an expression of the fact that goodness is not a merely relative term, but refers to something that is absolute and unchanging: otherwise it could not be the object of knowledge.

To the idea that virtue is knowledge and that virtue is teachable, Plato seems to have clung, as also to the idea that no one does evil knowingly and willingly. When a man chooses that which is *de facto* evil, he chooses it *sub specie boni:* he desires something which he imagines to be good, but which is, as a matter of fact, evil. Plato certainly allowed for the headstrong character of appetite, which strives to carry all before it, sweeping the charioteer along with it in its mad onrush to attain that which appears to it as a good; but if the bad horse overpowers the resistance of the charioteer, it can, on Plato's principles, only be because either the charioteer has no knowledge of the true good or because his knowledge of the good is obscured for the time being by the onrush of passion. It might well seem that such a doctrine, inherited from Socrates, conflicts with Plato's obvious admission of moral responsibility, but it is open to Plato to reply that a man who knows what is truly good may allow his judgment to be so obscured by passion, at least temporarily, that the apparent good appears to him as a true good, although he is responsible for having allowed passion so to darken reason. If it be objected that a man may deliberately choose evil because it is evil, Plato could only answer that the man has said: "Evil, be thou my good." If he chooses what is really evil or harmful, knowing it to be ultimately such, that can only be because he, in spite of his knowledge, fixes his attention on an aspect of the object which appears to him as good. He may indeed be responsible for so fixing his attention, but, if he chooses, he can only choose *sub ratione boni*. A man might very well know that to murder his enemy will be ultimately harmful to him, but he chooses to do it all the same, since he fixes his attention on what appears to be the immediate good of satisfying his desire for revenge or of obtaining some benefit by the elimination of his enemy. (It might be remarked that the Greeks needed a clearer view of *Good* and *Right* and their relation to one another. The murderer may know very well that murder is wrong, but he chooses to commit is as being, *in some respects*, a *good*. The murderer who knew that murder was wrong might also know, of course, that "wrong" and "ultimately harmful or evil" were inseparable, but that would not take away the aspect of "goodness" [i.e. usefulness or desirability] attaching to the act. When we use the word "evil," we often mean "wrong," but when Plato said that no one willingly chooses to do what he knows to be evil, he did not mean that no one chooses to do what he knows to be wrong, but that no one deliberately chooses to do what he knows to be in all respects harmful to himself.)

In the *Republic*[10] Plato considers four chief or cardinal virtues—wisdom (Σοφία), courage or fortitude ('Ανδρεία), temperance (Σωφροσύνη) and justice (Δικαιοσύνη). Wisdom is the virtue of the rational part of the soul, courage of the spirited part, while temperance consists in the union of the spirited and appetitive parts under the rule of reason. Justice is a general virtue consisting in this, that every part of the soul performs its proper task in due harmony.

2. In the *Gorgias* Plato argues against the identification of good and evil with pleasure and pain, and against the "Superman" morality propounded by Callicles. Against Polus, Socrates has tried to show that to do an injustice, e.g. to play the part of the tyrant, is worse than to suffer injustice, since to do injustice makes one's soul worse, and this is the greatest evil that a man can suffer. Moreover, to do injustice and then to get off scot-free is the worst thing of all, because that only confirms the evil in the soul, whereas punishment may bring reformation. Callicles breaks in on the discussion in order to protest that Socrates is appealing "to the popular and vulgar notions of right, which are not natural, but only conventional":[11] to do evil may be disgraceful from the conventional standpoint, but this is simply herd-morality. The weak, who are the majority, club together to restrain "the stronger sort of men," and proclaim as *right* the actions that suit them, i.e. the members of the herd, and as *wrong* the actions that are harmful to them.[12] Nature, however, shows among both men and animals that "justice consists in the superior ruling and having more than the inferior."[13]

Socrates thanks Callicles for his frankness in openly stating his opinion that Might is Right, but he points out that if the weak majority do in fact tyrannise over the "strong," then they are actually the stronger and also are justified, on Callicles' own admission. This is not a mere verbal quibble, for if Callicles persists in maintaining his rejection of conventional morality, he must now show how the strong, the ruthless and unscrupulous individualist, is qualitatively "better" than the herd-man, and so has the right to rule. This Callicles tries to do by maintaining that his individualist is wiser than "the rabble of slaves and nondescripts," and so ought to rule and have more than his subjects. Irritated by Socrates' observation that, in this case, the physician should have more to eat and drink than anybody else, and the cobbler larger shoes than anybody, Callicles affirms that what he means is that those who are wise and courageous in the administration of the State ought to rule the State, and that justice consists in their having more than their subjects. Goaded by Socrates' question, whether the ruler should rule himself as well, Callicles roundly asserts that the strong man should allow his desires and passions full play. This gives Socrates his chance, and he compares Callicles' ideal man to a leaky cask: he is always filling himself with pleasure but never has enough: his life is the life of a cormorant not of a man. Callicles is prepared to admit that the scratcher who is constantly relieving his itch has a happy life, but he boggles at justifying the life of the catamite, and in the end is driven to admit a *qualitative* difference in pleasures. This leads to the conclusion that pleasure is subordinate to the good, and that reason must, therefore, be judge of pleasures and admit them only in so far as they are consonant with health and harmony and order of soul and body. It is thus not the intemperate man but the temperate man who is truly good and happy. The intemperate man does evil to himself, and Socrates drives home his point by the "Myth" of the impossibility of escaping judgment after death.[14]

3. Plato expressly rejects the maxim that one should do good to one's friends and evil to one's enemies. To do evil can never be good. In the first Book Polemarchus puts forward the theory that "it is just to do good to our friend if he is a good man, and to hurt our enemy if he is a bad man."[15] Socrates (understanding by "to hurt" to do real harm, and not simply to punish—which he regarded as remedial) objects that to hurt is to make worse, and, in respect of human excellence, that means less just, so that, according to Polemarchus, it pertains to the just man to make the unjust man worse. But this is obviously rather the work of the unjust man than of the just man.

Chapter Twenty-Three

THE STATE

Plato's political theory is developed in close connection with his ethics. Greek life was essentially a communal life, lived out in the City-State and unthinkable apart from the City, so that it would not occur to any genuine Greek that a man could be a perfectly good man if he stood entirely apart from the State, since it is only in and through Society that the good life becomes possible for man—and Society meant the City-State. The rational analysis of this experimental fact results in the doctrine that organised Society is a "natural" institution, that man is essentially a social animal—a doctrine common to both Plato and Aristotle: the theory that Society is a necessary evil and results in the stunting of man's free development and growth would be entirely foreign to the genuine Greek. (It would, of course, be foolish to represent the Greek consciousness according to the analogy of the ant-heap or the beehive, since individualism was rife, showing itself both in the internecine wars between States and in the factions within the Cities themselves, e.g. in attempts on the part of an individual to establish himself as Tyrant; but this individualism was not a rebellion against Society as such—rather did it presuppose Society as an accepted fact.) For a philosopher like Plato, then, who concerned himself with man's happiness, with the truly good life for man, it was imperative to determine the true nature and function of the State. If the citizens were all morally bad men, it would indeed be impossible to secure a good State; but, conversely, if the State were a bad State, the individual citizens would find themselves unable to lead the good life as it should be lived.

Plato was not a man to accept the notion that there is one morality for the individual and another for the State. The State is composed of individual men and exists for the leading of the good life: there is an absolute moral code that rules all men and all States: expediency must bow the knee to Right. Plato did not look upon the State as a personality or organism that can or should develop itself without restraint, without paying any attention to the Moral Law: it is not the arbiter of right and wrong, the source of its own moral code, and the absolute justification of its own actions, be the latter what they may. This truth finds clear expression in the *Republic*. The interlocutors set out to determine the nature of justice, but at the close of the first Book Socrates declares that "I know not what justice is." [1] He then suggests in the second Book[2] that if they consider the State they will see the same letters "written larger and on a larger scale," for justice in the State "will be larger and more easily discernible." He proposes, therefore, that "we inquire into the nature of justice and injustice as appearing in the State first, and secondly in the individual, proceeding from the greater to the lesser and comparing them." The obvious implication of this is that the principles of justice are the same for individual and State. If the individual lives out his life as a member of the State, and if the justice of the one as of the other is determined by ideal justice, then clearly neither the individual nor the State can be emancipated from the eternal code of justice.

Now, it is quite obvious that not every actual Constitution or every Government embodies the ideal principle of Justice; but Plato was not concerned to determine what empirical States *are* so much as what the State *ought* to be, and so, in the *Republic*, he sets himself to discover the Ideal State, the pattern to which every actual State ought to conform itself, so far as it can. It is true that in the work of his old age, the *Laws*, he makes some concessions to practicability; but his general purpose remained that of delineating the norm or ideal, and if empirical States do not conform to the ideal, then so much the worse for the empirical States. Plato was profoundly convinced that Statesmanship is, or should be, a science; the Statesman, if he is to be truly such, must know what the State is and what its life ought to be; otherwise he runs the risk of bringing the State and its citizens to shipwreck and proves himself to be not a Statesman but a bungling "politician." Experience had taught him that actual States were faulty, and he turned his back on practical political life, though not without the hope of sowing the seeds of true statesmanship in those who entrusted themselves to his care. In the seventh Letter Plato speaks of his sad experience, first with the Oligarchy of 404 and then with the restored Democracy, and adds: "The result was that I, who had at first been full of eagerness for a public career, as I gazed upon the whirlpool of public life and saw the incessant movement of shifting currents, at last felt dizzy . . . and finally saw clearly in regard to all States now existing that without exception their system of government is bad. Their constitutions are almost without redemption, except through some miraculous plan accompanied by good luck. Hence I was forced to say in praise of the correct philosophy that it affords a vantage-point from which we can discern in all cases what is just for communities and for individuals; and that accordingly the human race will not be free of evils until either the stock of those who rightly and truly follow philosophy acquire political authority, or the class who have power in the cities be led by some dispensation of providence to become real philosophers." [3]

I shall outline Plato's political theory, first as it appears in the *Republic,* and then as it appears in the *Statesman* and the *Laws.*

1. The Republic

1. The State exists in order to serve the wants of men. Men are not independent of one another, but need the aid and co-operation of others in the production of the necessaries of life. Hence they gather associates and helpers into one dwelling-place "and give this joint dwelling the name of City." [4] The original end of the city is thus an economic end, and from this follows the principle of the division and specialisation of labour. Different people have different natural endowments and talents and are fitted to serve the community in different ways: moreover, a man's work will be superior in quality and also in quantity if he works at one occupation alone, in accordance with his natural gifts. The agricultural labourer will not produce his own plough or mattock, but they will be produced for him by others, by

those who specialise in the production of such instruments. Thus the existence of the State, which at present is being considered from the economic viewpoint, will require the presence of husbandmen, weavers, shoemakers, carpenters, smiths, shepherds, merchants, retail traders, hired labourers, etc. But it will be a very rude sort of life that is led by these people. If there is to be a "luxurious" city, something more will be required, and musicians, poets, tutors, nurses, barbers, cooks, confectioners, etc., will make their appearance. But with the rise of population consequent on the growing luxury of the city, the territory will be insufficient for the city's needs, and some of the neighbour's territory will have to be annexed. Thus Plato finds the origin of war in an economic cause. (Needless to say, Plato's remarks are not to be understood as a justification of aggressive war: for his remarks on this subject see the section on war under the heading of the *Laws*.)

2. But, if war is to be pursued, then, on the principle of the division and specialisation of labour, there will have to be a special class of guardians of the State, who will devote themselves exclusively to the conduct of war. These guardians must be spirited, gifted with the θυμοειδές element; but they must also be philosophic, in the sense of knowing who the true enemies of the State are. But if the exercise of their task of guardianship is to be based on knowledge, then they must undergo some process of education. This will begin with music, including narrative. But, says Plato, we will scarcely permit the children of the State to receive into their minds at their most impressionable age opinions the reverse of those which they should entertain when they are grown to manhood.[5] It follows, then, that the legends about the gods, as retailed by Hesiod and Homer, will not be taught to children or indeed admitted into the State, since they depict the gods as indulging in gross immorality, taking various forms, etc. Similarly, to assert that the violation of oaths and treaties was brought about by the gods is intolerable and not to be admitted. God is to be represented, not as the author of all things, whether good or bad, but only of such things as are good.[6]

It is to be noted in all this how, though Socrates starts off the discussion by finding the origin of the State in the need of supplying the various natural wants of man and asserts the economic origin of the State, the interest soon shifts to the problem of education. The State does not exist simply in order to further the economic needs of men, for man is not simply "Economic Man," but for their happiness, to develop them in the good life, in accordance with the principles of justice. This renders education necessary, for the members of the State are rational beings. But it is not any kind of education that will do, but only education to the true and the good. Those who arrange the life of the State, who determine the principles of education and allot the various tasks in the State to its different members, must have knowledge of what is really true and good—in other words, they must be philosophers. It is this insistence on truth that leads Plato to the, as it appears to us, rather extraordinary proposal to exclude epic poets and dramatists from the ideal State. It is not that Plato is blind to the beauties of Homer or Sophocles: on the contrary, it is just the fact that the poets make use of beautiful language and imagery which renders them so dangerous in Plato's eyes. The beauty and charm of their words are, as it were, the sugar which obscures the poison that is imbibed by the simple. Plato's interest is primarily ethical: he objects to the way the poets speak about the gods, and the way in which they portray immoral characters, etc. In so far as the poets are to be admitted at all into the ideal State, they must set themselves to produce examples of good moral character, but, in general, epic and dramatic poetry will be banished from the State, while lyric poetry will be allowed only under the strict supervision of the State authorities. Certain harmonies (the Ionian and Lydian) will be excluded as effeminate and convivial. (We may think that Plato exaggerated the bad results that would follow from the admission of the great works of Greek literature, but the principle that animated him must be admitted by all who seriously believe in an objective moral law, even if they quarrel with his particular applications of the principle. For, granted the existence of the soul and of an absolute moral code, it is the duty of the public authorities to prevent the ruin of the morality of the members of the State so far as they can, and so far as the particular acts of prevention employed will not be productive of greater harm. To speak of the absolute rights of Art is simply nonsense, and Plato was quite justified in not letting himself be disturbed by any such trashy considerations.)

Besides music, gymnastics will play a part in the education of the young citizens of the State. This care of the body, in the case of those who are to be guardians of the State and athletes of war, will be of an ascetic character, a "simple, moderate system," not calculated to produce sluggish athletes, who "sleep away their lives and are liable to most dangerous illnesses if they depart, in ever so slight a degree, from their customary regimen," but rather "warrior athletes, who should be like wakeful dogs, and should see and hear with the utmost keenness." [7] (In these proposals for the State education of the young, both physically and mentally, Plato is anticipating what we have seen realised on a great scale, and which, we recognise, may be used for bad ends as well as for good. But that, after all, is the fate of most practical proposals in the political field, that while they may be used for the benefit of the State, i.e. its true benefit, they may also be abused and applied in a way that can only bring harm to the State. Plato knew that very well, and the selection of the rulers of the State was a matter of great concern to him.)

3. We have then so far two great classes in the State—the inferior class of artisans and the superior class of guardians. The question arises, who are to be the rulers of the State. They will, says Plato, be carefully chosen from the class of guardians. They are not to be young: they must be the best men of their class, intelligent and powerful, and careful of the State, loving the State and regarding the State's interests as identical with their own—in the sense, needless to say, of pursuing the true interests of the State without thought of their own personal advantage or disadvantage.[8] Those, then, who from childhood up have been observed to do that which is best for the State, and never to have deserted this line of conduct, will be chosen as rulers of the State. They will be the perfect guardians, in fact the only people who are rightly entitled to the name of "guardian": the others, who have hitherto been termed guardians, will be called "auxiliaries," having it as their office to support the decisions of the rulers.[9] (Of the education of the rulers I shall treat shortly.)

The conclusion is, therefore, that the ideal State will consist of three great classes (excluding the slave class, of whom more later), the artisans at the bottom, the Auxiliaries or military class over them, and the Guardians or Guardian at the top. However, though the Auxiliaries occupy a more honourable position than the artisans, they are not to be savage animals, preying on those beneath them, but even if stronger than their fellow-citizens, they will be their friendly allies, and so it is most necessary to ensure that they should have the right education and mode of life. Plato says that they should possess no private property of their own, but should receive all necessaries from their fellow-citizens. They should have a common mess and live together like soldiers in a camp: gold and silver they should neither handle nor touch. "And this will be their salvation and the salvation of the State." [10] But if they once start amassing property, they will very soon turn into tyrants.

4. It will be remembered that Plato set out at the beginning of the dialogue to determine the nature of justice, and that having found the task difficult, the suggestion was made that they might be able to see more clearly what justice is if they examined it as it exists in the State. At the present point of the discussion, when the different classes of the State have been outlined, it becomes possible to behold justice in the State. The wisdom of the State resides in the small class of rulers or Guardians, the courage of the State in the Auxiliaries, the temperance of the State consists in the due subordination of the governed to the governing, the justice of the State in this, that everyone attends to his own business without interfering with anyone else's. As the individual is just when all the elements of the soul function properly in harmony and with due subordination of the lower to the higher, so the State is just or righteous when all the classes, and the individuals of which they are composed, perform their due functions in the proper way. Political injustice, on the other hand, consists in a meddling and restless spirit, which leads to one class interfering with the business of another class. [11]

5. In the fifth Book of the *Republic* Plato treats of the famous proposal as to "community" of wives and children. Women are to be trained as men: in the ideal State they will not simply stay at home and mind the baby, but will be trained in music and gymnastics and military discipline just like men. The justification of this consists in the fact that men and women differ simply in respect to the parts they play in the propagation of the species. It is true that woman is weaker than man, but natural gifts are to be found in

both sexes alike, and, as far as her nature is concerned, the woman is admissible to all pursuits open to man, even war. Duly qualified women will be selected to share in the life and official duties of the guardians of the State. On eugenic principles Plato thinks that the marriage relations of citizens, particularly of the higher classes of the State, should be under the control of the State. Thus the marriages of Guardians or Auxiliaries are to be under the control of the magistrates, with a view not only to the efficient discharge of their official duties, but also to the obtaining of the best possible offspring, who will be brought up in a State nursery. But be it noted that Plato does not propose any complete community of wives in the sense of promiscuous free love. The artisan class retains private property and the family: it is only in the two upper classes that private property and family life is to be abolished, and that for the good of the State. Moreover, the marriages of Guardians and Auxiliaries are to be very strictly arranged: they will marry the women prescribed for them by the relevant magistrates, have intercourse and beget children at the prescribed times and not outside those times. If they have relations with women outside the prescribed limits and children result, it is at least hinted that such children should be put out of the way.[12] Children of the higher classes, who are not suitable for the life of those classes, but who have been "legitimately" born, will be relegated to the class of the artisans.

(Plato's proposals in this matter are abhorrent to all true Christians. His intentions were, of course, excellent, for he desired the greatest possible improvement of the human race; but his good intentions led him to the proposal of measures which are necessarily unacceptable and repugnant to all those who adhere to Christian principles concerning the value of the human personality and the sanctity of human life. Moreover, it by no means follows that what has been found successful in the breeding of animals, will also prove successful when applied to the human race, for man has a rational soul which is not intrinsically dependent on matter but is directly created by Almighty God. Does a beautiful soul always go with a beautiful body or a good character with a strong body? Again, if such measures were successful—and what does "successful" mean in this connection?—in the case of the human race, it does not follow that the Government has the right to apply such measures. Those who to-day follow, or would like to follow, in the footsteps of Plato, advocating, e.g. compulsory sterilisation of the unfit, have not, be it remembered, Plato's excuse, that he lived at a period anterior to the presentation of the Christian ideals and principles.)

6. In answer to the objection that no city can, in practice, be organised according to the plans proposed, "Socrates" replies that it is not to be expected that an ideal should be realised in practice with perfect accuracy. Nevertheless he asks, what is the smallest change that would enable a State to assume this form of Constitution? and he proceeds to mention one—which is neither small nor easy—namely, the vesting of power in the hands of the philosopher-king. The democratic principle of government is, according to Plato, absurd: the ruler must govern in virtue of knowledge, and that knowledge must be knowledge of the truth. The man who has knowledge of the truth is the genuine philosopher. Plato drives home his point by the simile of the ship, its captain and crew.[13] We are asked to imagine a ship "in which there is a captain who is taller and stronger than anyone else in the ship, but he is a little deaf and is short-sighted, and his knowledge of navigation is not much better." The crew mutiny, take charge of the ship and, "drinking and feasting, they continue their voyage with such success as might be expected of them." They have, however, no idea of the pilot's art or of what a true pilot should be. Thus Plato's objection to democracy of the Athenian type is that the politicians really do not know their business at all, and that when the fancy takes the people they get rid of the politicians in office and carry on as though no special knowledge were required for the right guidance of the ship of State. For this ill-informed and happy-go-lucky way of conducting the State, he proposes to substitute rule by the philosopher-king, i.e. by the man who has real knowledge of the course that the ship of State should take, and can help it to weather the storms and surmount the difficulties that it encounters on the voyage. The philosopher will be the finest fruit of the education provided by the State: he, and he alone, can, as it were, draw the outline of the concrete sketch of the ideal State and fill up that outline, because he has acquaintance with the world of Forms and can take them as his model in forming the actual State.[14]

Those who are chosen out as candidates or possible rulers will be educated, not only in musical harmony and gymnastics, but also in mathematics and astronomy. They will not, however, be trained in mathematics merely with a view to enabling them to perform the calculations that everyone ought to learn to perform, but rather with a view to enabling them to apprehend intelligible objects—not "in the spirit of merchants or traders, with a view to buying or selling," nor only for the sake of the military use involved, but primarily that they may pass "from becoming to truth and being," [15] that they may be drawn towards truth and acquire the spirit of philosophy.[16] But all this will merely be a prelude to Dialectic, whereby a man starts on the discovery of absolute being by the light of reason only, and without any assistance of the senses, until he "attains at last to the absolute good by intellectual vision and therein reaches the limit of the intellectual world." [17] He will thus have ascended all the steps of the "Line." The chosen rulers of the State, therefore, or rather those who are chosen as candidates for the position of Guardians, those who are "sound in limb and mind" and endowed with virtue, will be gradually put through this course of education, those who have proved themselves satisfactory by the time they have reached the age of thirty being specially selected for training in Dialectic. After five years spent in this study they will "be sent down into the den and compelled to hold any military or other office which the young are qualified to hold," in order that they may get the necessary experience of life and show whether, when confronted with various temptations, "they will stand firm or flinch." [18] After fifteen years of such probation those who have distinguished themselves (they will then be fifty years old) will have reached the time "at which they must raise the eye of the soul to the universal light which lightens all things, and behold the absolute good; for that is the pattern according to which they are to order the State and lives of individuals, and the remainder of their own lives too, making philosophy their chief pursuit; but when their turn comes, toiling also at politics and ruling for the public good, not as if they were doing some great thing, but of necessity; and when they have brought up others like themselves and left them in their place to be governors of the State, then they will depart to the Islands of the Blest and dwell there; and the city will give them public memorials and sacrifices and honour them, if the Pythian oracle consent, as demi-gods, and at any rate as blessed and divine." [19]

7. In the eighth and ninth Books of the *Republic* Plato develops a sort of philosophy of history. The perfect State is the aristocratic State; but when the two higher classes combine to divide the property of the other citizens and reduce them practically to slavery, aristocracy turns into timocracy, which represents the preponderance of the spirited element. Next the love of wealth grows, until timocracy turns into oligarchy, political power coming to depend on property qualifications. A poverty-stricken class is thus developed under the oligarchs, and in the end the poor expel the rich and establish democracy. But the extravagant love of liberty, which is characteristic of democracy, leads by way of reaction to tyranny. At first the champion of the common people obtains a bodyguard under specious pretences; he then throws off pretence, executes a *coup d'état* and turns into a tyrant. Just as the philosopher, in whom reason rules, is the happiest of men, so the aristocratic State is the best and happiest of States; and just as the tyrannical despot, the slave of ambition and passion, is the worst and most unhappy of men, so is the State ruled by the tyrant the worst and most unhappy of States.

2. *The Statesman (Politicus)*

1. Towards the close of the *Statesman*, Plato shows that the science of politics, the royal and kingly science, cannot be identical with e.g. the art of the general or the art of the judge, since these arts are ministerial, the general acting as minister to the ruler, the judge giving decisions in accordance with the laws laid down by the legislator. The royal science, therefore, must be superior to all these particular arts and sciences, and may be defined as "that common science which is over them all, and guards the laws, and all things that there are in the State, and truly weaves them all into one." [20] He distinguishes this science of the monarch or ruler from tyranny, in that the latter rests merely on compulsion, whereas the rule of the true king and statesman is "the voluntary management of voluntary bipeds." [21]

2. "No great number of persons, whoever they may be, can have political knowledge or order a State wisely," but "the

true government is to be found in a small body, or in an individual," [22] and the ideal is that the ruler (or rulers) should legislate for individual instances. Plato insists that laws should be changed or modified as circumstances require, and that no superstitious regard for tradition should hamper an enlightened application to a changed condition of affairs and fresh needs. It would be just as absurd to stick to obsolete laws in the face of new circumstances, as it would be for a doctor to insist on his patient keeping to the same diet when a new one is required by the changed conditions of his health. But as this would require divine, rather than human, knowledge and competence, we must be content with the second-best, i.e. with the reign of *Law*. The ruler will administer the State in accordance with fixed Law. The Law must be absolute sovereign, and the public man who violates law should be put to death. [23]

3. Government may be government by one, by few, or by many. If we are speaking of well-ordered governments, then that of the one, monarchy, is the best (leaving out of account the ideal form, in which the monarch legislates for individual cases), that of the few the second-best, and that of the many the worst. If, however, we are speaking of lawless governments, then the worst is government by the one, i.e. tyranny (since that can do the most harm), the second-worst that by the few, and the least bad that by the many. Democracy is thus, according to Plato, "the worst of all lawful governments, and the best of all lawless ones," since "the government of the many is in every respect weak and unable to do either any great good or any great evil when compared with the others, because in such a State the offices are parcelled out among many people." [24]

4. What Plato would think of demagogic Dictators is clear from his remarks on tyrants, as also from his observations on the politicians who are devoid of knowledge and who should be called "partisans." These are "upholders of the most monstrous idols, and themselves idols; and, being the greatest imitators and magicians, they are also Sophists *par excellence*." [25]

3. The Laws

1. In the composition of the *Laws* Plato would seem to have been influenced by personal experiences. Thus he says that perhaps the best conditions for founding the desired Con-

stitution will be had if the enlightened Statesman meets with an enlightened and benevolent tyrant or sovereign, since the despot will be in a position to put the suggested reforms into practice.[26] Plato's (unhappy) experience at Syracuse would have shown him at least that there was a better hope of realising the desired constitutional reforms in a city ruled over by one man than in a democracy such as Athens. Again, Plato was clearly influenced by the history of Athens, its rise to the position of a commercial and maritime empire, its fall in the Peloponnesian war. For in Book Four of the *Laws* he stipulates that the city shall be about eighty stadia from the sea—although even this is too near—i.e. that the State should be an agrarian, and not a commercial State, a producing, and not an importing, community. The Greek prejudice against trade and commerce comes out in his words, that "The sea is pleasant enough as a daily companion, but has a bitter and brackish quality; for it fills the streets with merchants and shopkeepers, and begets in the souls of men unfaithful and uncertain ways—making the State unfaithful and unfriendly both to her own citizens and also towards the rest of men." [27]

2. The State must be a true Polity. Democracy, oligarchy and tyranny are all undesirable because they are class-States, and their laws are passed for the good of particular classes and not for the good of the whole State. States which have such laws are not real polities but parties, and their notion of justice is simply unmeaning.[28] The government is not to be entrusted to any one because of considerations of birth or wealth, but for personal character and fitness for ruling, and the rulers must be subject to the law. "The State in which the law is above the rulers, and the rulers are the inferior of the law, has salvation and every blessing which the gods can confer." Plato here re-emphasises what he has already said in the *Statesman*.

The State exists, then, not for the good of any one class of men, but for the leading of the good life, and in the *Laws* Plato reasserts in unambiguous terms his conviction as to the importance of the soul and the tendance of the soul. "Of all the things which a man has, next to the gods, his soul is the most divine and the most truly his own," and "all the gold which is under or upon the earth is not enough to give in exchange for virtue." [29]

3. Plato had not much use for enormous States, and he

fixes the number of the citizens at the number 5,040, which "can be divided by exactly fifty-nine divisors" and "will furnish numbers for war and peace, and for all contracts and dealings, including taxes and divisions." [30] But although Plato speaks of 5,040 citizens, he also speaks of 5,040 houses, which would imply a city of 5,040 families rather than individuals. However that may be, the citizens will possess house and land, since, though Plato expressly clings to communism as an ideal, he legislates in the *Laws* for the more practical second-best. At the same time he contemplates provisions for the prevention of the growth of a wealthy and commercial State. For example, the citizens should have a currency that passes only among themselves and is not accepted by the rest of mankind. [31]

4. Plato discusses the appointment and functions of the various magistrates at length: I will content myself with mentioning one or two points. For example, there will be thirty-seven guardians of the law (νομοφύλακες), who will be not less than fifty years old when elected and will hold office up to their seventieth year at the latest. "All those who are horse or foot soldiers, or have taken part in war during the age for military service, shall share in the election of magistrates." [32] There shall also be a Council of 360 members, also elected, ninety from each property-class, the voting being designed apparently in such a way as to render unlikely the election of partisans of extreme views. There will be a number of ministers, such as the ministers who will have care of music and gymnastics (two ministers for each, one to educate, the other to superintend the contests). The most important of the ministers, however, will be the minister of education, who will have care of the youth, male and female, and who must be at least fifty years old, "the father of children lawfully begotten, of both sexes, or of one at any rate. He who is elected, and he who is the elector, should consider that of all the great offices of the State this is the greatest"; the legislator should not allow the education of children to become a secondary or accidental matter. [33]

5. There will be a committee of women to superintend married couples for ten years after marriage. If a couple have not had any children during a period of ten years, they should seek a divorce. Men must marry between the ages of thirty and thirty-five, girls between sixteen and twenty (later eighteen). Violations of conjugal fidelity will be punishable.

The men will do their military service between the ages of twenty and sixty; women after bearing children and before they are fifty. No man is to hold office before he is thirty and no woman until she is forty. The provisions concerning the superintendence of married relations by the State are hardly acceptable to us; but Plato doubtless considered them the logical consequence of his conviction that "The bride and bridegroom should consider that they are to produce for the State the best and fairest specimens of children which they can." [34]

6. In Book Seven Plato speaks of the subject of education and its methods. He applies it even to infants, who are to be rocked frequently, as this counteracts emotions in the soul and produces "a peace and calm in the soul." [35] From the age of three to the age of six boys and girls will play together in the temples, supervised by ladies, while at the age of six they will be separated, and the education of the two sexes will be conducted in isolation, though Plato does not abandon his view that girls should have more or less the same education as boys. They will be educated in gymnastics and music, but the latter will be carefully watched over, and a State anthology of verse will be composed. Schools will have to be built, and paid teachers (foreigners) will be provided: children will attend daily at the schools, where they will be taught not only gymnastics and music, but also elementary arithmetic, astronomy, etc.

7. Plato legislates for the religious festivals of the State. There will be one each day, that "one magistrate at least will sacrifice daily to some god or demigod on behalf of the city and citizens and their possessions." [36] He legislates, too, on the subject of agriculture and of the penal code. In regard to the latter Plato insists that consideration should be paid to the psychological condition of the prisoner. His distinction between βλάβη and ἀδικία[37] amounts pretty well to our distinction between a civil action and a criminal action.

8. In the tenth Book Plato lays down his famous proposals for the punishment of atheism and heresy. To say that the universe is the product of the motions of corporeal elements, unendowed with intelligence, is atheism. Against this position Plato argues that there must be a source of motion, and that ultimately we must admit a self-moving principle, which is soul or mind. Hence soul or mind is the source of the

cosmic movement. (Plato declares that there must be more than one soul responsible for the universe, as there is disorder and irregularity as well as order, but that there may be more than two.)

A pernicious heresy is that the gods are indifferent to man.[38] Against this Plato argues:

(a) The gods cannot lack the power to attend to small things.

(b) God cannot be too indolent or too fastidious to attend to details. Even a human artificer attends to details.

(c) Providence does not involve "interference" with law. Divine justice will at any rate be realised in the succession of lives.

A still more pernicious heresy is the opinion that the gods are venal, that they can be induced by bribes to condone injustice.[39] Against this Plato argues that we cannot suppose that the gods are like pilots who can be induced by wine to neglect their duty and bring ship and sailors to ruin, or like charioteers who can be bribed to surrender the victory to other charioteers, or like shepherds who allow the flock to be plundered on condition that they share in the spoils. To suppose any of these things is to be guilty of blasphemy.

Plato suggests penalties to be inflicted on those proved guilty of atheism or heresy. A morally inoffensive heretic will be punished with at least five years in the House of Correction, where he will be visited by members of the "Nocturnal Council," who will reason with him on the error of his ways. (Presumably those guilty of the two graver heresies will receive a longer term of imprisonment.) A second conviction will be punished with death. But heretics who also trade on the superstition of others with a view to their own profits, or who found immoral cults, will be imprisoned for life in a most desolate part of the country and will be cast out unburied at death, their families being treated as wards of the State. As a measure of safety Plato enacts that no private shrines or private cults are to be permitted.[40] Plato observes that before proceeding to prosecute an offender for impiety, the guardians of the law should determine "whether the deed has been done in earnest or only from childish levity."

9. Among the points of law dwelt on in Books Eleven and Twelve we may mention the following as of interest:

(a) It would be an extraordinary thing, says Plato, if any

well-behaved slave or freeman fell into the extremes
of poverty in any "tolerably well-ordered city or
government." There will, therefore, be a decree against
beggars, and the professional beggar will be sent
out of the country, "so that our country may be
cleared of this sort of animal." [41]

(b) Litigiousness or the practice of conducting lawsuits
with a view to gain, and so trying to make a court
a party to injustice, will be punishable by death.[42]

(c) Embezzlement of public funds and property shall
be punished by death if the offender is a citizen,
since, if a man who has had the full benefit of the
State-education behaves in this way, he is incurable.
If, however, the offender is a foreigner or a slave,
the courts will decide the penalty, bearing in mind
that he is probably not incurable.[43]

(d) A Board of εὔθυνοι will be appointed to audit the
accounts of the magistrates at the end of their terms
of office.[44]

(e) The Nocturnal Council (which is to meet early in the
morning before the business of the day begins) will
be composed of the ten senior νομοφύλακες, the minister and ex-ministers of education, and ten co-opted
men between the ages of thirty and forty. It will consist of men who are trained to see the One in the
Many, and who know that virtue is one (i.e. they
will be men trained in Dialectic) and who have
also undergone training in mathematics and astronomy, that they may have a firmly-grounded conviction
as to the operation of divine Reason in the world.
Thus this Council, composed of men who have a
knowledge of God and of the ideal pattern of goodness, will be enabled to watch over the Constitution
and be "the salvation of our government and of our
laws." [45]

(f) In order to avoid confusion, novelties and restlessness,
no one will be permitted to travel abroad without
sanction of the State, and then only when he is over
forty years of age (except, of course, on military
expeditions). Those who go abroad will, on their
return, "teach the young that the institutions of other
States are inferior to their own." [46] However, the
State will send abroad "spectators," in order to see

if there is anything admirable abroad which might
with profit be adopted at home. These men will be
not less than fifty or more than sixty years old, and
on their return they must make a report to the
Nocturnal Council. Not only will visits of citizens to
foreign countries be supervised by the State, but
also visits of travellers from abroad. Those who come
for purely commercial reasons will not be encouraged
to mix with the citizens, while those who come for
purposes approved of by the Government will be
honourably treated as guests of the State.[47]

10. *Slavery.* It is quite clear from the *Laws* that Plato
accepted the institution of slavery, and that he regarded the
slave as the property of his master, a property which may
be alienated.[48] Moreover, while in contemporary Athens the
children of a marriage between a slave woman and a freeman seem to have been considered as free, Plato decrees
that the children always belong to the master of the slave
woman, whether her marriage be with a freeman or a freed-
man.[49] In some other respects, too, Plato shows himself
severer than contemporary Athenian practice, and fails to
give that protection to the slave that was accorded by
Athenian law.[50] It is true that he provides for the protection
of the slave in his public capacity (e.g. whoever kills a
slave in order to prevent the latter giving information concerning an offence against the law, is to be treated as though
he had killed a citizen),[51] and permits him to give information in murder cases without being submitted to torture;
but there is no explicit mention of permission to bring a
public prosecution against a man guilty of ὕβρις against his
slave, which was permitted by Attic law. That Plato disliked the free-and-easy way in which the slaves behaved in
democratic Athens appears from the *Republic*,[52] but he
certainly did not wish to advocate a brutal treatment of the
slave. Thus in the *Laws*, although he declares that "slaves
ought to be punished as they deserve, and not admonished
as if they were freemen, which will only make them con-
ceited," and that "the language used to a servant ought
always to be that of command, and we ought not to jest
with them, whether they are females or males"; he expressly
says that "we should tend them carefully, not only out of
regard to them, but yet more out of respect to ourselves.
And the right treatment of slaves is not to maltreat them,

and to do them, if possible, even more justice than those who are our equals; for he who really and naturally reverences justice and really hates injustice, is discovered in his dealings with that class of man to whom he can easily be unjust." [53] We must, therefore, conclude that Plato simply accepted the institution of slavery, and, in regard to the treatment of slaves, that he disliked Athenian laxity on the one hand and Spartan brutality on the other.

11. *War.* In the first Book of the *Laws,* Cleinias the Cretan remarks that the regulations of Crete were designed by the legislator with a view to war. Every city is in a natural state of war with every other, "not indeed proclaimed by heralds, but everlasting." [54] Megillus, the Lacedaemonian, agrees with him. The Athenian Stranger, however, points out (*a*) that, in regard to external or international war, the best legislator will endeavour to prevent it occurring in his State, or, if it does arise, will endeavour to reconcile the warring factions in an abiding friendship, and (*b*), that in regard to external or international war, the true statesman will aim at the best. Now, the happiness of the State, secured in peace and goodwill, is the best. No sound legislator, therefore, will ever order peace for the sake of war, but rather, if he orders war it will be for the sake of peace.[55] Thus Plato is not at all of the opinion that Policy exists for the sake of War, and he would scarcely sympathise with the virulent militarists of modern times. He points out that "many a victory has been and will be suicidal to the victors, but education is never suicidal." [56]

12. When man reflects on human life, on man's good and on the good life, as Plato did, he clearly cannot pass by man's social relations. Man is born into a society, not only into that of the family but also into a wider association, and it is in that society that he must live the good life and attain his end. He cannot be treated as though he were an isolated unit, living to himself alone. Yet, although every thinker who concerns himself with the humanistic viewpoint, man's place and destiny, must form for himself some theory of man's social relations, it may be well that no theory of the State will result, unless a somewhat advanced political consciousness has gone before. If man feels himself as a passive member of some great autocratic Power—the Persian Empire, for example—in which he is not called upon to play any active role, save as taxpayer or soldier, his political con-

sciousness is scarcely aroused: one autocrat or another, one empire or another, Persian or Babylonian, it may make very little difference to him. But when a man belongs to a political community in which he is called upon to shoulder his burden of responsibility, in which he has not only duties but also rights and activities, then he will become politically conscious. To the politically unconscious man the State may appear as some thing set over against him, alien if not oppressive, and he will tend to conceive his way of salvation as lying through individual activity and perhaps through cooperation in other societies than that of the reigning bureaucracy: he will not be immediately stimulated to form a theory of the State. To the politically conscious man, on the other hand, the State appears as a body in which he has a part, as an extension in some sort of himself, and so will be stimulated—the reflective thinker, that is to say—to form a theory of the State.

The Greeks had this political consciousness in a very advanced degree: the good life was to them inconceivable apart from the Πόλις. What more natural, then, than that Plato, reflecting on the good life in general, i.e. the good life of man as such, should reflect also on the State as such, i.e. the ideal Πόλις? He was a philosopher and was concerned, not so much with the ideal Athens or the ideal Sparta, as with the ideal City, the Form to which the empirical States are approximations. This is not, of course to deny that Plato's conception of the Πόλις was influenced to a great extent by the practice of the contemporary Greek City-State —it could not be otherwise; but he discovered principles which lie at the basis of political life, and so may truly be said to have laid the foundations of a *philosophical* theory of the State. I say a "philosophical" theory of the State, because a theory of immediate reform is not general and universal, whereas Plato's treatment of the State is based on the nature of the State as such, and so it is designed to be universal, a character which is essential for a philosophic theory of the State. It is quite true that Plato dealt with reforms which he thought to be necessitated by the actual conditions of the Greek States, and that his theory was sketched on the background of the Greek Πόλις; but since he meant it to be universal, answering to the very nature of political life, it must be allowed that he sketched a philosophical theory of the State.

The political theory of Plato and Aristotle has indeed formed the foundation for subsequent fruitful speculation on the nature and characteristics of the State. Many details of Plato's *Republic* may be unrealisable in practice, and also undesirable even if practicable, but his great thought is that of the State as rendering possible and as promoting the good life of man, as contributing to man's temporal end and welfare. This Greek view of the State, which is also that of St. Thomas, is superior to the view which may be known as the liberal idea of the State, i.e. the view of the State as an institution, the function of which is to preserve private property and, in general, to exhibit a negative attitude towards the members of the State. In practice, of course, even the upholders of this view of the State have had to abandon a completely *laissez-faire* policy, but their theory remains barren, empty and negative in comparison with that of the Greeks.

However, it may well be that individuality was insufficiently stressed by the Greeks, as even Hegel notes. ("Plato in his *Republic* allows the rulers to appoint individuals to their particular class, and assign to them their particular tasks. In all these relations there is lacking the principle of subjective freedom." Again, in Plato "the principle of subjective freedom does not receive its due.")[57] This was brought into strong light by the theorists of the modern era who stressed the Social Contract theory. For them men are naturally atoms, separate and disunited, if not mutually antagonistic, and the State is merely a contrivance to preserve them, so far as may be, in that condition, while at the same time providing for the maintenance of peace and the security of private property. Their view certainly embodies truth and value, so that the individualism of thinkers like Locke must be combined with the more corporate theory of the State upheld by the great Greek philosophers. Moreover, the State which combines both aspects of human life must also recognise the position and rights of the supernatural Society, the Church. Yet we have to be careful not to allow insistence on the rights of the Church and the importance of man's supernatural end to lead us to minimise or mutilate the character of the State, which is also a "perfect society," having man's temporal welfare as its end.

Chapter Twenty-Four

PHYSICS OF PLATO

1. The physical theories of Plato are contained in the *Timaeus*, Plato's only "scientific" dialogue. It was probably written when Plato was about seventy years old, and was designed to form the first work of a trilogy, the *Timaeus*, the *Critias*, and the *Hermocrates*.[1] The *Timaeus* recounts the formation of the material world and the birth of man and the animals; the *Critias* tells how primitive Athens defeated the invaders from mythical Atlantis, and then was itself overwhelmed by flood and earthquake; and it is conjectured that the *Hermocrates* was to deal with the rebirth of culture in Greece, ending with Plato's suggestions for future reform. Thus the Utopian State or Socratic Republic[2] would be represented in the *Critias* as something realised in the past, while practical reforms for the future would be proposed in the *Hermocrates*. The *Timaeus* was actually written, the *Critias* breaks off before completion, and was left unfinished, while the *Hermocrates* was never composed at all. It has been very reasonably suggested that Plato, conscious of his advancing age, dropped the idea of completing his elaborate historical romance and incorporated in the *Laws* (Books 3 ff.) much of what he had wanted to say in the *Hermocrates*.[3]

The *Timaeus* was thus written by way of preface to two politico-ethical dialogues, so that it would be hardly correct to represent Plato as having suddenly conceived an intense interest in natural science in his old age. It is probably true that he was influenced by the growing scientific interest in the Academy, and there can be little doubt that he felt the

necessity of saying something about the material world, with
a view to explaining its relation to the Forms; but there is
no real reason for supposing that the centre of Plato's interest
underwent a radical shift from ethical, political and metaphysical themes to questions of natural science. As a matter
of fact, he says expressly in the *Timaeus* that an account
of the material world cannot be more than "likely," that we
should not expect it to be exact or even altogether self-
consistent,[4] phrases which clearly indicate that in Plato's
eyes Physics could never be an exact science, a science in the
true sense. Nevertheless, some account of the material universe was called for by the peculiar character of the Platonic
theory of Ideas. While the Pythagoreans held that things are
numbers, Plato held that they participate in numbers (retaining his dualism), so that he might justly be expected to
proffer some explanation from the physical standpoint of
how this participation comes to be.

Plato doubtless had another important reason for writing
the *Timaeus*, namely to exhibit the organised Cosmos as the
work of Intelligence and to show that man partakes of both
worlds, the intelligible and the sensible. He is convinced
that "mind orders all things," and will not agree "when an
ingenious individual (Democritus?) declares that all is disorder":[5] on the contrary, soul is "the oldest and most divine
of all things," and it is "mind which ordered the universe." [6]
In the *Timaeus*, therefore, Plato presents a picture of the
intelligent ordering of all things by Mind, and exhibits the
divine origin of man's immortal soul. (Just as the entire
universe comprises a dualism of the intelligible and eternal
on the one hand, and the sensible and fleeting on the other,
so man, the microcosm, comprises a dualism of eternal soul,
belonging to the sphere of Reality, and body which passes
and perishes.) This exhibition of the world as the handiwork
of Mind, which forms the material world according to the
ideal pattern constitutes an apt preface to the proposed extended treatment of the State, which should be rationally
formed and organised according to the ideal pattern and
not left to the play of irrational and "chance" causes.

2. If Plato thought of his physical theories as a "likely
account" (εἰκότες λόγοι), are we thereby compelled to
treat the whole work as "Myth"? First of all, the theories of
Timaeus, whether myth or not, must be taken as Plato's
theories: the present writer entirely agrees with Professor

Cornford's rejection of Professor A. E. Taylor's notion that the *Timaeus* is a "fake" on Plato's part, a statement of "fifth-century Pythagoreanism," "a deliberate attempt to amalgamate Pythagorean religion and mathematics with Empedoclean biology," [7] so that "Plato was not likely to feel himself responsible for the details of any of his speaker's theories." Apart from the inherent improbability of such a fake on the part of a great and original philosopher, already advanced in years, how is it that Aristotle and Theophrastus and other ancients, as Cornford points out, have left us no hint as to the faked character of the work? If this was its real character, they cannot all have been ignorant of the fact; and can we suppose that, if they were aware of such an interesting fact, they would all have remained absolutely silent on the point? It is really too much to ask us to believe that the true character of the *Timaeus* was first revealed to the world in the twentieth century. Plato certainly borrowed from other philosophers (particularly the Pythagoreans), but the theories of Timaeus are Plato's own, whether borrowed or not.

In the second place, although the theories put into the mouth of Timaeus are Plato's own theories, they constitute, as we have seen, a "likely account," and should not be taken as meant to be an exact and scientific account—for the very simple fact that Plato did not consider such an exact scientific account to be possible. He not only says that we should remember that we "are only human," and so should accept "the likely story and look for nothing further" [8]—words which might imply that it is just human frailty which renders true natural science impossible; but he goes further than that, since he expressly refers this impossibility of an exact natural science to "the nature of the subject." An account of what is only a likeness "will itself be but likely": "what becoming is to being, that is belief to truth." [9] The theories are put forward, therefore, as "likely" or probable; but that does not mean that they are "mythical" in the sense of being consciously designed to symbolise a more exact theory that, for some reason or other, Plato is unwilling to impart. It may be that this or that feature of the *Timaeus* is conscious symbolism, but we have to argue each case on its own merits, and are not justified in simply dismissing the whole of the Platonic Physics as Myth. It is one thing to say: "I do not think an exact account of the material world possible, but the following account is as likely or more likely than any other"; and it is another thing to say: "I put forward the following account as a mythical, symbolic and pictorial expression of an exact account which I propose to keep to myself." Of course, if we care to call a confessedly "probable" account "Myth," then the *Timaeus* is certainly Myth; but it is not Myth (in its entirety at least) if by "Myth" you mean a symbolic and pictorial representation of a truth clearly perceived by the author but kept to himself. Plato means to do the best he can, and says so.

3. Plato sets out to give an account of the generation of the world. The sensible world is becoming, and "that which becomes must necessarily become through the agency of some cause." [10] The agent in question is the divine Craftsman or Demiurge. He "took over" [11] all that was in discordant and unordered motion, and brought it into order, forming the material world according to an eternal and ideal pattern, and fashioning it into "a living creature with soul and reason" [12] after the model of the ideal Living Creature, i.e. the Form that contains within itself the Forms of "the heavenly race of gods, the winged things which fly through the air, all that dwells in the water, and all that goes on foot on the dry earth." [13] As there is but one ideal living Creature, the Demiurge made but one world.[14]

4. What was the motive of the Demiurge in so acting? The Demiurge is good and "desired that all things should come as near as possible to being like himself," judging that order is better than disorder, and fashioning everything for the best.[15] He was limited by the material at his disposal, but he did the best he could with it, making it "as excellent and perfect as possible."

5. How are we to regard the figure of the Demiurge? He must at least represent the divine Reason which is operative in the world; but he is not a Creator-God. It is clear from the *Timaeus* that the Demiurge "took over" a pre-existing material and did his best with it: he is certainly not said to have created it out of nothing. "The generation of this cosmos," says Plato, "was a mixed result of the combination of Necessity and Reason," [16] Necessity being also called the Errant Cause. The word "Necessity" naturally suggests to us the reign of fixed law, but this is not precisely what Plato meant. If we take the Democritean or Epicurean view of the universe, according to which the world is built up out of atoms

without the aid of Intelligence, we have an example or what Plato meant by Necessity, i.e. the *purposeless*, that which was not formed by Intelligence. If we also bear in mind that in the Atomistic System the world owes its origin to the "chance" collision of atoms, we can more easily see how Plato could associate Necessity with Chance or the Errant Cause. For us these may seem to be opposed notions, but for Plato they were akin, since they both denote that in which Intelligence and conscious Purpose have no share. Thus it is that in the *Laws* Plato can speak of those who declare that the world originated "not by the action of mind, or of any God, or from art, but by nature and chance" (φύσει καὶ τύχῃ) or of necessity (ἐξ᾽ ἀνάγκης).[17] Such a view of the universe is characterised by Aristotle[18] as the ascription of the world to Spontaneity (τὸ αὐτόματον), though inasmuch as motion is due to the previous motion of another atom, one could also say that the universe is due to Necessity. Thus the three notions of "spontaneously" and "by chance" and "of necessity" were allied notions. The elements, if considered as left to themselves, as it were, proceed spontaneously or by chance or necessarily, according to the point of view taken; but they do not subserve *purpose* unless the operation of Reason is introduced. Plato can, therefore, speak of Reason "persuading" necessity, i.e. making the "blind" elements subserve design and conscious purpose, even though the material is partly intractable and cannot be fully subordinated to the operation of Reason.

The Demiurge was, then, no Creator-God. Moreover, Plato most probably never thought of "chaos" as ever existing in actual fact, in the sense of there having been an historical period when the world was simply a disorderly chaos. At any rate this was the tradition of the Academy with but very few dissentient voices (Plutarch and Atticus). It is true that Aristotle takes the account of the world's formation in the *Timaeus* as an account of formation in time (or at least criticises it as so interpreted), but he expressly mentions that the members of the Academy declared that in describing the world's formation they were merely doing so for purposes of exposition, in order to understand the universe, without supposing that it ever really came into existence.[19] Among Neo-Platonists Proclus gave this interpretation[20] and Simplicius.[21] If this interpretation is correct, then the Demiurge is still less like a Creator-God: he is a

symbol of the Intelligence operative in the world, the King
of heaven and earth of the *Philebus*.[22] Moreover, it is to be
noted that in the *Timaeus* itself Plato asserts that "it is hard
to find the maker and father of the universe, and having
found him it is impossible to speak of him to all." [23] But if
the Demiurge is a symbolic figure, it may also be that the
sharp distinction implied in the *Timaeus* between the
Demiurge and the Forms is only a pictorial representation.
In treating of the Forms I inclined towards what might
be called a Neo-Platonic interpretation of the relation between Mind, the Forms and the One, but I admitted that it
might be that the Forms were Ideas of Mind or Intelligence. In any case it is not necessary to suppose that the
picture of the Demiurge as a Divine Craftsman outside
the world and also entirely distinct from the Forms is to
be taken literally.

6. What did the Demiurge "take over"? Plato speaks of
the "Receptacle—as it were, the nurse—of all Becoming." [24]
Later he describes this as "Space, which is everlasting, not
admitting destruction; providing a situation for all things
which come into being, but itself apprehended without the
senses by a sort of bastard reasoning, and hardly an object
of belief." [25] It appears, therefore, that Space is not that
out of which the primary elements are made, but that *in
which* they appear. It is true that Plato makes a comparison
with gold out of which a man moulds figures;[26] but he goes
on to say that Space "never departs at all from its own
character. For it is ever receiving all things, and never in
any way whatsoever takes on any character which is like
any of the things that enter it." [27] It is probable, then, that
Space or the Receptacle is not the matter out of which the
primary qualities are made, but that in which they appear.

Plato remarks that the four elements (earth, air, fire and
water) cannot be spoken of as substances, since they are
constantly changing: "for they slip away and do not wait
to be described as 'that' or 'this' or by any phrase that
exhibits them as having permanent being." [28] They are
rather to be termed *qualities*, which make their appearance
in the Receptacle, "in which (ἐν ᾧ) all of them are always
coming to be, making their appearance and again vanishing
out of it." [29] The Demiurge thus "took over" (*a*) the
Receptacle, "a kind of thing invisible and characterless,
all-receiving, partaking in some very puzzling way of the

intelligible and very hard to apprehend," [30] and (*b*) the primary qualities, which appear in the Receptacle and which the Demiurge fashions or builds up after the model of the Forms.

7. The Demiurge proceeds to confer geometrical shapes on the four primary elements. Plato only takes things as far back as triangles, choosing the right-angled isosceles (half-square) and the right-angled scalene or half-equilateral, from which are to be built up the square and equilateral faces of the solids.[31] (If anyone asks why Plato makes a beginning with triangles, he answers that "the principles yet more remote, God knows and such men as are dear to Him." [32] In the *Laws*[33] he indicates that it is only when the third dimension is reached that things become "perceptible to sense." It is sufficient, therefore, for purposes of exposition to start with the surface or second dimension, and leave the remoter principles alone.) The solids are then constructed, the cube being assigned to earth (as the most immobile or hard to move), the pyramid to fire (as the "most mobile," having "the sharpest cutting edges and the sharpest points in every direction"), the octahedron to air, and the icosahedron to water.[34] These bodies are so small that no single one of them is perceptible by us, though an aggregate mass is perceptible.

The elementary solids or particles may be, and are, transformed into one another, since water, for example, may be broken down into its constituent triangles under the action of fire, and these triangles may recombine in Space into the same figure or into different figures. Earth, however, is an exception because, although it may be broken up, its constituent triangles (isosceles or half-square, from which the cube is generated) are peculiar to it alone, so that earth-particles "can never pass into any other kind." [35] Aristotle objects to this exception made in favour of earth, on the ground that it is unreasonable and unsupported by observation.[36] (The particles are spoken of as "motions or powers," [37] and in the state of separation they have "some vestiges of their own nature." [38] Thus Ritter says that "Matter may be defined as that which acts in space." [39]) From the primary elements come substances as we know them: e.g. copper is "one of the bright and solid kinds of water," containing a particle of earth, "which, when the two substances begin to be separated again by the action of time," appears by itself on the surface as verdigris.[40] But Plato observes that to enumerate the genesis and nature of substances is not much more than a "recreation," a "sober and sensible pastime" that affords innocent pleasure.[41]

8. The Demiurge is depicted as creating the World-Soul (though it is unlikely that Plato meant this to be taken literally, for in the *Phaedrus* it is stated that soul is uncreated[42]), which is a mixture composed of (*a*) Intermediate Existence (i.e. intermediate between the Indivisible Existence of the Forms and the Divisible Existence or Becoming of purely sensible things); (*b*) Intermediate Sameness; and (*c*) Intermediate Difference.[43] As immortal souls are also fashioned by the Demiurge from the same ingredients as the World-Soul,[44] it follows that the World-Soul and all immortal souls share in both worlds—in the unchanging world, inasmuch as they are immortal and intelligible, and in the changing world, inasmuch as they are themselves living and changing. The stars and planets have intelligent souls which are the celestial gods,[45] made by the Demiurge and having assigned to them the office of fashioning the mortal parts of the human soul and the human body.[46] It would appear from the *Phaedrus* that human souls never really had a beginning, and Proclus interprets Plato in this sense, though it is true that in the *Laws* the question seems to be left open.[47]

As to the traditional Greek deities, whose genealogies were narrated by the poets, Plato remarks that "to know and to declare their generation is too high a task for us"; it is best to "follow established usage." [48] Plato seems to have been agnostic as regards the existence of the anthropomorphic deities,[49] but he does not reject them outright, and in the *Epinomis*[50] the existence of invisible spirits (who were to play a large part in post-Aristotelian Greek philosophy), in addition to that of the celestial gods, is envisaged. Plato, therefore, upholds the traditional worship, though he places little reliance on the stories of the generation and genealogy of the Greek deities, and was probably doubtful if they really existed in the form in which the Greeks popularly conceived them.

9. The Demiurge, having constructed the universe, sought to make it still more like its pattern, the Living Creature or Being. Now, the latter is eternal, but "this character it was not possible to confer completely on the generated things.

But he took thought to make a certain moving likeness
of eternity; and, at the same time that he ordered the
Heaven, he made, of eternity that abides in unity, an
everlasting likeness moving according to number—that which
we have named Time." [51] Time is the movement of the
sphere, and the Demiurge gave man the bright Sun to
afford him a unit of time. Its brightness, relative to that of
the other celestial bodies, enables man to differentiate day
and night.

10. One cannot enter into details concerning the formation of the human body and its powers, or of the animals,
etc. It must suffice to point out how Plato stresses finality,
as in his quaint observation that "the gods, thinking that
the front is more honourable and fit to lead than the back,
gave us movement for the most part in that direction." [52]

The conclusion of the whole account of the formation of
the world is that "having received its full complement of
living creatures, mortal and immortal, this world has thus
become a visible living creature embracing all things which
are visible, an image of the intelligible, a perceptible god,
supreme in greatness and excellence, in beauty and perfection, this Heaven, one and single in its kind." [53]

Chapter Twenty-Five

ART

1. Beauty

1. Had Plato any appreciation of natural beauty? There is not an abundance of material from which to form an opinion. However, there is a description of natural scenery at the beginning of the *Phaedrus*,[1] and there are some similar remarks at the beginning of the *Laws*,[2] though in both cases the beauty of the scene is appreciated rather from a utilitarian standpoint, as a place of repose or as a setting for a philosophic discussion. Plato had, of course, an appreciation of human beauty.

2. Had Plato any real appreciation of Fine Art? (This question only arises because of his dismissal of dramatists and epic poets from the Ideal State on moral grounds, which might be held to imply that he lacked any real appreciation of literature and art.) Plato dismissed most of the poets from the *Republic* owing to metaphysical and, above all, moral considerations; but there certainly are not wanting indications that Plato was quite sensible of the charm of their compositions. While the words at the beginning of *Republic* 398 would not appear to be entirely sarcastic, in No. 383 of the same dialogue Socrates affirms that "although we praise much in Homer, this we shall not praise, the sending by Zeus of a lying dream to Agamemnon." Similarly, Plato makes Socrates say: "I must speak, although the love and awe of Homer, which have possessed me from youth, deter me from doing so. He seems to be the supreme teacher and leader of this fine tragic band, but a man should

not be reverenced before the truth and I must needs speak
out." [3] Again, "We are ready to acknowledge that Homer
is the greatest of poets and first of tragedy writers; but we
must recognise that hymns to the gods and praises of the
good are the only poetry which ought to be admitted into
our State." [4] Plato expressly says that if only poetry and the
other arts will prove their title to be admitted into a well-
ordered State, "we shall be delighted to receive her, knowing
that we ourselves are very susceptible of her charms; but
we may not on that account betray the truth." [5]

Bearing these points in mind, it seems impossible to write
Plato down as a Philistine in regard to the arts and literature. And if it be suggested that his tributes of appreciation
to the poets are but the grudging tributes of convention, we
may point to Plato's own artistic achievement. If Plato himself had shown in no degree the spirit of the artist, it might
be possible to believe that his remarks concerning the charms
of the poets were due simply to convention or were even
sarcastic in tone; but when we consider that it is the author
of the *Symposium* and the *Phaedo* who speaks, it is really
too much to expect anyone to believe that Plato's condemnation, or at least severe restriction, of art and literature
was due to aesthetic insensibility.

3. What was Plato's theory of Beauty? That Plato regarded beauty as objectively real, is beyond all question.
Both in the *Hippias Maior* and in the *Symposium* it is assumed that all beautiful things are beautiful in virtue of
their participation in the universal Beauty, Beauty itself.
So when Socrates remarks "Then beauty, too, is something
real," Hippias replies, "Real, why ask?" [6]

The obvious consequence of such a doctrine is that there
are degrees of beauty. For if there is a real subsistent Beauty
then beautiful things will approximate more or less to this
objective norm. So in the *Hippias Maior* the notion of relativity is introduced. The most beautiful ape will be ugly
in comparison with a beautiful man, and a beautiful porridge-
pot will be ugly in comparison with a beautiful woman. The
latter in turn will be ugly in comparison with a god. Beauty
itself, however, in virtue of a participation in which all
beautiful things are beautiful, cannot be supposed to be
something which "may just as well be called ugly as beautiful." [7] Rather is it "not partly beautiful and partly ugly;
not at one time beautiful and at another time not; not

beautiful in relation to one thing and deformed in relation to another; not here beautiful and there ugly, not beautiful in the estimation of some people and deformed in that of others; ... but ... eternally self-subsistent and monoeidic with itself." [8]

It follows also that this supreme Beauty, as being absolute and the source of all participated beauty, cannot be a beautiful *thing*, and so cannot be material: it must be supersensible and immaterial. We can see at once, then, that if true Beauty is supersensible, beautiful works of art or literature will, apart from any other consideration, necessarily occupy a comparatively low step on the ladder of beauty, since they are material, where as Beauty itself is immaterial; they appeal to the senses, while absolute Beauty appeals to the intellect (and indeed to the rational will, if we bring into consideration the Platonic notion of Eros). Now, no one will wish to question the sublimity of Plato's idea of the ascent from the things of sense to the "divine and pure, the monoeidic beautiful itself"; but a doctrine of supersensible beauty (unless it is purely analogical) makes it very difficult to form any definition of beauty which will apply to the beautiful in all its manifestations.

The suggestion is offered in the *Hippias Maior* [9] that "whatever is useful is beautiful." Thus efficiency will be beauty: the efficient trireme or the efficient institution will be beautiful in virtue of its efficiency. But in what sense, then, can the Supreme Beauty be thought of as useful or efficient? It ought, if the theory is to be consistent, to be Absolute Usefulness or Efficiency—a difficult notion to accept, one might think. Socrates, however, introduces a qualification. If it is the useful or efficient which is beautiful, is it that which is useful for a good or for a bad purpose or for both? He will not accept the idea that what is efficient for an evil purpose is beautiful, and so it must be that the useful for a good purpose, the truly profitable, is the beautiful. But if the beautiful is the profitable, i.e. that which *produces* something good, then beauty and goodness cannot be the same, any more than the cause and its product can be the same. But since Socrates is unable to accept the conclusion that what is beautiful is not at the same time good, he suggests that the beautiful is that which gives pleasure to the eye or ear—e.g. beautiful men and colour-patterns and pictures and statues, beautiful voices and music and poetry and prose. This definition is, of course, not quite consistent with the characterisation of supreme Beauty as immaterial, but, quite apart from that fact, it is involved in another difficulty. That which gives pleasure through sight cannot be beautiful simply because it comes through *sight*, for then a beautiful tone would not be beautiful; nor can a tone be beautiful precisely because it gives pleasure to the sense of *hearing*, since in that case a statue which is seen but not heard, would not be beautiful. The objects, therefore, which cause aesthetic pleasure of sight or hearing must share some common character which makes them beautiful, which belongs to them both. What is this common character? Is it perhaps "Profitable pleasure," since the pleasures of sight and hearing are "the most harmless and the best of pleasures?" If this be so, then, says Socrates, we are back in the old position that beauty cannot be good nor the good beautiful.

If anything like the foregoing definition of beauty were maintained, it would be inconsistent with Plato's general metaphysical position. If Beauty is a transcendental Form, how can it possibly be that which gives pleasure to the senses of sight and hearing? In the *Phaedrus*[10] Plato declares that beauty alone, in distinction from wisdom, has the privilege of manifesting itself to the senses. But does it manifest itself through what is itself beautiful or not? If the latter, how can there be a real manifestation? If the former, then do the sensible manifesting beauty and the supersensible manifested beauty unite in a common definition or not? And if so, in what definition? Plato does not really offer any definition that will cover both types of beauty. In the *Philebus* he speaks of true pleasure as arising from beautiful shapes and colours and sounds and goes on to explain that he is referring to "straight lines and curves" and to "such sounds as are pure and smooth and yield a single pure tone." These "are not beautiful relatively to anything else but in their own proper nature." [11] In the passage in question Plato distinguishes between the pleasure attaching to the perception of beauty and beauty itself, and his words must be read in connection with his statement[12] that "measure and symmetry everywhere pass into beauty and virtue," which implies that beauty consists in μετριότης καὶ συμμετρία. Perhaps this is as near as Plato ever comes to offering a definition of beauty that would apply to sensible and to

supersensible beauty (he certainly assumed that there are
both, and that the one is a copy of the other); but if we
take into account the remarks on beauty scattered about in
the dialogues, it is probable that we must admit that Plato
wanders "among so many conceptions, among which it is
just possible to say that the identification of the Beautiful
with the Good prevails," [13] though the definition offered in
the *Philebus* would seem to be the most promising.

2. Plato's Theory of Art

1. Plato suggests that the *origin* of art is to be sought in
the natural instinct of expression. [14]

2. In its metaphysical aspect or its essence, art is *imitation*.
The Form is exemplary, archetypal; the natural object is an
instance of μίμησις. Now, the painting of a man, for example, is the copy or imitation of a natural, particular man.
It is, therefore, the imitation of an imitation. Truth, however,
is to be sought properly in the Form; the work of the
artist accordingly stands at two removes from the truth.
Hence Plato, who was above all things interested in truth, was
bound to depreciate art, however much he might feel the
beauty and charm of statues, painting or literature. This
depreciatory view of art comes out strongly in the *Republic*,
where he applies it to the painter and the tragic poet, etc. [15]
Sometimes his remarks are a little comical, as when he
observes that the painter does not even copy objects accurately, being an imitator of appearance and not of fact. [16]
The painter who paints a bed, paints it only from one point
of view, as it appears to the senses immediately: the poet
portrays healing, war and so on, without any real knowledge
of the things of which he is speaking. The conclusion is
that "imitative art must be a long way from truth." [17] It is
"two grades below reality, and quite easy to produce without any knowledge of the truth—for it is mere semblance and
not reality." [18] The man who gives up his life to producing this shadow of reality has made a very bad bargain.

In the *Laws* there appears what is perhaps a somewhat
more favourable judgment concerning art, though Plato has
not altered his metaphysical position. When saying that the
excellence of music is not to be estimated merely by the
amount of sense-pleasure it occasions, Plato adds that the
only music which has real excellence is the kind of music

"which is an imitation of the good." [19] Again, "those who seek for the best kind of song and music, ought not to seek for that which is pleasant, but for that which is true; and the truth of imitation consists, as we were saying, in rendering the thing imitated according to quantity and quality." [20] He thus still clings to the concept of music as imitative ("everyone will admit that musical compositions are all imitative and representative"), but admits that imitation may be "true" if it renders the thing imitated as best as it can in its own medium. He is ready to admit music and art into the State, not only for educative purposes, but also for "innocent pleasure";[21] but he still maintains the imitation-theory of art, and that Plato's idea of imitation was somewhat narrow and literal must be clear to anyone who reads the second Book of the *Laws* (though it must be admitted, I think, that to make *music* imitative implies a widening of imitation to include symbolism. That music is imitative is, of course, a doctrine common to both the *Republic* and the *Laws*). It is through this concept of imitation that Plato arrives at the qualities of a good critic, who must (*a*) know of what the imitation is supposed to be; (*b*) know whether it is "true" or not; and (*c*) know whether it has been well executed in words and melodies and rhythms.[22]

It is to be noted that the doctrine of μίμησις would indicate that for Plato art definitely has its own sphere. While ἐπιστήμη concerns the ideal order and δόξα the perceptible order of natural objects, εἰκασία concerns the imaginative order. The work of art is a product of imagination and addresses itself to the emotional element in man. It is not necessary to suppose that the imitative character of art maintained by Plato *essentially* denoted mere photographic reproduction, in spite of the fact that his words about "true" imitation indicate that this is what he was often thinking of. For one thing, the natural object is not a photographic copy of the Idea, since the Idea belongs to one order and the perceptible natural object belongs to another order, so that we may conclude by analogy that the work of art need not necessarily be a mere reproduction of the natural object. It is the work of imaginative creation. Again, Plato's insistence on the imitative character of music makes it very difficult, as I have mentioned, to suppose that imitation meant essentially mere photographic reproduction. It is rather imag-

inative symbolism, and it is precisely because of this fact
that it does not assert truth or falsehood, but is imaginative
and symbolic and wears the glamour of beauty, that it
addresses itself to the emotional in man.

Man's emotions are varied, some being profitable, others
harmful. Reason, therefore, must decide what art is to be
admitted and what is to be excluded. And the fact that
Plato definitely admits forms of art into the State in the
Laws shows that art occupies a particular sphere of human
activity, which is irreducible to anything else. It may not
be a high sphere, but it is a sphere. This is borne out by
the passage in which Plato, after referring to the stereo-
typed character of Egyptian art, remarks that "if a person
can only find in any way the natural melodies, he should
confidently embody them in a fixed and legal form." [23] It
must, however, be admitted that Plato does not realise—
or, if he does realise, does not sufficiently exhibit—the specifically disinterested character of aesthetic contemplation in
itself. He is much more concerned with the educational and
moral effects of art, effects which are irrelevant, no doubt,
to aesthetic contemplation as such, but which are none the
less real, and which must be taken into account by anyone
who, like Plato, values moral excellence more than aesthetic
sensibility. [24]

3. Plato recognises that the popular view of art and music
is that they exist to give pleasure, but it is a view with
which he will not agree. A thing can only be judged by
the standard of pleasure when it furnishes no utility or
truth or "likeness" (reference to imitation), but exists solely
for the accompanying charm. [25] Now, music, for instance, is
representative and imitative, and good music will have "truth
of imitation": [26] therefore music, or at least good music,
furnishes a certain kind of "truth," and so cannot exist solely
for the sake of the accompanying charm or be judged of by
the standard of sense-pleasure alone. The same holds good
for the other arts. The conclusion is that the various arts
may be admitted into the State, provided that they are kept
in their proper place and subordinated to their educative
function, this function being that of giving *profitable* pleasure. That the arts do not, or should not, give pleasure, Plato
by no means intends to assert: he allows that in the city
there should be "a due regard to the instruction and amusement which the Muses give," [27] and even declares that "every

man and boy, free and slave, both sexes, and the whole city, should never cease charming themselves with the strains of which we have spoken, and that there should be every sort of change and variation of them in order to take away the effect of sameness, so that the singers may always have an appetite for their hymns and receive pleasure from them." [28]

But though Plato in the *Laws* allows for the pleasurable and recreative functions of art, the "innocent pleasure" [29] that it affords, he most certainly stresses its educative and moral function, its character of providing profitable pleasure. The attitude displayed towards art in the *Laws* may be more liberal than that shown in the *Republic*, but Plato's fundamental attitude has not changed. As we have seen when treating of the State, a strict supervision and censorship of art is provided for in both dialogues. In the very passage in which he says that due regard should be paid to the instruction and amusement given by the Muses, he asks if a poet is to be allowed to "train his choruses as he pleases, without reference to virtue or vice." [30] In other words, the art admitted into the State must have that remote relation to the Form ("truth of imitation" *via* the natural object) which is possible in the creations of the imagination. If it has not got that, then the art will be not only unprofitable but also bad art, since good art must have this "truth of imitation," according to Plato. Once more, then, it becomes clear that art has a function of its own, even if not a sublime one, since it constitutes a rung on the ladder of education, fulfils a need of man (expression) and affords recreation and innocent amusement, being the expression of a definite form of human activity—that of the creative imagination (though "creative" must be understood in connection with the doctrine of imitation). Plato's theory of art was doubtless sketchy and unsatisfactory, but one can hardly be justified in asserting that he had no theory at all.

Note on the Influence of Plato

1. The example of Plato is an influence by itself. His life was one of utter devotion to truth, to the attainment of abiding, eternal and absolute truth, in which he firmly and constantly believed, being ready to follow, as Socrates was, wherever reason might lead. This spirit he endeavoured to

stamp upon the Academy, creating a body of men who, under the ascendency of a great teacher, would devote themselves to the attainment of Truth and Goodness. But though he was a great speculative philosopher, devoted to the attainment of truth in the intellectual sphere, Plato, as we have seen, was no mere theorist. Possessed of an intense moral earnestness and convinced of the reality of absolute moral values and standards, he urged men to take thought for their dearest possession, their immortal soul, and to strive after the cultivation of true virtue, which alone would make them happy. The good life, based on an eternal and absolute pattern, must be lived both in private and in public, realised both in the individual and in the State: as relativistic private morality was rejected, so was the opportunist, superficial, self-seeking attitude of the sophistic "politician" or the theory that "Might is Right."

If man's life *ought* to be lived under the dominion of reason according to an ideal pattern, in the world as a whole we must acknowledge the actual operation of Mind. Atheism is utterly rejected and the order in the world is ascribed to Divine Reason, ordering the cosmos according to the ideal pattern and plan. Thus that which is realised in the macrocosm, e.g. in the movements of heavenly bodies, should also be realised in man, the microcosm. If man does follow reason and strives to realise the ideal in his life and conduct, he becomes akin to the Divine and attains happiness in this life and the hereafter. Plato's "otherworldliness" did not spring from a hatred of this life, but was rather a consequence of his convinced belief in the reality of the Transcendent and Absolute.

2. Plato's personal influence may be seen from the impression he made on his great pupil, Aristotle. Witness the latter's verses to the memory

Of that unique man
Whose name is not to come from the lips of the wicked.
Theirs is not the right to praise him—
Him who first revealed clearly
By word and by deed
That he who is virtuous is happy.
Alas, not one of us can equal him.[31]

Aristotle gradually separated himself from some of the Platonic doctrines that he had held at first; but, in spite of his growing interest in empirical science, he never abandoned metaphysics or his belief in the good life culminating in true wisdom—in other words, he never abandoned altogether the legacy of Plato, and his philosophy would be unthinkable apart from the work of his great predecessor.

3. Of the course of Platonism in the Academy and in the Neo-Platonic School I shall speak later. Through the Neo-Platonists Platonism made its influence felt on St. Augustine and on the formative period of mediaeval thought. Indeed, although St. Thomas Aquinas, the greatest of the Schoolmen, adopted Aristotle as "the Philosopher," there is much in his system that can be traced back ultimately to Plato rather than to Aristotle. Moreover, at the time of the Renaissance, the Platonic Academy of Florence endeavoured to renew the Platonic tradition, while the influence of the Platonic Republic may be seen in St. Thomas More's *Utopia* and Campanella's *City of the Sun*.

4. In regard to modern times, the influence of Plato may not be at first sight so obvious as it is in Antiquity and in the Middle Ages; but in reality he is the father or grandfather of all spiritualist philosophy and of all objective idealism, and his epistemology, metaphysics and politico-ethics have exercised a profound influence on succeeding thinkers, either positively or negatively. In the contemporary world we need only think of the inspiration that Plato has afforded to thinkers like Professor A. N. Whitehead or Professor Nicolai Hartmann of Berlin.

5. Plato, who stands at the head of European philosophy, left us no rounded system. That we do not possess his lectures and a complete record of his teaching in the Academy, we naturally regret, for we would like to know the solution of many problems that have puzzled commentators ever since; but, on the other hand, we may in a real sense be thankful that no cut and dried Platonic system (if ever there was such) has come down to us, a system to be swallowed whole or rejected, for this fact has enabled us to find in him, more easily perhaps than might otherwise be the case, a supreme example of the philosophic spirit. If he has not left us a complete system, Plato has indeed left us the example of a way of philosophising and the example of a life devoted to the pursuit of the true and the good.

Chapter Twenty-Six

THE OLD ACADEMY

The Platonic philosophy continued to exercise a profound influence throughout Antiquity; we must, however, distinguish various phases in the development of the Platonic School. The old Academy, which consisted of disciples and associates of Plato himself, held more or less to the dogmatic content of the Master's philosophy, though it is noticeable that it was the "Pythagorean" elements in the thought of Plato that received particular attention. In the Middle and New Academies an anti-dogmatic sceptical tendency is at first predominant, though it later gives way before a return to dogmatism of an eclectic type. This eclecticism is very apparent in Middle Platonism, which is succeeded at the close of the period of ancient philosophy by Neo-Platonism, an attempt at a complete synthesis of the original content of Platonism with those elements which had been introduced at various times, a synthesis in which those traits are stressed which are most in harmony with the general spirit of the time.

The Old Academy includes, together with men like Philippus of Opus, Heraclides Ponticus, Eudoxus of Cnidus, the following successors to Plato in the headship of the School at Athens: Speusippus (348/7-339/8), Xenocrates (339/8-315/4), Polemon (315/4-270/69) and Crates (270/69-265/4).

Speusippus, Plato's nephew and immediate successor as Scholarch, modified the Platonic dualism by abandoning the Ideas as distinct from τὰ μαθηματικά and making Real-

ity to consist in mathematical numbers.¹ The Platonic
Number-Ideas were thus dismissed, but the essential
χωρισμός remained. By his admission of scientific perception
(ἐπιστημονικὴ αἴσθησις) Speusippus is sometimes said to
have given up the Platonic dualism of knowledge and
perception,² but it must be remembered that Plato had
himself gone some way towards admitting this, inasmuch
as he allowed that λόγος and αἴσθησις co-operate in the
apprehension of the atomic idea.

It is difficult to tell exactly what the members of the Old
Academy taught, since (unless Philippus of Opus wrote the
Epinomis) no whole work of theirs has come down to us,
and we have only the remarks of Aristotle and the testimony of other ancient writers to rely on. But apparently
Speusippus held that substances proceed from the One
and the absolute Many, and he placed the Good or
τελεία ἕξις at the end of the process of becoming and not
at the beginning, arguing from the development of plants
and animals. Among the animate beings that proceed from
the One is the invisible Reason or God,³ which he probably
also identified with the World-Soul. (Possibly this might
afford an argument in favour of a "Neo-Platonic" interpretation of Plato.) As for human souls, these are immortal in
their entirety. We may note that Speusippus interpreted the
account of "creation" in the *Timaeus* as a mere form of
exposition and not as meant to be an account of an actual
creation in time: the world has no beginning in time. The
traditional gods he interpreted as physical forces, and thus
brought upon himself a charge of atheism.⁴

Xenocrates of Chalcedon, who succeeded Speusippus as
Scholarch, identified the Ideas with mathematical numbers,
and derived them from the One and the Indeterminate
Duality (the former being Νοῦς or Zeus, the father of the
gods, the latter being the feminine principle, the mother
of the gods).⁵ The World-Soul, produced by the addition
of the Self and the Other to number, is a self-moved number.
Distinguishing three worlds—the sub-lunar, the heavenly,
and the super-celestial—Xenocrates filled all three worlds with
"demons," both good and bad. This doctrine of evil demons
enabled him to explain the popular myths, in which evil
actions are ascribed to "gods," and the existence of immoral
cults, by saying that the evil actions were the acts of
evil demons, and that the immoral cults were directed to

these demons and not to the gods.[6] In company with his predecessor, Xenocrates held that even the irrational parts of the soul (which was not created in time) survive after death, and, together with his successor, Polemon, he deprecated the consumption of fleshmeat on the ground that this might lead to the dominion of the irrational over the rational. Like Speusippus and Crantor (and in opposition to Aristotle), Xenocrates understood the priority of the simple over the composite in the *Timaeus* to be a logical and not a temporal priority.[7] (The Περὶ ἀτόμων γραμμῶν, attributed to Aristotle, was directed against Xenocrates' hypothesis of tiny invisible lines, which he employed as an aid in the deduction of dimensions from numbers.)

Heraclides Ponticus adopted from the Pythagorean Ecphantus the theory that the world is composed of particles which he called ἄναρμοι ὄγκοι probably meaning that they are separated from one another by space. From these material particles the world was composed through the operation of God. The soul is therefore corporeal (consisting of aether, an element added to the others by Xenocrates). While asserting the diurnal revolution of the earth on its axis, Heraclides also held that Mercury and Venus revolve round the sun, and he seems to have suggested that the earth may do likewise.

One of the most celebrated mathematicians and astronomers of Antiquity is *Eudoxus* (c. 497-355 B.C.). Philosophically speaking, he is noteworthy for having held (a) that the Ideas are "mixed" with things,[8] and (b) that pleasure is the highest good.[9]

The first commentary on Plato's *Timaeus* was written by *Crantor* (c. 330-270), in which he interpreted the account of "creation" as a timeless and not as a temporal event. It is depicted as taking place in time simply for the purpose of logical schematism. In this interpretation Crantor was in accord, as we have seen, with both Speusippus and Xenocrates. In his Περὶ Crantor upheld the doctrine of the moderating of the passions (Metriopathy) in opposition to the Stoic ideal of Apathy.[10]

Appendix One

SOME ABBREVIATIONS
USED IN THIS VOLUME

AËTIUS. Collectio placitorum (philosophorum).

ALBINUS. Didask. (Didaskalikos).

AMMIANUS MARCELLINUS. Rerum gest. (Rerum gestarum libri 18).

AUGUSTINE. Contra Acad. (Contra Academicos).
    C.D. (De Civitate Dei).

BURNET. E.G.P. (Early Greek Philosophy).
    G.P., I. (Greek Philosophy. Part I, Thales to Plato).

CAPITOLINUS, JULIUS. Vit. M. Ant. (Vita Marci Antonini Pii).

CHALCIDIUS. In Tim. (Commentary on Plato's *Timaeus*).

CICERO. Acad. Prior. (Academica Priora).
    Acad. Post. (Academica Posteriora).
    Ad Att. (Letters to Atticus).
    De Div. (De Divinatione).
    De Fin. (De Finibus).
    De Nat. D. (De Natura Deorum).
    De Off. (De Officiis).
    De Orat. (De Oratore).
    De Senect. (De Senectute).
    Somn. Scip. (Somnium Scipionis).
    Tusc. (Tusculanae Disputationes).

CLEMENS ALEXANDRINUS. Protrep. (Protrepticus).
    Strom. (Stromata).

DAMASCIUS. Dubit. (Dubitationes et solutiones de primis principiis).

DIOGENES LAËRTIUS. Lives of the Philosophers.

EPICTETUS. Disc. (Discourses).

 Ench. (Enchiridion).

EUDEMUS. Phys. (*Physics,* of which only fragments remain).

EUNAPIUS. Vit. Soph. (Lives of the Sophists).

EUSEBIUS. Hist. Eccl. (Historia Ecclesiastica).

 Prep. Evan. (Preparatio Evangelica).

GELLIUS, AULUS. Noct. Att. (Noctes Atticae).

GREGORY OF NAZIANZEN. adv. Max. (adversus Maximum).

HIPPOLYTUS. Ref. (Refutationis omnium haeresium libri X).

JOSEPHUS. Ant. Jud. (Jewish Antiquities).

LACTANTIUS. Div. Inst. (Institutiones divinae).

LAMPRIDIUS. Alex. (Life of Alexander Severus).

 Aurel. (Life of Aurelian).

LUCIAN. De morte Peregr. (De morte Peregrini).

MARCUS AURELIUS. Med. (Meditations or To Himself).

MAXIMUS OF TYRE. Diss. (Dissertationes).

ORIGEN. c. Cels. (Contra Celsum).

P.G. Patrologia Graeca (ed. Migne).

P.L. Patrologia Latina (ed. Migne).

PHILO. De conf. ling. (De confusione linguarum).

 De gigant. (De gigantibus).

 De human. (De humanitate).

 De migrat. Abrah. (De migratione Abrahami).

 De mutat. nom. (De mutatione nominum).

 De opif. mundi (De opificio mundi).

 De post. Caini (De posteritate Caini).

 De somn. (De somniis).

 De vita Mos. (De vita Moysis).

 Leg. alleg. (Legum allegoriarum libri).

 Quis rer. div. her. (Quis rerum divinarum heres sit).

 Quod Deus sit immut. (Quod Deus sit immutabilis).

PHOTIUS. Bibliotheca (about A.D. 857).

PLUTARCH. Cat. Mai. (Cato Maior).

 De anim. proc. (De animae procreatione in Timaeo).

 De comm. notit. (De communibus notitiis adversus Stoicos).

 De def. orac. (De defectu oraculorum).

 De gloria Athen. (Bellone an pace clariores fuerint Athenienses).

 De Is. et Osir. (De Iside et Osiride).

 De prim. frig. (De primo frigido).

 De ser. num. vind. (De sera numinis vindicta).

 De sol. animal. (De sollertia animalium).

De Stoic repug. (De repugnantiis Stoicis).

Non p. suav. (Ne suaviter quidem vivi posse secundum Epicurum).

PSEUDO-PLUTARCH. Strom. (Fragments of the stromateis conserved in Eusebius' *Preparatio Evangelica*).

PORPHYRY. Isag. (Isagoge, i.e. introd. to Aristotle's *Categories*).

PROCLUS. De Prov. (De providentia et fato et eo quod in nobis).

In Alcib. (Commentary on *Alcibiades* I of "Plato").

In Remp. (Commentary on *Republic* of Plato).

In Parmen. (Commentary on *Parmenides* of Plato).

In Tim. (Commentary on *Timaeus* of Plato).

Instit. Theol. (Institutio Theologica).

Theol. Plat. (In Platonis Theologiam).

SENECA. Nat. Quaest. (Naturalium Quaestionum libri VII).

SEXTUS EMPIRICUS. adv. math. (Adversus mathematicos).

Pyrr. Hyp. (Pyrrhonenses Hypotyposes).

SIMPLICIUS. In Arist. Categ. (Commentary on Aristotle's *Categories*).

Phys. (Commentary on Aristotle's *Physics*).

STACE, W. T. Crit. Hist. (A Critical History of Greek Philosophy).

STOBAEUS. Flor. (Florilegium).

TACITUS. Ann. (Annales).

Hist. (Historiae).

THEOPHRASTUS. Phys. Opin. (Physicorum Opiniones).

XENOPHON. Cyneg. (Cynegeticus).

Mem. (Memorabilia).

Appendix Two

A NOTE ON SOURCES

Since on the one hand some philosophers did not write at all, while on the other hand the works of many philosophers who did not write have been lost, we have to rely in very many cases on the testimony of later writers for information as to the course of Greek philosophy.

The chief source of knowledge in the ancient world concerning the pre-Socratic philosophy was the work of Theophrastus entitled *Physicorum Opiniones*, a work which, unfortunately, we possess only in fragmentary form. Theophrastus' work became the source of various other compilations, epitomes or "doxographies," in some of which the opinions of the philosophers were arranged according to theme, while in others the opinions were set forth under the names of the respective philosophers. Of the former type were the *Vetusta Placita*, written by an unknown disciple of Poseidonius in the first half of the first century A.D. We do not possess this work, but that it existed and that it was based on Theophrastus' work, has been shown by Diels. The *Vetusta Placita* in turn formed the main source of the so-called *Aëtii Placita* or Συναγωγὴ τῶν ᾿Αρεσκόντων (about A.D. 100). Aetiüs' work in turn served as a basis for the *Placita philosophorum* of the Pseudo-Plutarch (compiled about A.D. 150), and the doxographical extracts given by John Stobaeus (A.D. fifth century) in the first book of his *Eclogae*. These two last works are the most important doxographical compilations which we possess, and it has become evident that the main ultimate source for both was the work of Theophrastus, which was also ultimately the chief, though not the only, source for the first book of Hippolytus' *Refutation of all heresies* (in which the subject-matter is arranged under the names of the respective philosophers concerned), and for the fragments, falsely attributed to Plutarch, which are quoted in the *Preparatio Evangelica* of Eusebius.

Further information on the opinions of Greek philosophers is provided by such works as the *Noctes Atticae* of Aulus Gellius (about A.D. 150), the writings of philosophers like Plutarch, Cicero and Sextus Empiricus, and the works of the Christian Fathers and early Christian writers. (Care must be exercised, however, in the use of such historical sources, since, for example, Cicero drew his knowledge of early Greek philosophers from intermediate sources, while Sextus Empiricus was mainly concerned to support his own sceptical position by drawing attention to the contradictory opinions of the dogmatic philosophers. In regard to Aristotle's testimony as to the opinions of his predecessors we must not forget that Aristotle tended to look on earlier philosophies simply from the viewpoint of his own system and to see in them preparatory work for his own achievement. His attitude on this matter was doubtless largely justified, but it does mean that he was not always concerned to give what we should consider a purely objective and scientific account of the course of philosophic thought.) The commentaries composed by authors of Antiquity on the works of eminent philosophers are also of considerable importance, for instance, the commentary by Simplicius on the Physics of *Aristotle*.

In regard to the lives of the philosophers the most important work which we possess is that of Diogenes Laërtius (A.D. third century). This work is a compilation of material taken from various sources and is of very unequal merit, much of the biographical material being anecdotal, legendary and valueless in character, "tall stories" and different, sometimes contradictory, accounts of an event being included by the author, accounts which he had collected from previous writers and compilers. On the other hand it would be a great mistake to allow the unscientific character of the work to obscure its importance and very real value. The indices of the works of the philosophers are important, and we are indebted to Diogenes for a considerable amount of valuable information on the opinions and lives of the Greek philosophers. In assessing the historical value of Diogenes' statements it is obviously necessary to know (as far as this is posible) the particular source to which he was indebted on any given occasion, and no little painstaking and fruitful labour has been expended by scholars, in order to attain this knowledge.

For the chronology of the Greek philosphers the chief source is the *Chronica* of Apollodorus, who based the first part of his chronicle on the *Chronographia* of Eratosthenes of Cyrene (third century before Christ), but added a supplement, carrying it down to about the year 110 B.C. Apollodorus had not, of course, exact material at his disposal, and he had recourse to the arbitrary method of linking up some event of importance which was supposed to have occurred during the period of a philosopher's life, with the philosopher's prime or ἀκμὴ (taken as the fortieth year) and then reckoning backward to the date of the philosopher's birth. Similarly, it was taken as a general rule that a disciple was forty years younger than his master. Accuracy, therefore, was not to be expected.

(On the general subject of sources see e.g. Ueberweg-Praechter, *Die Philosophie des Altertums*, pp. 10-26 (Apollodorus' Chronicle is given on pp. 667-71), A. Fairbanks, *The First Philosophers of Greece*, pp. 263-88, L. Robin, *Greek Thought and the Origins of the Scientific Spirit*, pp. 7-16, and the *Stellenregister* to Diels' *Fragmente der Vorsokratiker*.

Appendix Three

A FEW BOOKS

1. *General Histories of Greek Philosophy*

ADAMSON, R. (ed. Sorley and Hardie). The Development of
Greek Philosophy. London, 1908.

BENN, A. W. The Greek Philosophers. London, 1914.

BRÉHIER, E. Histoire de la philosophie. Tome I. Paris, 1943.

BURNET, J. Greek Philosophy, Part I. Thales to Plato.
Macmillan.

(This scholarly work is indispensable to the student).

ERDMANN, J. E. A History of Philosophy, vol. I. Swan
Sonnenschein, 1910.

(Erdmann was an eminent historian of the Hegelian
School.)

GOMPERZ, TH. Greek Thinkers, 4 vols. (Trs. L. Magnus.)
John Murray.

ROBIN, L. La pensée grecque et les origines de l'esprit scien-
tifique. Paris, 1923.

Greek Thought and the Origins of the Scientific Spirit
London, 1928.

RUGGIERO, G. DE. La filosofia greca. 2 vols. Bari, 1917.

(Professor de Ruggiero writes from the viewpoint of an
Italian Neo-Hegelian.)

STACE, W. T. A Critical History of Greek Philosophy. Macmillan, 1920.

STENZEL, J. Metaphysik des Altertums. Berlin, Oldenbourg,
1929.

(Particularly valuable for the treatment of Plato.)

STOCKL, A. A Handbook of the History of Philosophy. Part I.

Pre-Scholastic Philosophy. Trs. by T. A. Finlay, S.J. Dublin, 1887.

UEBERWEG-PRAECHTER. Die Philosophie des Altertums. Berlin, Mittler, 1926.

WERNER, C. La philosophie grecque. Paris, Payot, 1938.

ZELLER, E. Outlines of the History of Greek Philosophy. Kegan Paul, 1931.

(Revised by W. Nestle, translated by L. R. Palmer.)

2. *Pre-Socratic Philosophy*

The best collection of the fragments of the pre-Socratics is to be found in Hermann Diels' *Vorsokratiker,* fifth edition. Berlin, 1934-5.

BURNET, J. Early Greek Philosophy. Black, 3rd edition, 1920; 4th edition, 1930.

(This extremely useful work includes very many fragments.)

COVOTTI, A. I Presocratici. Naples, 1934.

FAIRBANKS, A. The First Philosophers of Greece. London, 1898.

ZELLER, E. A History of Greek Philosophy from the earliest period to the time of Socrates. Trs. S. F. Alleyne. 2 vols. Longmans, 1881.

3. *Plato*

The Works of Plato are published, under the editorship of J. Burnet, in the *Oxford Classical Texts.* A well-known translation, in five volumes, is that by B. Jowett, O.U.P., 3rd edition, 1892. There are also more literal translations.

ARCHER-HIND, R. D. The Timaeus of Plato. Macmillan, 1888.

CORNFORD, F. M. Plato's Theory of Knowledge. Kegan Paul, 1935.

(A translation of the *Theaetetus* and *Sophist,* with commentary.)

Plato's Cosmology. Kegan Paul, 1937.

(A translation of the *Timaeus,* with running commentary.)

Plato and Parmenides. Kegan Paul, 1939.

(Translation of the *Parmenides,* with commentary and discussion.)

The Republic of Plato. Translated with Introduction and Notes. O.U.P.

DEMOS, R. The Philosophy of Plato. Scribners, 1939.

DIÈS, AUGUSTE. Autour de Platon. Beauchesne, 1927.
　　Platon. Flammarion, 1930.
FIELD, G. C. Plato and his Contemporaries. Methuen, 1930.
GROTE, C. Plato and the other Companions of Socrates.
　　John Murray, 2nd edition, 1867.
HARDIE, W. F. R. A Study in Plato. O.U.P., 1936.
HARTMANN, N. Platons Logik des Seins. Giessen, 1909.
LODGE, R. C. Plato's Theory of Ethics. Kegan Paul, 1928.
LUTOSLAWSKI, W. The Origin and Growth of Plato's Logic.
　　London, 1905.
MILHAUD, G. Les philosophes-géomètres de la Grèce. 2nd
　　edition, Paris, 1934.
NATORP, P. Platons Ideenlehre. Leipzig, 1903.
NETTLESHIP, R. L. Lectures on the Republic of Plato. Mac-
　　millan, 1898.
RITTER, C. The Essence of Plato's Philosophy. George Allen
　　& Unwin, 1933.
　　　(Translated by Adam Alles.)
　　Platon, sein Leben, seine Schriften, seine Lehre. 2 vols.
　　Munich, 1910 and 1923.
ROBIN, L. La théorie Platonicienne des idées et des nombres.
　　Paris, 1933.
　　Platon. Paris, 1936.
　　La physique de Platon. Paris, 1919.
SHOREY, P. The Unity of Plato's Thought. Chicago, 1903.
STENZEL, J. Plato's Method of Dialectic. O.U.P., 1940.
　　　(Translated by D. G. Allan.)
　　Zahl und Gestalt bei Platon und Aristoteles. 2nd edition.
　　Leipzig, 1933.
　　Platon der Erzieher. 1928.
　　Studien zur Entwicklung der Platonischen Dialektik. Bres-
　　lau, 1917.
STEWART, J. A. The Myths of Plato. O.U.P., 1905.
　　Plato's Doctrine of Ideas. O.U.P., 1909.
TAYLOR, A. E. Plato, the Man and his Work. Methuen, 1926.
　　　(No student of Plato should be unacquainted with this
　　　masterly work.)
　　A Commentary on Plato's Timaeus. O.U.P., 1928.
　　Article on Plato in Encyc. Brit., 14th edition.
　　Platonism and its Influence. U.S.A. 1924 (Eng. Harrap).
WILAMOWITZ-MOELLENDORF, U. VON. Platon. 2 vols. Berlin,
　　1919.
ZELLER, E. Plato and the Older Academy. Longmans, 1876.
　　　(Translated by S. F. Alleyne and A. Goodwin.)

NOTES

CHAPTER ONE

¹ Hegel, *Hist. Phil.*, I, p. 17.
² *Proleg.*, p. 2 (Mahaffy).
³ A. N. Whitehead, *Process and Reality*, p. 18. Needless to say, the antihistorical attitude is not Professor Whitehead's own attitude.
⁴ N. Hartmann, *Ethics*, I, p. 119.
⁵ Hegel, *Hist. Phil.*, I, p. 12.
⁶ *Hist. Phil.*, III, p. 552.
⁷ Cf. *The Unity of Philosophical Experience*.
⁸ *De Verit.*, 22, 2, ad 1.
⁹ J. Maréchal, S.J., *Le Point de Départ de la Metaphysique: Cahier V.*
¹⁰ Pref. to 1st Ed. of *Critique of Pure Reason*.
¹¹ *Hist. Phil.*, I, p. 149.
¹² Burnet, *G.P.*, I, p. 9.

CHAPTER TWO

¹ "It was in Ionia that the new Greek civilisation arose: Ionia in whom the old Aegean blood and spirit most survived, taught the new Greece, gave her coined money and letters, art and poesy, and her shipmen, forcing the Phoenicians from before them, carried her new culture to what were then deemed the ends of the earth." Hall, *Ancient History of the Near East*, p. 79.
² For what Julius Stenzel calls *Vortheoretische Metaphysik* cf. Zeller, *Outlines*, Introd. ss 3; Burnet, *E.G.P.*, Introd.; Ueberweg-Praechter, pp. 28-31; Jaeger, *Paideia;* Stenzel, *Metaphysik des Altertums*, I, pp. 14 ff., etc.
³ *E.G.P.*, pp. 17-18.
⁴ "*Nel sesto secolo A.C. ci si presenta, in Grecia, uno dei fenomeni meravigliosi della coltura umana. La Scuola di Mileto crea la ricerca scientifica: e le linee fondamentali, stabilite in quei primi albori, si*

perpetuano attraverso le generazioni e i secoli." Aurelio Covotti, *I Presocratici,* p. 31 (Naples, 1934).

[5] As Dr. Praechter points out (p. 27), the religious conceptions of the Orient, even if they had been taken over by the Greeks, would not explain the peculiar characteristic of Greek philosophy, free speculation on the essence of things. As for Indian philosophy proper, it would not appear to be earlier than the Greek.

[6] *Outlines of the History of Greek Philosophy,* by Eduard Zeller, 13th edit., revised by Nestle, translated by L. R. Palmer, pp. 2-3.

[7] 425-7.

[8] 1224.

[9] *The Legacy of the Ancient World,* p. 83, note 2.

[10] From Benjamin Jowett's translation of Thucydides (Oxford Un. Press).

[11] The German word *Urstoff* is here employed, simply because it expresses the notion of primitive element or substrate or "stuff" of the universe in one short word.

CHAPTER THREE

[1] *Hist.,* I, 74.

[2] Diog. Laërt., *Lives of the Philosophers,* 1, 22-4.

[3] *Metaphysics* (trans. by J. A. Smith and W. D. Ross).

[4] *De Anima,* A 5, 411 a 7; 2, 405 a 19.

[5] So Aëtius, I, 7, XI (D. 11 A 23).

[6] Cicero: *De Nat. D.,* I, 10, 25 (D. *ibid.*).

[7] *Metaph.,* 983 b 18.

[8] *Phys. Opin.,* fr. 2 (D. 12 A 9). Cf. Ps. Plut. *Strom.,* 2 (D. 12 A 10).

[9] Frag. 1.

[10] Frags. 1-3.

[11] Frag. 1.

[12] D. 12 A 17. Simpl. *Phys.,* 1121, 5: Aët. II, 1, 3: Cic. *De Nat. D.,* 1, 10, 25: Aug. *C.D.,* viii, 2.

[13] Cf. Hippol., *Ref.,* 16, 2 (D. 12 A 11).

[14] Frag. 5. Ps. Plut. *Strom.,* 2 (D. 12 A 10).

[15] Ps. Plut. *Strom.,* fr. 2 (D. 12 A 10).

[16] Frag. 2.

[17] Hippol. *Ref.,* i, 7 (D. 13 A 7).

[18] (Plut., *De prim. frig.,* 947 f.), Frag. 1.

[19] *G.P.,* I, p. 9.

[20] *Outlines,* p. 31.

CHAPTER FOUR

[1] *"Ben, invero, possono dirsi romanzi, le loro 'Vite.' "* Covotti, *I Presocratici,* p. 66.

[2] Cf. Diog. Laërt., 8, 8.

³ Polybius, ii, 39 (D. 14, 16).

⁴ Stace, *Critical History of Greek Philosophy*, p. 33.

⁵ ap. Gell., iv, II, 5 (D. 14, 9).

⁶ *E.G.P.*, p. 93, note 5.

⁷ *Metaphysik des Altertums, Teil I*, p. 42.

⁸ *Somn. Scip.*, I, 14, 19 (D. 44 A 23).

⁹ Ueberweg-Praechter, p. 69.

¹⁰ D. 21 a.

¹¹ *Metaph.*, 985, b 23-6.

¹² It seems certain that the Pythagorean acoustic ratios were ratios of lengths and not of frequencies, which the Pythagoreans would hardly be in a position to measure. Thus the longest harpstring was called ἡ ὑπάτη, though it gave our "lowest" note and frequency, and the shortest was called ἡ νεάτη, though it gave our "highest" note and frequency.

¹³ *Metaph.*, 985, b 31-986 a 3.

¹⁴ *Metaph.*, 986 a 17-21.

¹⁵ Cf. art. *Pythagoras*, Enc. Brit., 14th edit., by Sir Thos. Little Heath.

¹⁶ Stöckl, *Hist. Phil.*, I, p. 48 (trans. by Finlay, 1887).

¹⁷ *Metaph.*, 1092, b 10-13.

¹⁸ Stöckl, *Hist. Phil.*, I, pp. 43-9.

¹⁹ *E.G.P.*, p. 107.

²⁰ Philolaus (as we learn from the fragments) insisted that nothing could be known, nothing would be clear or perspicuous, unless it had or was number.

²¹ Cf. Arist. *Physics*, 203 a 10-15.

²² *In Eukleiden*, Friedlein, 65, 16-19.

²³ Heath, *art. cit.*

²⁴ Cf. the words of the Russian philosopher, Leo Chestov: "It has happened more than once that a truth has had to wait for recognition whole centuries after its discovery. So it was with Pythagoras' teaching of the movement of the earth. Everyone thought it false, and for more than 1,500 years men refused to accept this truth. Even after Copernicus savants were obliged to keep this new truth hidden from the champions of tradition and of sound sense." Leo Chestov, *In Job's Balances*, p. 168 (trans. by C. Coventry and Macartney).

²⁵ As a matter of fact the Pythagorean mathematisation of the universe cannot really be regarded as an "idealisation" of the universe, since they regarded number geometrically. Their identification of things and numbers is thus not so much an idealisation of things as a materialisation of numbers. On the other hand, in so far as "ideas," such as justice, are identified with numbers, one may perhaps speak with justice of a tendency towards idealism. The same theme recurs in the Platonic idealism.

It must, however, be admitted that the assertion that the Pythagoreans effected a geometrisation of number would scarcely hold good for the later Pythagoreans at least. Thus Archytas of Tarentum, a friend of Plato, was clearly working in the very opposite direction (cf. Diels, B 4), a tendency to which Aristotle, believing in the separation and irreducible character of both geometry and arithmetic, firmly objected. On the whole it might be better perhaps to speak of a Pythagorean discovery (even if incompletely analysed) of *isomorphisms* between arithmetic and geometry rather than of an interreduction.

CHAPTER FIVE

[1] Frag. 121.

[2] Frag. 39.

[3] Frags. 42, 40, 129 (latter doubtful, acc. to D.).

[4] Frags. 58, 79, 9, 119.

[5] Frag. 14.

[6] Frags. 123, 93, 1 (cf. 17, 34). Cf. Diog. Laërt., 9, 6.

[7] *E.G.P.*, p. 132.

[8] Cf. Frags. 12 and 91.

[9] *Crat.* 402 a.

[10] *De Caelo*, 298 b 30 (III, i).

[11] Heraclitus does indeed teach that Reality is constantly changing, that it is its essential nature to change; but this should not be interpreted as meaning that for him there is no changing Reality at all. Heraclitus has often been compared to Bergson, but Bergson's thought too has, not infrequently, been grossly, if understandably, misinterpreted.

[12] Frag. 50.

[13] Frag. 80.

[14] Numenius. Frag. 16, apud Chalcidium, c. 297 (D. 22 A 22).

[15] Frag. 51.

[16] Hegel, *Hist. Phil.*, I.

[17] Frag. 65.

[18] Diog. Laërt., 9, 8-9.

[19] Frag. 30.

[20] Frag. 90.

[21] Diog. Laërt., 9, 11.

[22] Frag. 54.

[23] Frag. 51.

[24] Frags. 60, 36.

[25] Frags. 58, 61, 37.

[26] Frag. 102.

[27] Frag. 32.

[28] Frag. 96.

[29] Frag. 118.

[30] Frags. 77, 36.

[31] Frag. 94.

[32] *Soph.*, 242 d.

[33] Cf. *E.G.P.*, pp. 159-60.

[34] *De def. orac.*, 415 f.
[35] *Hist. Phil.*, I, pp. 297-8.

CHAPTER SIX

[1] Frag. 15. One might compare the words of Epicharmus (Frag. 5): "For the dog seems to the dog to be the most beautiful creature, and the ox to the ox, the donkey to the donkey, and the swine to the swine."
[2] Frags. 23 and 26.
[3] *Metaph.*, A 5, 986 b 18.
[4] Diog. Laërt., 9, 21.
[5] Frag. 8.
[6] Frag. 8.
[7] *E.G.P.*, p. 182.
[8] *Crit. Hist.*, pp. 47 and 48.
[9] *Crit. Hist.*, pp. 49-52.
[10] Frag. 7.
[11] *Metaph.*, 986 b 18-21.
[12] Frag. 9. (Simplic. *Phys.*, 109, 34).

CHAPTER SEVEN

[1] *Parmen.*, 128 b.
[2] Procl., *in Parmen.*, 694, 23 (D. 29 A 15).
[3] Frags. 1, 2.
[4] Frag. 3.
[5] Arist., *Phys.*, H, 5,250 a 19; Simplic., 1108, 18 (D. 29 A 29).
[6] Arist., *Phys.*, Δ 3,210 b 22; 1,209 a 23. Eudem., *Phys.*, *Frag.* 42 (D. 29 A 24).
[7] Arist., *Phys.*, Z 9,239 b 9; 2,233 a 21; *Top.*, Θ 8,160 b 7.
[8] Arist., *Phys.*, Z 9,239 b 14.
[9] Arist., *Phys.*, Z 9,239 b 30.
[10] Arist., *Phys.*, Z 9,239 b 33.
[11] Ross, *Physics*, p. 660.

CHAPTER EIGHT

[1] Diog. Laërt., 8, 54.
[2] Diog. Laërt., 8, 69.
[3] Diog. Laërt., 8, 71. (The great Germanic classical poet Hölderlin wrote a poem on the legendary death of Empedocles, also an unfinished poetic play.)
[4] Frag. 11.
[5] Frag. 14.
[6] Frag. 8.
[7] Frag. 7 (ἀγέννητα i.e. στοιχεῖα).

[8] This theme of an unending cyclic process reappears in the philosophy of Nietzsche under the name of the Eternal Recurrence.

[9] Frag. 27.

[10] Frag. 20.

[11] Frag. 117.

[12] Frag. 105.

[13] Frag. 141.

[14] Arist., *De An.*, 427 a 21. Theoph., *de sensu*, 1 ff. Plat., *Tim.*, cf. 67 c ff. (D. 31 A 86).

CHAPTER NINE

[1] Anax. is said to have had property at Claz. which he neglected in order to follow the theoretic life. Cf. Plato, *Hipp. M.*, 283 a.

[2] *Phaedrus*, 270 a.

[3] *Apol.*, 26 d.

[4] Frag. 17.

[5] Frag. 10.

[6] *De Gen. et corr.*, Γ, 1, 314 a 24. *De Caelo*, Γ, 3, 302 a 28.

[7] Frag. 1.

[8] Frag. 11.

[9] Frag. 8.

[10] *G.P.*, I., pp. 77-8.

[11] Cf. Zeller, *Outlines*, p. 62; Stace, *Crit. Hist.*, pp. 95 ff.; Covotti, *I Presocratici*, ch. 21.

[12] Hegel, *Hist. Phil.*, I, p. 319.

[13] Frag. 12.

[14] Frag. 12.

[15] Frag. 14.

[16] *Crit. Hist.*, p. 99.

[17] *Metaph.*, A 3, 984 b 15-18.

[18] *Metaph.*, A 4, 985 a 18-21.

[19] *Phaedo*, 97 b 8.

CHAPTER TEN

[1] Epicurus, for instance, denied his existence, but it has been suggested that this denial was due to Epicurus' determination to claim originality.

[2] *E.G.P.*, p. 331.

[3] Aët., i, 3, 18 and 12, 6 (D. 68 A 47).

[4] *De Fato*, 20, 46 and *De Fin.*, i, 6, 17 (D. 68 A 47 and 56).

[5] *De An.*, A, 2, 403 b 28 ff.

[6] Frag. 2 (Aët., 1, 25, 4).

[7] *Phys.*, Θ i, 252 a 32; *De Caelo*, Γ 2, 300 b 8; *Metaph.*, A, 4, 985 b 19-20.

[8] *De Caelo*, Γ 4, 303 a 8.

CHAPTER ELEVEN

¹ *Philosophy during the Tragic Age of the Greeks*, in sect. 3.

CHAPTER TWELVE

¹ *Outlines*, p. 76.
² In using the term "Sophism" I do not mean to imply that there was any Sophistic system: the men whom we know as the Greek Sophists differed widely from one another in respect both of ability and of opinions: they represent a trend or movement, not a school.
³ *Antigone*, 332 ff.
⁴ Zeller, *Outlines*, p. 77.
⁵ Xen., *Cyneg.*, 13, 8 (D. 79, 2 a).
⁶ Hegel, *Hist. Phil.*, I, p. 354.
⁷ *Protag.*, 313 c 5-6.
⁸ *Protag.*, 312 a 4-7.

CHAPTER THIRTEEN

¹ *Protag.*, 309 c; *Rep.*, 600 c; Diog. Laërt., 9, 50 ff.
² *Plato*, p. 236, note.
³ Frag. 1.
⁴ *Theaet.*, 151 e, 152 a.
⁵ Arist., *Metaph.*, B 2, 997 b 32-998 a 6.
⁶ *Theaet.*, 166 ff.
⁷ Frag. 4.
⁸ *G.P.*, I, p. 117.
⁹ Aristoph., *Clouds*, 112 ff., 656-7.
¹⁰ Diog. Laërt., 9, 53 ff.
¹¹ Arist., *Rhet.*, 5, 1407 b 6.
¹² *Clouds*, 658 ff., 847 ff.
¹³ 366 c ff.
¹⁴ Frag. 5.
¹⁵ Cf. *Crat.*, 384 b.
¹⁶ Cf. *Protag.*, 337 a f.
¹⁷ *Outlines*, pp. 84-5.
¹⁸ Frag. 3.
¹⁹ 337 d, 2-3.
²⁰ Cf. Frags. 1, 3.
²¹ Aristotle or Theophrastus?
²² Cf. Zeller, *Outlines*, p. 87.
²³ Frag. 23 (Plut., *de gloria Athen.*, 5, 348 c).
²⁴ *Gorgias*, 482 e ff.
²⁵ Frags. 3 and 4.
²⁶ Alcidamas of Elaea. Cf. Aristot., *Rhet.*, III, 3, 1406 b; 1406 a. Schol. on I 13, 1373 b.
²⁷ *Outlines*, p. 88.
²⁸ *Rep.*, 338 c.

[29] Cf. Plut., apud Diels. Frag. 44 and 87 A 6.

[30] Ueberweg-Praechter, p. 122.

CHAPTER FOURTEEN

[1] *Apol.*, 17 d.

[2] Cf. Diog. Laërt. (Thus Praechter says roundly: *Der Vater des Sokrates war Bildhauer*, p. 132.)

[3] *Euthyphro*, 10 c.

[4] Diog. Laërt. remarks that "Some say that the Graces in the Akropolis are his work."

[5] *Theaet.*, 149 a.

[6] Taylor, *Socrates*, p. 38.

[7] "All the great buildings and works of art with which Athens was enriched in the Periclean age, the Long Walls which connected the city with the port of Peiraeus, the Parthenon, the frescoes of Polygnotus, were begun and completed under his eyes." *Socr.*, p. 36.

[8] *Sympos.*, 215 b 3 ff.

[9] *Clouds*, 362 (cf. *Sympos.*, 221).

[10] It is true, however, that the history of mysticism does record instances of prolonged ecstatic states. Cf. Poulain, *Grâces d' oraison*, p. 256.

[11] *Phys. Opin.*, fr. 4.

[12] *Phaedo*, 97-9.

[13] *Socr.*, p. 67.

[14] *Clouds*, 94.

[15] *Apol.*, 19.

[16] *Apol.*, 19.

[17] *Apol.*, 20 ff.

[18] *Apol.*, 28 e. Burnet suggests that the fighting at the foundation of Amphipolis (some fifteen years earlier) may be referred to.

[19] *Der echte und der Xenophontische Sokrates*, Berlin, 1893, 1901.

[20] *Die Lehre des Sokrates als sozialesreform system. Neuer Versuch zur Lösung des Problems der sokratischen Philosophie.* München, 1895.

[21] "While it is quite impossible to regard the Socrates of Aristophanes and the Socrates of Xenophon as the same person, there is no difficulty in regarding both as distorted images of the Socrates we know from Plato. The first is legitimately distorted for comic effect, the latter, not so legitimately, for apologetic reasons." Burnet, *G.P.*, I, p. 149.

[22] Cf. pp. 245-7 of this book; *v.* also Cornford's *Plato's Cosmology*, where he discusses Professor Taylor's theory.

[23] *Plato and his Contemporaries*, p. 228, Methuen, 1930. Cf. Field's summary of the evidence on the Socratic question, pp. 61-3.

[24] 314 c, καλοῦ καὶ νέου γεγονότος.

[25] Cf. article by R. Hackforth on Socrates in *Philosophy* for July 1933.

[26] A. D. Lindsay in Introd. to *Socratic Discourses* (Everyman), p. viii.

[27] *Metaph.*, M. 1078 b 27-9.

[28] The early dialogues of Plato, which may safely be considered "Socratic" in character, generally end without any determinate and positive result having been attained.

[29] *Mem.*, 1, 1, 16.

[30] *Mem.*, 4, 2, 14 ff.

[31] *Metaph.*, A 987 b 1-3.

[32] *Metaph.*, M 1,078 b 17-19.

[33] *Apol.*, 36.

[34] Xen., *Mem.*, 1, 1, 16; *Apol.*, 36.

[35] *Eth. Nic.*, 1145 b.

[36] *Crit. Hist.*, pp. 147-8. Professor Stace considers, however, that "Aristotle's criticism of Socrates is unanswerable."

[37] Xen., *Mem.*, IV, 4, 19 ff.

[38] Not all thinkers have been willing to admit that human nature *is* constant. But there is no real evidence to show that "primitive" man differed essentially from modern man; nor have we justification for supposing that a type of man will arise in the future who will be *essentially* different from the man of to-day.

[39] *Mem.*, 1, 2, 9; 3, 9, 10.

[40] *Mem.*, 1, 3, 2.

[41] *Mem.*, 1, 4, 5, 7.

[42] *Mem.*, 1, 4, 8.

[43] Ueb.-Praechter, p. 145; *der eigentliche Begründer der Teleologie in der Betrachtung der Welt.*

[44] Cf. e.g. *Mem.*, I, 1, 10-16.

[45] It is, as Burnet observes, a caricature which—like any caricature, if it is to have point—possesses a foundation in fact.

[46] Diog. Laërt., 2, 40.

[47] i, 173.

[48] Cf. *Apol.*, 36 a (the reading of which is not absolutely certain), and Diog. Laërt., 2, 41. Burnet and Taylor, understanding Plato as saying that Socrates was condemned by a majority of 60 votes, suppose that the voting was 280 to 220, out of a jury of 500.

[49] Diog. Laërt. (2, 42) says that the majority was 80 votes in excess of the first majority. According to Burnet and Taylor, the second voting would thus be 360 in favour of the death penalty as against 140.

[50] This remark is not meant to prejudice my view that the theory of Forms is not to be ascribed to Socrates.

[51] *Phaedo*, 118.

CHAPTER FIFTEEN

[1] Ueberweg-Praechter, p. 155.

[2] Gell, *Noct. Att.*, 6, 10.

[3] Diog. Laërt., 2, 106.

[4] Cf. Diog. Laërt., 2, 108.

[5] *Möglichkeit und Wirklichkeit*, Berlin, 1938.

[6] Diog. Laërt., 2, 115. Senec., *Ep.* 9, 3.

[7] Diog. Laërt., 6, 1.

[8] It has been suggested that it was Diogenes who founded the Cynic School or "Movement," and not Antisthenes: Arist. refers to the followers of Antisthenes as Ἀντισθενείοι (*Metaph.*, 1043 b 24). But the nickname of "Cynics" seems to have been accepted, only in the time of Diogenes and Arist.'s use of the term Ἀντισθενείοι would not appear to prove anything against Antisthenes having been the real fountain-head of the Cynic School.

[9] Simplic. in Arist., *Categ.*, 208, 29 f.; 211, 17 f.

[10] Plat., *Soph.*, 251 b; Arist., *Metaph.*, Δ 29, 1024 b 32-25 a 1.

[11] Arist., *Top.*, A xi, 104 b 20; *Metaph.*, Δ 29, 1024 b 33-4.

[12] Cf. Vita Antisth., apud Diog. Laërt.

[13] Cf. Cic., *De Nat.*, 1, 13, 32; Clem. Alex., *Protrep.*, 6, 71, 2; *Strom.*, 5, 14, 108, 4.

[14] Dion. Chrys., 8, 2.

[15] Diog. Laërt., 6, 20.

[16] Diog. Laërt., 6, 72.

[17] Diog. Laërt., *Lives of Crates and Hipparchia*.

[18] Dates from Heinrich von Stein's *De philos. Cyrenaica*, part I, *De Vita Aristippi*, Gött, 1858.

[19] Cf. Sext. Emp. *adv. mathemat.*, 7, 191 ff.

[20] Diog. Laërt., 2, 86 ff.

[21] Diog. Laërt., 2, 75.

[22] Diog. Laërt., 2, 97; Cic., *De Nat. D.*, 1, 1, 12.

[23] Diog. Laërt., 2, 94-6.

[24] Cic., *Tusc.*, 1, 34, 83.

[25] Diog. Laërt., 2, 96 f.; Clem. Alex., *Strom.*, 2, 21, 130, 7 f.

CHAPTER SIXTEEN

[1] Diog. Laërt., 9, 34 f. Cf. Burnet, *G.P.*, I, p. 195.

[2] According to Diog. Laërt. (9, 35), quoting Favorinus, Democritus ridiculed the assertions of Anaxagoras concerning Mind.

[3] Frag. 9.

[4] Frag. 9.

[5] Frag. 11.

[6] Frag. 125.

[7] Frag. 171. (Almost "fortune.")

[8] Frag. 189.

[9] Frag. 69.

[10] Frag. 37.

[11] Frag. 154.

CHAPTER SEVENTEEN

¹ Diog. Laërt., 3, 4.
² Diog. Laërt., 3, 5.
³ *Metaph.*, A 6, 987 a 32-5.
⁴ Diog. Laërt., 3, 6.
⁵ At least, this is what the reference to Potidaea (*Charmides*, 153) implies.
⁶ *Ep.* 7, 324 b 8-326 b 4.
⁷ *Apol.*, 34 a 1, 38 b 6-9.
⁸ *Phaedo*, 59 b 10.
⁹ *Ep.*, 7, 324 a 5-6.
¹⁰ Diog. Laërt., 3, 19-20.
¹¹ *Ep.* 7, 341 c 4-d 2; *Ep.* 2, 314 c 1-4.
¹² *Uno et octogesimo anno scribens est mortuus.* Cic., *De Senect.*, 5, 13.

CHAPTER EIGHTEEN

¹ *Plato*, p. 10.
² Ueberweg-Praechter, p. 195. Dr. Praechter's invaluable work does not, of course, represent the hypercritical fashion of the time of Ueberweg.
³ *Plato*, p. 13.
⁴ Ueberweg-Praechter, p. 199.
⁵ *Plato*, p. 13.
⁶ Arist., *Rhet.*, 1415 b 30.
⁷ *Topics* A 5, 102 a 6; E 5, 135 a 13; Z 6, 146 a 22.
⁸ *Aristotle*, e.g. p. -32. Cf. Diog. Laërt., 3, 37. Taylor (*Plato*, p. 497) thinks that Diog. only means that Philippus transcribed the *Epinomis* from wax tablets.
⁹ Ritter accepts *Epistles* 3 and 8 and the main narrative of 7.
¹⁰ Cf. Ueberweg-Praechter, pp. 199-218.
¹¹ Arist., *Pol.*, B 6, 1264 b 27.
¹² Diog. Laërt., 3, 38.
¹³ *Plato*, p. 18.
¹⁴ *Meno*, 90 a.
¹⁵ 17 ff.
¹⁶ *Polit.*, 284 b 7 ff., 286 b 10.
¹⁷ K. Fr. Hermann.
¹⁸ Cf. the words of Dr. Praechter, *Platon ist ein Werdender gewesen sein Leben lang.* Ueberweg-Praechter, p. 260.

CHAPTER NINETEEN

¹ We do not thereby mean to imply that Plato had not made up his mind as to the status of sense-perception long before he wrote the *Theaetetus* (we have only to read the *Republic*, for instance,

or consider the genesis and implications of the Ideal Theory): we refer rather to systematic consideration in published writings.

[2] 151 e 2-3.

[3] 152 c 5-7.

[4] 185 c 4-e 2.

[5] 208 c 7-8.

[6] 208 c 7-e 4.

[7] *Rep.*, 509 d 6-511 e 5.

[8] On the left side of the line are states of mind: on the right side are corresponding objects. In both cases the "highest" are at the top. The very close connection between the Platonic epistemology and the Platonic ontology is at once apparent.

[9] *Rep.*, 509 e 1-510 a 3.

[10] *Rep.*, 510 a 5-6.

[11] Plato's theory of art is discussed in a later chapter.

[12] *Rep.*, 510 b 4-6.

[13] *Rep.*, 510 e 2-511 a 1.

[14] Cf. W. R. F. Hardie, *A Study in Plato*, p. 52 (O.U.P., 1936).

[15] *Rep.*, 510 c.

[16] *Rep.*, 511 c 8-d 2.

[17] *Lectures on the Republic of Plato* (1898), pp. 252 f.

[18] 987 b 14 ff. Cf. 1059 b 2 ff.

[19] *Metaph.*, 1083 a 33-5.

[20] Cf. *Forms and Numbers, Mind*, Oct. 1926 and Jan. 1927. (Reprinted in *Philosophical Studies*.)

[21] *Rep.*, 510 c 2 ff.

[22] *Rep.*, 510 c 4-5.

[23] *Rep.*, 510 b 6-9.

[24] *Rep.*, 511 b 3-c 2.

[25] *Rep.*, 533 c 8.

[26] *Epin.*, 990 c 5-991 b 4.

[27] Cf. Taylor, *Plato*, p. 501.

[28] *Metaph.*, 992 a 20 ff.

[29] *Metaph.*, 992 a 20-1.

[30] *Rep.*, 514 a 1-518 d 1.

[31] Nettleship, *Lectures on the Republic of Plato*, p. 260.

[32] *Rep.*, 517 b 8-c 4.

CHAPTER TWENTY

[1] Cf. Stace, *Critical History*, p. 191.

[2] *Rep.*, 596 a 6-7; cf. 507 ab.

[3] *Phaedo*, 102 b 1.

[4] *Metaph.*, A, 987 b 1-10; M, 1078 b 30-32.

[5] *Metaph.*, A, 991 b 2-3.

[6] *Phaedo*, 114 d 1-2.

[7] It is indeed the opinion of the writer that Aristotle, in his criticism of the Ideal Theory, scarcely does justice to Plato, but he would

ascribe this to the polemical attitude Aristotle came to adopt towards the theory rather than to any supposed imbecility.

[8] *Phaedo*, 65 c 2 ff.

[9] *Phaedo*, 100 b 5-7.

[10] Cf. *Phaedo*, 84 e 3-85 b 7.

[11] *Meno*, 81 a 5 ff.

[12] *Sympos.*, 210 e 1-212 a 7.

[13] *Hippias Maior*, 289 d 2-5.

[14] *Sympos.*, 209 e 5-210 a 4. Cf. 210 e 1-2.

[15] *Plato*, p. 229, note 1.

[16] *Sympos.*, 210 a 4 ff.

[17] *Rep.*, 509 b 6-10.

[18] These phrases occur in the *Phaedo*.

[19] 1218 a 24.

[20] *Metaph.*, 1091 b 13-15.

[21] *Metaph.*, 988 a 10-11.

[22] 517 b 7-c 4.

[23] *Rep.*, 509 b 6-10.

[24] *Rep.*, 526 e 3-4.

[25] *Tim.*, 28 c 3-5.

[26] Cf. *Ep.* 2, 314 b 7-c 4.

[27] *Tim.*, 30 b 6-c 1.

[28] *Ep.* 2, 312 e ff.

[29] *Ep.* 6, 323 d 2-6.

[30] *Rep.*, 532 a 5-b 2.

[31] *Rep.*, 532 c 5-6.

[32] *Rep.*, 529-30.

[33] *Sophist*, 248 e 6-249 a 2.

[34] *Zahl und Gestalt*, pp. 133 ff.

[35] Cf. Hardie, *A Study in Plato*, p. 75.

[36] *Phaedrus*, 247 c 6-8.

[37] 130 a 8 ff.

[38] *Plato's Method of Dialectic*, p. 55. (Trs. D. J. Allan, Oxford, Clarendon Press, 1940.)

[39] *Parm.*, 132 d 1 ff.

[40] *Sympos.*, 211 b 2 (μετέχοντα). In 212 a 4, sense-objects are spoken of as εἴδωλα, which implies "imitation."

[41] Proclus pointed out that the relation of a copy to its original is a relation not only of resemblance, but also of derivation-from, so that the relation is not symmetrical. Cf. Taylor, *Plato*, p. 358: "My reflection in the glass is a reflection of my face, but my face is not a reflection of it."

[42] 135 e 1-4.

[43] 241 a.

[44] *A Study in Plato*, p. 106.

[45] Cf. Chapter X, *Democritus*, in *Plato's Method of Dialectic*.

[46] *Soph.*, 259 e 5-6.

[47] To postulate Forms of Sitting and Flying may be a logical appli-

cation of Plato's principles, but it obviously raises great difficulties. Aristotle implies that the upholders of the Ideal Theory did not go beyond postulating Ideas of natural substances (*Met.*, 1079 a). He also asserts that according to the Platonists there are no Ideas of Relations, and implies that they did not believe in Ideas of Negation.

[48] 249 b 2-3.

[49] 249 d 3-4.

[50] Cf. 253 b 8 ff.

[51] *Philebus*, 16 d 7-e 2.

[52] *Tim.*, 30 a 4-5.

[53] *Rep.*, 597 b 5-7.

[54] *Rep.*, 517 c 4.

[55] *Rep.*, 509 b 6-10.

[56] The fact that Plato speaks of God as "king" and "truth," while the Idea of the Good is "the source of truth and reason," suggests that God or Reason is *not* to be identified with the Good. A Neo-Platonic interpretation is rather implied.

[57] *Phil.*, 30 c 2-e 2.

[58] *Phil.*, 28 c 6 ff.

[59] *Tim.*, 29 e 1-30 a 7.

[60] Though in *Timaeus*, 37 c, the "Father" means the Demiurge.

[61] The Neo-Platonists held that the Divine Reason was not ultimate, but proceeded from the One.

[62] *Soph.*, 248 e 6-249 d 4.

[63] 249 a 4-7.

[64] 245 c 5-246 a 2.

[65] My debt to Professor Taylor's treatment of the topic will be obvious to all those who have read his articles in *Mind* (Oct. 1926 and Jan. 1927). Cf. Appendix to *Plato*.

[66] *Metaph.*, A, 6, 9; M and N.

[67] 990 c 5-991 b 4.

[68] *Rep.*, 546 c.

[69] *Expositio*, ed. Hiller, 43, 5-45, 8.

[70] *Metaph.*, 987 b 21-2.

[71] *Plato*, p. 225.

[72] *Critical Hist.*, pp. 190-1.

[73] *The Essence of Plato's Philosophy*, p. 11.

[74] Cf. *Philebus*, 51 b 9-d 1.

[75] *Sympos.*, 210 d 3-5.

[76] Cf. *Phaedo*.

[77] Cf. *Phaedrus*.

[78] *Sympos.*, 179 a 7-8.

[79] 201 d 8 ff.

[80] 206 a 7-207 a 4.

[81] 52 a 1-4.

[82] Stéphane Mallarmé, *Poems*. (Trans. by Roger Fry. Chatto & Windus, 1936.)

CHAPTER TWENTY-ONE

[1] 279 b 8-c 3.
[2] 896 a 1-2.
[3] 46 d 5-7.
[4] 85 e 3-86 d 4, 93 c 3-95 a 2.
[5] *Tim.*, 86 b ff.
[6] *Laws*, 775 b ff.
[7] *Tim.*, 86 d 7-e 3.
[8] Bk. 4.
[9] Cf. Cic., *Tusc. Disp.*, 4, 5, 10. (In this passage Cicero refers to *two* parts, the rational and the non-rational parts.)
[10] *Tim.*, 69 d 6-70 a 7.
[11] *Tim.*, *ibid.*
[12] *Tim.*, 69 c 2-e 4.
[13] 246 a 6 ff.
[14] 246 a 4-6.
[15] 41 c 6-42 e 4, 69 b 8-c 8.
[16] Cf. St. Aug.: *Homo anima rationalis est mortali atque terreno utens corpore.* (*De moribus Ecc. cath.*, I, 27.)
[17] Letter to unknown correspondent about 1680, Duncan, *Philosophical Works of Leibniz*, p. 9.
[18] 70 d 7-72 e 2.
[19] 72 e 3-77 d 5.
[20] I do not mean to imply an acceptance of the Kantian Critique, but simply to point out that, even on Plato's assumption, his conclusion is not the only one possible.
[21] 77.
[22] 78 b 4-80 e 1.
[23] 86 e 6-88 b 8.
[24] 103 c 10-107 a 1.
[25] 608 d 3-611 a 2.
[26] 245 c 5 ff.
[27] Cf. *Laws*, 896 a 1-b 3.
[28] *Rep.*, 498 b 3-d 6.
[29] 492 e 8-11.
[30] Duncan, p. 9.
[31] *Essence*, p. 282.
[32] *Theaet.*, 191 c 8 and ff.; *Phil.*, 33 c 8-34 c 2.

CHAPTER TWENTY-TWO

[1] 21 c 1-8.
[2] Cf. 51.
[3] 61 b 4 ff.
[4] 62 c 1-4.
[5] *Theaet.*, 176 a 5-e 4.
[6] *Theaet.*, 176 b 1-3.

[7] *Rep.*, 613 a 7-b 1.

[8] *Laws*, 715 e 7-717 a 3.

[9] *Protag.*, 330 c 3 ff.

[10] *Rep.*, Bk. 4.

[11] *Gorgias*, 482 e 3-5.

[12] The resemblance to the opinions of Nietzsche is obvious, though Nietzsche's idea was very far from being that of the political and licentious tyrant.

[13] 483 d 5-6.

[14] *Gorgias*, 523 ff.

[15] *Rep.*, 335 a 7-8.

CHAPTER TWENTY-THREE

[1] 354 c 1.

[2] 368 e 2-369 a 3.

[3] *Ep.* 7, 325 d 6-326 b 4.

[4] *Rep.*, 369 c 1-4.

[5] 377 a 12-c 5.

[6] 380 a 5-c 3.

[7] 403 e 11-404 b 8.

[8] 412 c 9-413 c 7.

[9] 414 b 1-6.

[10] 417 a 5-6.

[11] 433 a 1 and ff.

[12] 461 c 4-7.

[13] 488 a 1-489 a 2.

[14] Plato, like Socrates, considered the "democratic" practice of choosing magistrates, generals, etc., by lot or according to their rhetorical ability, irrational and absurd.

[15] 525 b 11-c 6.

[16] 527 b 9-11.

[17] 532 a 7-b 2.

[18] 539 e 2-540 a 2.

[19] 540 a 7-c 2.

[20] 305 e 2-4.

[21] 276 e 10-12.

[22] 297 b 7-c 2.

[23] 297 e 1-5.

[24] 303 a 2-8.

[25] 303 b 8-c 5.

[26] 709 d 10-710 b 9.

[27] 705 a 2-7.

[28] 715 a 8-b 6.

[29] 726 a 2-3, 728 a 4-5.

[30] 737 e 1-738 b 1.

[31] 742 a 5-6.

[32] 753 b 4-7.

[33] 765 d 5-766 a 6.
[34] 783 d 8-e 1.
[35] 790 c 5-791 b 2.
[36] 828 b 2-3.
[37] 861 e 6 ff.
[38] 899 d 5-905 d 3.
[39] 905 d 3-907 d 1.
[40] 909 d 7-8.
[41] 936 c 1-7.
[42] 937 d 6-938 c 5.
[43] 941 c 4-942 a 4.
[44] 945 b 3-948 b 2.
[45] 960 e 9 ff.
[46] 951 a 2-4.
[47] 949 e 3 ff.
[48] Cf. 776 b 5-c 3.
[49] 930 d 1-e 2.
[50] Cf. *Plato and Greek Slavery*, Glenn R. Morrow, in *Mind*, April 1939, N.S. vol. 48, No. 190.
[51] 872 c 2-6.
[52] *Rep.*, 563.
[53] 776 d 2-718 a 5.
[54] 626 a 2-5.
[55] 628 c 9-e 1.
[56] 641 c 2-7.
[57] Hegel, *The Philosophy of Right*, sect. 299 and sect. 185. Trans. Professor S. W. Dyde. (George Bell & Sons, 1896.)

CHAPTER TWENTY-FOUR

[1] Cf. *Tim.*, 27 ab.
[2] 26 c 7-e 5.
[3] See Introd. to Professor Cornford's edition of *Timaeus*.
[4] Cf. 27 d 5-28 a 4 and 29 b 3-d 3. This was a consequence of the epistemological and ontological dualism, which Plato never abandoned.
[5] *Philebus*, 28 c 6-29 a 5.
[6] *Laws*, 966 d 9-e 4.
[7] *A Commentary on Plato's Timaeus*, pp. 18-19.
[8] *Tim.*, 29 d 1-3.
[9] *Tim.*, 29 c 1-3.
[10] 28 c 2-3.
[11] 30 a 3-4.
[12] 30 b 1-c 1.
[13] 39 e 3-40 a 2.
[14] 31 a 2-b 3.
[15] 29 e 3-30 a 6.
[16] 47 e 5-48 a 2.

[17] *Laws*, 889 c 4-6.
[18] *Physics*, B. 4, 196 a 25.
[19] *De Caelo*, 279 b 33.
[20] i, 382; iii, 273.
[21] *Phys.*, 1122, 3.
[22] 28 c 7-8.
[23] 28 c 3-5.
[24] 49 a 5-6.
[25] 52 a 8-b 2.
[26] 50 a 5-b 5.
[27] 50 b 7-c 2.
[28] 49 e 2-4.
[29] 49 e 7-50 a 1.
[30] 51 a 7-b 1.
[31] Cf. 53 c 4 ff.
[32] 53 d 6-7.
[33] 894 a 2-5.
[34] 55 d 6 ff.
[35] 56 d 5-6.
[36] *De Caelo*, 306 a 2.
[37] 56 c 4.
[38] 53 b 2.
[39] *Essence*, p. 261.
[40] 59 c 1-5.
[41] 59 c 5-d 2.
[42] 246 a 1-2.
[43] 35 a 1 ff. Cf. *Proclus*, ii, 155, Cornford's *Timaeus*, pp. 59 ff.
[44] 41 d 4 ff.
[45] 39 e 10-42 a 1.
[46] Cf. 41 a 7-d 3, 42 d 5-e 4.
[47] 781 e 6-782 a 3.
[48] *Tim.*, 40 d 6-41 a 3.
[49] Cf. *Phaedrus*, 246 c 6-d 3.
[50] 984 d 8-e 3.
[51] *Tim.*, 37 d 3-7.
[52] *Tim.*, 45 a 3-5.
[53] *Tim.*, 92 c 5-9.

CHAPTER TWENTY-FIVE

[1] 230 b 2 ff.
[2] 625 b 1-c 2.
[3] 595 b 9-c 3.
[4] 607 a 2-5.
[5] 607 c 3-8.
[6] H.M., 287 c 8-d 2.
[7] H.M., 289 c 3-5.
[8] Sympos., 211 a 2-b 2.

[9] 295 c 1 ff.
[10] 250 d 6-8.
[11] 51 b 9-c 7.
[12] *Phil.*, 64 e 6-7.
[13] *Aesthetic*, by Benedetto Croce, pp. 165-6. (2nd edit., trs. by Douglas Ainslie, Macmillan, 1929.)
[14] Cf. *Laws*, 653-4, 672 b 8-c 6.
[15] *Rep.*, 597 c 11 and ff.
[16] *Rep.*, 597 e 10 ff.
[17] *Rep.*, 598 b 6.
[18] *Rep.*, 598 e 6-599 a 3.
[19] *Laws*, 668 a 9-b 2.
[20] *Laws*, 668 b 4-7.
[21] *Laws*, 670 d 6-7.
[22] *Laws*, 669 a 7-b 3.
[23] 657 b 2-3.
[24] For further treatment of Plato's philosophy of art, see e.g. Professor R. G. Collingwood's article, "Plato's Philosophy of Art," in *Mind* for April 1925.
[25] *Laws*, 667 d 9-e 4.
[26] 668 b 4-7.
[27] 656 c 1-3.
[28] 665 c 2-7.
[29] 670 d 7.
[30] 656 c 5-7.
[31] Arist., Frag. 623. (Rose, 1870.)

CHAPTER TWENTY-SIX

[1] Frag. 42, a-g.
[2] So Praechter, p. 343.
[3] Frag. 38-9.
[4] Cic., *De Nat. D.*, 1, 13, 32.
[5] Frag. 34 ff.
[6] Frag. 24 ff.
[7] Frag. 54.
[8] *Metaph.*, A 9, 991 a 8-19.
[9] *Eth. Nic.*, 1101 b 27 ff.; 1172 b 9 ff.
[10] Cic., *Acad.*, 2, 44, 135; *Tusc.*, 3, 6, 12.